Assessment for Learning in Higher Education

"An invaluable guide for practitioners, quality assurers, university managers and students themselves who wish to better understand the importance of assessment for learning."

Professor Sally Brown

Assessment for Learning in Higher Education is a practical guide to Assessment for Learning (AfL); a term that has become internationally accepted in Higher Education and features in the learning and teaching strategies of many universities. It is also mandated by official bodies such as QAA in the UK. Many staff in Higher Education are uncertain about how to implement AfL, especially in times of increasingly constrained resources and this vital new guide provides solutions that make best use of assessment as a tool for learning.

This book provides an important and accessible blend of practical examples of AfL in a variety of subject areas. The authors present practical, jargon-free, often small-scale and eminently 'do-able' ideas that will make its introduction achievable. The book provides practical case examples backed up by relevant theory for both new lecturers and more experienced staff who may be interested in embedding AfL principles and practice into their university teaching. AfL approaches go beyond minor adaptations to teaching practice, and signify a shift in the foundations of thinking about assessment. With this in mind there is guidance on the development of effective learning environments and communities through the use of:

- collaboration and dialogue;
- authentic assessment;
- formative assessment;
- peer and self-assessment;
- student development for the long-term;
- innovative approaches to effective feedback.

Assessment for Learning in Higher Education fills a vital gap in assessment literature and as AfL is increasingly on the Higher Education agenda, with the promotion of assessment as a tool for learning, this book will become an essential handbook to guide all academic practitioners.

Kay Sambell is Professor of Learning and Teaching at Northumbria University, UK. **Liz McDowell** is Professor in Academic Practice at Northumbria University, UK. **Catherine Montgomery** is Principal Lecturer in Education at Northumbria University, UK.

Assessment for Learning in Higher Education

Kay Sambell, Liz McDowell
and Catherine Montgomery

Routledge
Taylor & Francis Group

LONDON AND NEW YORK

First published 2013
by Routledge
2 Park Square, Milton Park, Abingdon, Oxon OX14 4RN

Simultaneously published in the USA and Canada
by Routledge
711 Third Avenue, New York, NY 10017

Routledge is an imprint of the Taylor & Francis Group, an *informa* business

British Library Cataloguing in Publication Data
A catalogue record for this book is available from the British Library

Library of Congress Cataloging-in-Publication Data
Sambell, Kay.
Assessment for learning in higher education / Kay Sambell, Liz McDowell,
Catherine Montgomery.
p. cm.
1. Education, Higher–Evaluation–Methodology. 2. Universities and
colleges–Examinations. I. McDowell, Liz. II. Montgomery, Catherine, 1962–
III. Title.
LB2366.S26 2012
378.166–dc23
2012007999

ISBN: 978–0–415–58657–3 (hbk)
ISBN: 978–0–415–58658–0 (pbk)
ISBN: 978–0–203–81826–8 (ebk)

Typeset in Garamond
by Keystroke, Station Road, Codsall, Wolverhampton

MIX
Paper from
responsible sources
FSC www.fsc.org FSC® C004839

Printed and bound in Great Britain by
TJInternational Ltd, Padstow, Cornwall

Contents

Author biographies

Professor Kay Sambell

Kay Sambell is currently Professor of Learning and Teaching in the School of Health, Community and Education Studies at Northumbria University. A committed university teacher with over twenty years' classroom experience, she continues to work with large groups of students, putting new pedagogic principles into practice. In 2002 she was awarded a National Teaching Fellowship for her research and development work on innovative assessment to support student learning. Kay has directed a wide range of funded learning and teaching initiatives, developing, researching and sharing practical, evidence-informed ideas about improving student learning. In 2005 she became a Director of Northumbria University's Centre for Excellence in Assessment for Learning, where she led on student engagement and enhancement. She has been a keynote speaker and presenter at a range of national and international conferences dedicated to the scholarship of teaching and learning in Higher Education.

Professor Liz McDowell

Liz McDowell is currently Professor in Academic Practice at Northumbria University. She has been engaged in research on assessment over the last twenty years with a particular focus on the relationships between assessment and learning in Higher Education. She is the founder of a series of well-regarded conferences on assessment, subsequently promoted jointly with EARLI, the European Association for Research in Learning and Instruction. In 2004 Liz led a cross-disciplinary team in a successful bid for an award of national centre for excellence (CETL) in assessment and became Director of the CETL in Assessment for Learning at Northumbria University. Liz's interest in researching assessment is closely linked to a commitment to making a difference to assessment in practice. She has been an adviser, consultant and keynote speaker in universities in the UK and beyond and engaged in many research and development projects. In recognition of this she has been awarded a National Teaching Fellowship.

Dr Catherine Montgomery

Catherine Montgomery is currently Principal Lecturer in Education at Northumbria University and was Associate Director for Research in Northumbria's CETL in Assessment for Learning. Catherine was appointed to the CETL in 2006 and led a research team aiming to establish the impact of the introduction of AfL approaches and innovations across all the Schools of Northumbria University. Over four years this involved twenty-four projects of varying sizes and types, using different methodological approaches, ranging from large-scale quantitative projects (e.g. 700 questionnaires) to more qualitative analyses of one specific module site and focusing on gaining different sightings of Assessment for Learning in context. Catherine's particular interest in the socio-cultural aspects of Assessment for Learning stem from her disciplinary background in Sociolinguistics and her research in international education. Catherine was awarded a National Teaching Fellowship in 2010.

Preface

Professor Sally Brown

At a time of ever-increasing global competitiveness for students in Higher Education (HE), the way in which we can best engage, educate and satisfy students has become an issue of real urgency. At the heart of the staff–student relationship is the issue of assessment and most specifically, how we can move students towards being active partners in knowledge creation through the kinds of activities we engage in with them through their assignments.

The seventy-four UK Centres for Excellence in Teaching and Learning which were set up through a fiercely competitive national bidding process have had a significant effect on the learning and teaching context not just in the UK but also internationally and none more so than the Assessment for Learning CETL, from which this book stems. Building on a long-standing international reputation for scholarship in the field of assessment at the University of Northumbria, particularly its co-leadership of the European Association for Research on Learning and Instruction (EARLI) conferences on assessment, the Northumbria CETL has pioneered a powerful approach to integrating assessment fully within the curriculum, to ensure that assessment is *for* not just *of* learning.

This book interrogates key questions associated with assessment including:

- How can the links between the curriculum and assessment be made truly productive?
- How can students be supported to take seriously and gain a better understanding of the feedback they receive?
- How can assessment be used to motivate learning and channel student behaviours in positive directions?
- How much do students' beliefs about assessment influence their behaviour?
- How can we make assessment tasks more purposive and authentic?
- How can assessment foster personal development and employability?

In proposing some answers to these questions, the authors draw heavily on authentic voices of both students and staff who have worked with the CETL team on projects and research, and these provide the central strength of the volume.

It has been a privilege over the years to work with and alongside the authors and the rest of the CETL team and to recognise the importance of their work. This text will make an invaluable guide for practitioners, quality assurers, university managers and students themselves who wish to better understand the importance of assessment for learning, and it will further scholarship in the field significantly.

I commend the volume to you.

Sally Brown
Emeritus Professor, Leeds Metropolitan University, Adjunct Professor at the University of the Sunshine Coast, Queensland, James Cook University and University of Central Queensland, and Visiting Professor at the University of Plymouth and Liverpool John Moores University

Acknowledgements

Academics whose innovative practice helped inform the examples in this guide include: Elise Alexander, Linda Allin, Mandy Asghar, Victoria Bazin, Peter Beven, Erik Bohemia, Mike Calvert, Gillian Davison, Greta Defeyter, Lesley Fishwick, Mel Gibson, Linda Graham, Jackie Harvey, Junxia Hou, Tim Howarth, Mike Jeffries, Pam Knights, Sue Lampitt, Tony Mellor, Stephen Merry, Catherine Montgomery, Paul Orsmond, Roger Penlington, Ali Pickard, Sue Robson, Alistair Sambell, Kay Sambell, Julie Scanlon, Chris Tuffnell, Delia Wakelin, Howard Wickes, Rosie White.

Particular thanks are due, too, to Sally Brown and Mel Gibson for their invaluable comments on early drafts of the book and to Angelina Wilson for her involvement as CETL research assistant and for helping us to prepare the text.

Introduction

This book is a practical guide to Assessment for Learning (AfL) in Higher Education. We have designed the book specifically to help busy practitioners – including experienced and new lecturers, educational developers, senior management teams, academic support teams, graduate tutors and so on – to put AfL into practice.

The book has been created by three experts in the field of assessment in an attempt to address some of the assessment quandaries that many of us face on a day-to-day basis. The challenges associated with assessment are often referred to by practitioners in the following sorts of ways, as outlined in the quotes below . . .

Voicing the issues

What are your assessment challenges? Perhaps . . .

> *". . . marking, marking, marking! How do I get time to mark everything that comes in – and give my students feedback?"*

> *"How do I answer that student question 'Do we need this for the exam?'"*

> *"How often do I read a good paraphrase of what is in the key texts when I really want to know what the student made of the topic?"*

> *"Why do good and conscientious students fall at assessment hurdles? They don't seem to understand what they are supposed to do."*

> *"Students are always wanting more feedback but I'm not sure that half of them even read it!"*

> *"Students are very dependent, beforehand they want to know exactly what to put into their assignment and afterwards they want to know precisely where they 'lost' marks."*

You may well recognize the assessment challenges referred to above and could, probably, list even more. The aim of this book is to support practitioners who routinely encounter these kinds of issues, but who want to use AfL to improve the situation in ways which promote effective learning. Those new to teaching in Higher Education will find the book an excellent resource as a strong foundation for practice right from the start. More experienced colleagues will find ideas that will endorse and refresh their practice, finding special value in finding new ideas that are not often shared beyond a specific disciplinary community.

How to use this book

The book seeks to support busy practitioners by drawing on up-to-date practice and research in assessment in Higher Education. In it, we intend to share different ways of thinking about assessment and ways of putting them into practice.

Each chapter, like this Introduction, will be opened by a section which voices the issues by expressing some key assessment challenges. The overall idea is that you will recognize the problems, the contexts, and the students, and be able to adopt or adapt to your own situation ideas about possible AfL ways forward.

Having highlighted some key concerns, each chapter then goes on to offer a brief overview of some important and influential theories and debates, based on research and scholarly work about the theory and practice of assessment in Higher Education. This serves to locate some common assessment dilemmas within a broader frame of reference, and briefly explains the thinking behind some of the 'problems', and behind some of the ways forward that are suggested in the name of AfL.

The bulk of each chapter, though, focuses on strategies for putting AfL into practice. Here the aim is to give suggestions for general tactics we can use to design AfL into our courses. Each chapter suggests three broad approaches. These are then illustrated by a number of 'real-life' examples of AfL in practice, drawn from university teachers working in different disciplines and courses. The aim here is to present a rich store of practicable examples, which emphasize the practical application of AfL ideas, in the hope that they offer inspiration for adapting similar approaches in your own context. The examples, presented in text boxes, are loosely based upon the actual practices of colleagues we have worked with, both in our Centre for Excellence in AfL and beyond. We are greatly indebted to the innovators on whose practice these examples are based. The examples we have selected are, however, deliberately brief and presented in a condensed, largely decontextualized format to help them perform this illustrative, thought-provoking function. To that end we acknowledge that we have chosen to foreground certain aspects to highlight key points, so the examples offer broad representations, rather than present a series of detailed, complex or situated case studies which aim for verisimilitude and the nuanced complexities of disciplinary differences.

Towards the end of each chapter we return to visit the prominent issues and challenges once more, in a section which offers a fully worked example of putting AfL into practice. These extended examples are based upon case studies of practice which took place under the auspices of our Centre for Excellence in AfL and which, as a consequence, were fully investigated by independent researchers. These case studies are included because they tend to reveal more of the complexity and detail of AfL. Above all, though, they are offered because they present illustrative quotations from important stakeholders in each instance, namely, the students who were involved. We believe it is always important and often salutary to try to consider students' perspectives on assessment. To that end, the book will often present 'real' students' views – and sometimes staff voices too – gathered as part of our research evidence, which emerge as voices that are threaded throughout the book. Where they appear, direct quotes from students or staff will be presented in italics.

Finally, each chapter closes with a short list of possible discussion points about the pertinent issues underpinning each chapter. The idea here is that they might function as talking points for course teams or groups of colleagues who wish to interrogate their own assessment practices and agree ways of redesigning them, if necessary. Alternatively, they may simply stimulate individual reflection.

The main chapters reflect the six core principles that we have identified in our model of AfL. As a consequence the book is organized around six chapters, which tie into these core principles, and explain and illuminate them. The whole book concludes with a final chapter which presents a manifesto. This aims to share, extend and consider how we might revolutionize assessment practice through a collective intent. The manifesto sketches out a strategic direction for those who are serious about developing AfL. As a public declaration of certain principles and beliefs, our manifesto suggests that AfL is much more than a set of tactics or techniques which can be adopted by teachers, and inflects more towards our view of AfL as a philosophy, which frames learning, and the associated staff–student and student–student relationships, in particular ways.

What is AfL and why is it important?

The term 'Assessment for Learning' or AfL is probably familiar to many. Assessment for Learning has become a popular term and a great deal of activity is centred on it. It features in the learning and teaching strategies of many UK universities and in the policies of the Quality Assurance Agency for Higher Education (QAA) in the UK. In a general sense, it is seen as an important way of improving and promoting student learning and, often, of ameliorating some of the problems and flashpoints that assessment in Higher Education all too commonly represents.

An introduction to Assessment for Learning: the impact of assessment

The most common way that people think about assessment is as a form of testing or evaluation. The aim is to identify what an individual knows and can do, normally describing it in the form of a mark or grade which counts towards an achievement record in an educational context. Identifying what an individual knows and can do is at the heart of all forms of assessment but some features, such as grading, mainly apply to summative assessment. The main purpose of summative assessment is to sum up what each individual achieves and provide this information in a way that is suitable for use beyond the programme, such as access to further stages of education or to employment. A second type of assessment, formative assessment, uses evaluations of what students know and can do in planning future learning activities and to help students to improve. Normally formative assessment informs students about outcomes and gives feedback to students so that they can understand the qualities of their current achievements and how they need to develop further. Assessment for learning encompasses both formative and summative assessment and in some applications the two may be indistinguishable. What underpins AfL is the principle that *all* assessment, within the overall package, should contribute to helping students to learn and to succeed.

Most undergraduate students and also postgraduates on taught Masters programmes experience a learning programme that is permeated throughout with assessment. They experience various types of course work: essays; reports; presentations; alongside end-point exams of various kinds. Assessment requirements and assessment outcomes are given prominence as students progress though their courses. However students are often dissatisfied with an experience that is centred on being assessed and undertaking tasks that have little meaning especially when compared to 'real life'. Typically students say things like:

"You are just churning things out so that you can be marked."

"You're doing an assignment that hundreds of students before you have done."

"What you write just goes into a black hole – nobody reads it."

Academic teachers design assessment that will require students to develop and demonstrate the skills, knowledge and understanding that are genuinely important in the subject. This is the principle of constructive alignment (Biggs and Tang, 2011) However, assessment as designed is not the same as assessment in practice. Students adapt their behaviour according to the assessment environment *as they see it*. There is a large body of empirical research in what is often termed 'approaches to learning' research (e.g. Marton, Hounsell and Entwistle, 1997) which provides us with a good understanding of how assessment impacts on students and their learning. It shows that students act on the basis of their own interpretations of requirements, considered within their individual and social contexts. Examples are students who put off learning then cram for the exam, or students who ignore feedback as irrelevant. The following comments are typical:

"You put your notes to one side after lectures and open them up just before the exam so that you can get as much stuff as possible into your head."

"By the time you get feedback it's hard to make anything of it – you're on to the next thing."

The decisions and assumptions that students individually or collectively make have been said to create a 'hidden curriculum' – a framework which represents what is important, what requirements mean and 'what you really have to do' (Sambell and McDowell, 1998). In this way assessment has an important impact on learning. This is often termed the 'backwash effect' (Biggs, 1996) where even end-point assessment affects the ways in which students go about learning since students often use the assessment system as a key indicator of what it is they are supposed to learn and how they are required to demonstrate their learning. One encouraging implication is that alterations to our assessment designs offer a useful way of positively influencing learning.

Our integrated model of AfL: an holistic approach

Much has been written about AfL, sometimes using alternative terms such as 'assessment as a tool for learning' or 'learning-oriented assessment'. As we have argued, in broad terms, AfL is widely seen as an important way in which to improve and promote student learning. Sometimes, however, AfL is approached in a rather fragmented way, with a narrow focus on one or two pertinent features, and often considering only one aspect of AfL, such as 'feedback'. This fragmented view of AfL can cause practitioners who wish to put AfL into practice to introduce a set of techniques, which they 'drop in' or 'bolt on' to their existing learning, teaching and assessment regimes.

By contrast, our view of AfL is an holistic model – almost like a philosophy. From this standpoint the model of AfL that we have developed represents an overall approach to assessment, rather than a set of techniques which can be 'dropped in'. Our model is based on a set of core conditions, or central principles, derived from research and practice, which underpin effective assessment practice in Higher Education. These can be seen represented in Figure I.1.

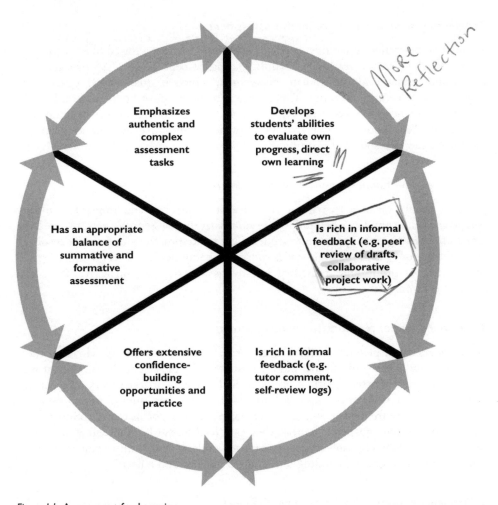

Figure I.1 Assessment for Learning

The six principles are outlined as follows:

1 Authentic assessment

When we assess student learning we must focus on what it is we really want students to achieve and avoid being driven too much by what is 'easy to assess' or the ways in which assessment has always been done in the subject. The content and methods of assessment should emphasize authenticity and complexity rather than reproduction of knowledge and reductive measurement. If we assess the genuine article we are also more likely to engage students because they can see that the tasks they are being asked to do are meaningful. Authentic assessment promotes much more active and student-led approaches to learning.

2 Balancing summative and formative assessment

Summative assessment must be carried out effectively but not allowed to dominate and drive the whole of the teaching, learning and assessment process. An over-focus on marks and grades leads to student engagement which is qualitatively different to engagement in genuine learning. Time, space and energy must be found to infuse the student experience with formative assessment and reduce the dominance of summative assessment. We should also seek ways in which summative as well as formative assessment can be a source of learning.

3 Creating opportunities for practice and rehearsal

Students should be able to try out their learning, practise and improve, building competence and confidence before they are summatively assessed. We need to avoid the situation where the first opportunity students get to do something and receive feedback and guidance on it is in the high-stakes context of being marked. It is possible to build in a variety of group and individual low-stakes activities within active and social learning environments.

4 Designing formal feedback to improve learning

Well-designed and planned feedback is essential to students' learning. However there are limitations in the conventional ways that universities provide feedback; often it is in the form of tutor-written feedback on individual students' marked work. We need to address the limitations of this approach by building in other kinds of formal feedback from tutors, more frequently and at earlier stages, so that, for instance, comments are received before the end-point, so that they can 'feed forward' (Hounsell et al., 2008) directly into refinements and revisions of future work. It is also important to draw on other sources of feedback including self- and peer review and reflection.

5 Designing opportunities for informal feedback

Active, collaborative and dialogic approaches to teaching, learning and assessment bring with them an intrinsic supply of feedback to benefit student learning. As students work together, discuss ideas and methods, and interact with teachers they can test out their own ideas and skills, see how other students go about things and begin to absorb the standards and requirements of their subjects. This type of feedback can also be generated through participation beyond the formal curriculum.

6 Developing students as self-assessors and effective lifelong learners

If students are to be active in their own learning they need to be able to make decisions for themselves, decide what approaches to take and evaluate their own progress. There should be opportunities for students to be active participants in assessment processes and develop assessment literacy. Ultimately, as graduates and professionals, students need to take over for themselves much of the assessment that lecturers currently do for them but be skilled at drawing on the resources of workplace colleagues to support their ongoing development.

How can the AfL framework help practitioners?

The principles have been extracted from evidence-based research and the vast body of published work on assessment in Higher Education, which busy teachers seldom have the luxury of reading. The idea is that, in distilling the key principles underpinning effective assessment and feedback practices, the model acts as a framework to be used by people who want to design good assessment and promote good learning. Indeed, our model has been used to guide the development of assessment practices across a wide range of subjects within our own university. Here, individuals and course teams have used our model of AfL as a conceptual framework which prompted them to consider addressing a whole set of interlinked AfL practices. Each principle or condition offered practitioners a set of issues or questions to consider in relation to the student experience of assessment. The evaluation and analysis of existing practices then generated new ways forward with the redesign of learning, teaching and assessment environments, so that the principles helped inform and guide the development of practice. Where assessment practices were re-engineered within our university, extensive case study research was undertaken to investigate the student response and the impacts on learning of AfL approaches. In this development we needed to be particularly aware of the resource constraints and the impact of large classes in many Higher Education contexts.

To enable readers to use the model, each chapter explains the thinking behind the interrelated elements of our model of AfL, and, most importantly, offers a range of practical strategies for putting the principles into practice, with a wealth of concrete examples. This is because, in our experience, whilst many lecturers endorse AfL principles, they often find it difficult to implement them in the current HE context. In this way the book tries to go beyond a statement of AfL principles, and seeks to illustrate ways in which they can be implemented despite sometimes challenging circumstances. It is worth re-emphasising, though, that rather than offering a set of tips or strategies, we offer the principles as aspects that are vital to consider. The six key principles that constitute effective AfL that we have identified need to be considered in combination in order to develop AfL environments. In practice, they overlap and inter-relate in an holistic way and are presented separately simply for convenience and clarity, to help academics think about and identify ways of improving their practice. In fact, they might best be thought of as different lenses through which to look at our assessment practices. So whilst particular applications of AfL may foreground one or two of the key aspects, the others also need to be kept in mind. Taken as a whole, they aim to promote worthwhile, long-lasting student learning, encouraging and supporting learners to take responsibility for, and exercise control over, their own learning. Accordingly it is important to bear in mind that this is not a menu from which to choose only one dish but a way of thinking about assessment that enables teaching teams to ensure that everything is working together and pulling in the same direction in support of student learning.

Theories and debates

Views of learning and the importance of learning communities

Anyone starting out in the use of AfL soon realizes that it is about more than a set of techniques that can simply be added into conventional approaches to teaching, learning and assessment. Minor adaptations to assessment practices can only go so far. Our model of AfL foregrounds the active involvement of students in the assessment process. AfL needs to operate within learning environments that are characterized by collaboration, social interaction, peer learning and methods such as enquiry-based or research-based learning. We believe that university, disciplinary and classroom assessment cultures play a major part in supporting or impeding learning. Lecturers can influence student learning by fostering physical, virtual and metaphoric AfL spaces that encourage active learning and the development of learning communities. AfL approaches accompany a necessary shift in learning relationships, with students becoming part of effective learning communities, involved in co-construction of knowledge, rather than passive recipients of teachers' knowledge. From our perspective, students benefit from encouragement to engage individually with learning activities and subject matter. We will argue that assessment can play a major role here. But students also benefit from engagement through participation and the development of identity. Pedagogic and assessment practices can be reconfigured to promote this, too.

Ideas about assessment relate very closely to ideas about learning. What we decide to assess indicates *what* we value in learning – the subject content, skills, qualities and so on. This is intrinsically linked to *how* we test or evaluate learning because assessment needs to enable the targeted learning and abilities to be demonstrated. Our integrated model of AfL is based within the social perspective on how people learn. This is often associated with the work of Vygotsky and work on communities of practice by Lave and Wenger (1991). The fundamental idea is that learning takes place in social and collaborative settings. Participation within a social group is not just an option for learning, as in conventional group work in HE, but essential. This way of learning is often compared to the learning of an apprentice who learns by contributing to the work of a community, acquiring knowledge and skills from senior colleagues, peers and others and, importantly, developing an identity as a practitioner.

These ideas have been translated into Higher Education contexts in the form of learning communities. Though there are different interpretations, it is almost always the case that learning communities incorporate active and collaborative learning activities within the curriculum and classroom. In Higher Education particular value is placed on disciplinary or subject-based communities: ' . . . a community focussed on academic content . . . allows [students] to further develop their identity and discover their voice as well as to integrate what they are learning into their world view and other academic and social experiences' (Zhao and Kuh, 2004: 117). Learning communities may also be seen to address perceived problems of isolation, lack of engagement and poor study practices amongst students, as proposed by Hughes (2011). However she regards knowledge-based identities, fostering engagement with academic knowledge, as the most important in generating learning.

The concept of 'student engagement' is closely related to that of learning communities and is widely used in the UK. In a recent substantial review of student engagement Trowler and Trowler (2010) define the term as fundamentally about student investment of time, effort and interest in their learning. They draw on the work of Chickering and Gamson (1987) to suggest key features of academic programmes that are positively linked to student engagement. Social and community-based features are prominent including: student–staff contact; active learning methods; prompt feedback; respect for diverse learning styles; and co-operation amongst students. They also report (2010: 12) that students who are unprepared academically benefit more than others from approaches that engage them in a learning community. Wiliam (2011) regards learning communities in the classroom as essential for formative assessment so that teachers and students can participate in clarifying learning intentions and success criteria. Furthermore, he suggests that participative classrooms can benefit from 'activating learners as instrumental resources for one another' (2011: 12). From a different perspective, Boekaerts and Minnaert (2003) use the term 'powerful learning environments' to denote active and participative approaches. They claim that these environments are extremely positive in engaging students and promoting better learning because they meet students' basic psychological needs for a sense of competence, autonomy and satisfying relationships.

The learning component of our model of AfL recognizes the emotional and affective dimensions of student learning and significance of communities, engagement and the development of learner identities. This is founded on a broad and complex understanding of how students learn which moves beyond the realm of the purely cognitive to acknowledge that learning is also a profoundly reflexive, social and emotional phenomenon.

Where did our model of AfL come from?

Our approach to AfL is evidence-based and founded on researching the experiences, perceptions and achievements of students and staff so that we know how assessment is working. In 2004 an interdisciplinary team of academics at Northumbria University made a bid for centre for excellence status to the Higher Education Funding Council for England (HEFCE). This bid was supported by more than ten years of research and development in assessment and, particularly, the impacts of assessment on student learning. We were awarded a Centre for Excellence in Assessment for Learning, known as CETL AfL. We developed the model as a basis for developing practice across the institution. The CETL AfL has enabled us to work with many lecturers and students both within our own university and beyond. Our approach to AfL helps to bridge the gap between theory and practice by highlighting some common issues and challenges which face practitioners and students, offering useful ways forward.

Chapter 1

Designing authentic assessment

The principle of authenticity is vitally important when it comes to designing effective Assessment for Learning environments. In this chapter we will explain why authenticity is so important for us to consider, so that assessment means more to students than just jumping through hoops.

This chapter covers:

- designing assessment tasks to promote deep, complex and worthwhile learning;
- creating tasks which students experience as meaningful and relevant in their own right;
- assessment which helps students develop a sense of 'really doing' the subject;
- assessment which students feel relates in some way to the real world;
- tasks which offer students a sense of personal involvement;
- challenges and issues in creating authentic assessment;
- strategies to promote learning communities via authentic assessment.

Voicing the issues

Karl is a second-year student who enjoys his electronic engineering course. He seems to relish the challenges that the degree offers and responds to most tasks with enthusiasm. His eagerness, though, wanes when he talks about the ways he studies a module when he knows his work will be assessed purely by an end-point exam.

Karl feels that exams are, as he puts it, unfair, because he thinks they don't give him a chance to show what he knows and how far he can apply ideas. Instead he feels that he must simply try to remember a set of facts and figures which he must recall when his lecturers demand. He explains:

> "Exams are not a normal way of working. Actually, when you think about it, they're rather pointless – they just say whether you're having a hard time remembering or an easy time remembering. So you revise in a way that means you just think 'Let me remember this for a short while'. You try and cram for an exam. When I know I have got an exam on a module I revise by writing down all the information I have to learn on post-it notes, which I stick up round the flat. The house gets covered with them! It's shallow learning which doesn't stick. Actually, you try to forget it before you take the next exam, because you don't want to get the two papers muddled up.

But it's odd, because normally, if you were in a working environment, say, and someone came to you with a problem to solve, you wouldn't necessarily have to know the stuff, and remember it, there and then. You'd say: 'Hang on a minute, I see there's an issue, so I'll go away and find out more about it, get to the bottom of what's going on here, and come back to you with a solution once I've talked to people and done some research'. That's the way of working you might use in a project-type assignment, where your lecturers ask you to work on something in a more realistic or relevant way. But not in an exam."

The example above illustrates one way in which, unfortunately, assessment can be detrimental to learning. The way that Karl talks about how he approaches learning when he knows he faces an end-point exam demonstrates the harmful influence that summative assessment can exert on learning. Whatever his lecturers may think, Karl's preconceptions and ideas about what an exam *really* tests, however ill-judged they may be, cause him to approach his studies in superficial or damaging ways. His comments about deliberately setting out to achieve 'shallow learning' exemplify this. So whilst his lecturers may argue that the exams they set are not simple memory tests, the fact remains that Karl's beliefs about exams exert a powerful influence over the sort of learning he sets out to achieve on specific modules. There are hints though, that when he faces a different assessment tasks such as a project his perceptions may be quite different.

One of the important issues that Karl raises is that, from his point of view, exams simply do not represent the sorts of tasks and activities he feels he would ever be asked to do in the workplace. Instead, they seem to be artificial, hoop-jumping exercises which he undertakes purely to accrue credit – in the form of marks. In this instance Karl feels assessment is somehow contrived, or false, rather than offering a relevant and meaningful insight into the sorts of skills, qualities and dispositions which will serve him well in the longer term. This all suggests that if we wish to promote lasting, worthwhile learning, we may need to think carefully about designing assessment. As we can see from Karl's comments, whether we like it or not, the assignments we set powerfully frame what students do, how they spend their time and, to a large degree, how they view the whole business of learning at university (Brown and Knight, 1994).

Theories and debates

There are substantial learning benefits to be gained by rethinking and redesigning summative assessment tasks and processes with a view to promoting and fostering deep, sustainable learning. Many researchers suggest it is vital that we carefully rethink summative assessment to ensure, as far as possible, it promotes positive messages about the type of learning we require. For example, Nicol (2009a: 5) advises that assessment tasks should 'engage students in deep rather than surface learning' and 'promote students' productive engagement in learning'. Often carefully designed 'authentic' assessment (Torrance, 1994) is regarded as one of the most powerful means we have to foster students' productive, worthwhile approaches to learning. For this reason the chapter aims to suggest strategies which help promote appropriate student learning by drawing attention to the design and development of authentic assessment tasks, arguing that we can make learning happen in productive ways if students find our assessment tasks inherently meaningful and relevant.

From the 1970s, research studies began to indicate that students' perceptions of the demands of assessment influenced their approaches to learning more heavily than teaching did. Snyder (1970), for instance, explored the ways in which the formal curriculum emphasized high-order educational goals, such as independent thinking, analysis, problem-solving ability and originality, but from the student viewpoint, assessment procedures often suggested that memorizing facts and theories were what was really needed to achieve success. Because of this, Ramsden (2003: 68) warns us that 'unsuitable assessment methods impose irresistible pressures on students to take the wrong approach to learning tasks'. In a similar vein, Gibbs and Simpson (2004: 25) draw attention to the influence of the design of assessment tasks on 'the quality of student engagement', highlighting the dangers of assessment designs which embody 'low level demands' and result in 'surface approaches to learning'.

We need to remain acutely sensitive to the possible 'backwash' effect that our assessment designs have on learning (Watkins, Dahlin and Eckholm, 2005). Higher Education claims, as a rule, to value and foster complex learning (Sadler, 2009), with an emphasis on helping students to integrate knowledge, develop sophisticated cognitive abilities and develop their lateral, imaginative, critical thinking skills. Consequently we need to consider how far our formal assessment tasks really encourage students to perceive, value and aspire to develop these qualities. Our own research (Sambell and McDowell, 1998; Sambell, McDowell and Brown, 1997) indicated that, from students' viewpoints, 'innovative' or 'alternative' assessments seemed to endorse deep approaches to learning. The issue of authenticity was particularly important to students and is the theme which is pursued in this chapter. Authenticity implies the use of activities that are inherently meaningful, interesting, relevant, and have long-term value. In our research, if students felt that they were required to undertake assessment tasks that seemed intrinsically useful and worthwhile, for example where they sought to communicate, discuss or defend their ideas, then they were more likely to invest effort in genuine, deep and lasting learning, rather than simply going through the motions, reproducing whatever information or answers they assumed their lecturers wanted to hear or see.

The concept of authenticity is, however, a relative one (Brown, Collins and Duguid, 1989; Collins, Brown and Newman, 1989). Authenticity can be seen as faithfulness to the discipline or subject area. From this perspective, we might try to design assessment to promote students' purposeful engagement with the subject matter and the methods of enquiry that are valued in particular academic disciplines. If, for example, we want our students to develop disciplinary identities and immerse themselves in ways of being, knowing and seeing which start to emulate the kinds of things that disciplinary experts do, we need to design assessment to be authentic in these kinds of ways. Here the sorts of questions we might ask about our assessment tasks include:

- How far do the tasks we set encourage students to genuinely understand the subject, so that they form a sense of thinking and practising (Meyer and Land, 2005) like an engineer, biologist, geographer, historian and so on, as opposed to juggling formulae or performing tasks in an isolated, formulaic or unconnected way? Ramsden (2003: 39) suggests that we may find students involved in 'imitation' rather than 'real' subjects, that is, learning processes which are only about passing tests and completing assignments with no personal relevance or bearing on the world their studies are supposed to explain.

- How far do the tasks make students feel they are really being required to act as a developing participant in the disciplinary community, as opposed to feeling they are being asked simply to be a student being made to produce an essay, or a poster, almost regardless of the disciplinary context?

Authenticity can also be seen in terms of applying learning to, or learning within, real-world contexts or practices beyond the academy. It is probably no surprise that much of the research work on authenticity to date has been conducted in professional education such as nursing (e.g. Gulikers, 2006), where the links between formal study, assessment and the real world of professional practice are explicit and clearly foregrounded. Questions about authenticity are, for instance, self-evidently of particular concern in competence-based assessment when the intention is to measure the skills and knowledge against a prescribed professional standard. In these kinds of situations any mismatch between what is taught and assessed in Higher Education and the skills required for the world of work is clearly problematic (Biemans et al., 2004). For instance, if unrealistic and de-contextualized settings are used to assess learning, so that the situations confronting students in assessment are not actually similar to those found embodied in the complexity of most workplaces, then learners' capacity for professional practice may not be appropriately developed.

However, as Boud and Hawke (2004) point out, the issues surrounding authenticity and competence-based assessment related to professional practice are undoubtedly wider and more challenging. This is largely because of the unintended side-effects of assessment tasks which students see as inauthentic. Boud and Hawke point out, for instance, that whilst some competence-based assessment tasks might well serve the purpose of validating particular skills and competences, they might actually also unintentionally neglect, or even militate against, others: most specifically, those that are useful for the longer term beyond graduation. For example:

- Assessment tasks might emphasize problem *solution* rather than problem *formulation*. However, professional practice and life in a complex and ever-changing world typically requires graduates to work in ill-defined areas of knowledge or constantly changing contexts, so needs people who can recognize and identify problems as situations shift, rather than people who only know how to work to specific and rigid rules.
- Learners might become encouraged to look to others (their assessors) to make judgements rather than developing their own ability to judge their own learning outcomes. This can be perceived as a problem because, if this is the case, learners do not develop the evaluative independence required of future work and life situations.
- Assessment tasks in universities often place a premium on individual achievement, thereby inadvertently implying that all collaboration is cheating. This might undermine learners in developing the capacity to work cooperatively. However, the ability to work effectively with and for others is a vital attribute in many 'real-life' scenarios (Bowden et al., 2000).

These, and other related issues have more general application to a range of university courses than might at first be supposed, across the whole spectrum, including students studying academic disciplines and not only those studying on professional programmes In all cases it is important whether students believe the assessment tasks being set on their university courses are authentic and realistic, or inauthentic, artificial and relatively meaningless beyond the immediate context of being tested and gaining marks.

To address these sorts of issues, researchers often suggest there is a need to re-engineer university assessment tasks with questions of authenticity firmly in mind. It is important, though, to recognize they are not advocating the total abandonment of competency standards or competency assessment. Nor are they asserting that certification is unimportant. Instead, they urge lecturers to *augment* their current assessment practices in order to develop more authentic approaches which will support the processes of learning that students need beyond the point of graduation. Boud (2000) calls this 'sustainable assessment', which he defines as 'assessment that meets the needs of the present without compromising the ability of students to meet their own future learning needs' (151).

This all means that, as far as possible, we must try to design assessment to foster the kinds of attitudes and dispositions, as well as the knowledge and skills, which learners need for the variety of situations they will be confronted with throughout their lives. So, from this viewpoint, authentic assessment might usefully be viewed as a matter of offering students opportunities which clearly signal to them the value and importance of developing as learners. In fact, Boud *et al.* (2010) argue that the first question we should actually ask of our assessment practice is: 'Does assessment do what we want it to do in terms of promoting the kinds of learning that are desired for the longer term?' This chapter argues that it is vital to think deeply about this question and consider how far assessment helps or hinders the promotion of a range of graduate attributes. This might mean, for example, designing assessment experiences which actively support the development of attributes which include but also go beyond the disciplinary expertise, content or technical knowledge that has traditionally formed the core of most university courses (Barrie, 2007).

Finally, assessment is arguably most productive in terms of promoting genuine, valued learning if it fosters individuals' own interests and concerns. There is a world of difference between students feeling they are doing an assessment because they are required to slavishly conduct an activity for the sole reason that their teachers require it, and one in which they feel a sense of ownership and responsibility. Assessments which feel meaningful and authentic in these sorts of ways can support high levels of motivation and improved educational outcomes, rather than assessments in which students feel that everyone's response must look the same and that require a routine, formulaic approach. Indeed, Davison's research (2011), which explored authenticity in the context of AfL as part of our CETL research programme, indicated that it was important for learning to become linked to students' personal interests or issues that the individual had identified for themselves. Furthermore, according to Nicol (2009a) a sense of personal involvement might also be linked to a student's capacity to choose, say, some elements of the topic studied and the method of assessment. This kind of ownership is most often found at undergraduate level in relation to the honours dissertation but we suggest that it can also infuse earlier stages of degree study.

In summary, AfL, then, places considerable importance on explicitly creating assessment environments which encourage students to engage in meaningful, worthwhile learning experiences. The issues that this chapter addresses, then, are about ways in which we can design assessment to promote student engagement by trying to offer authentic learning and assessment experiences.

Putting it into practice

There are many ways in which academic teachers have tried to make assessment feel more worthwhile and meaningful to students. They may try to develop the ways in which students see and experience the assessment tasks themselves. This might be done explicitly to challenge students' preconceptions about assessment: encouraging them to move away from simply reproducing knowledge. One way of doing this is to develop assessment tasks that overtly make clear the requirement to engage in deep, active approaches to learning. Another way of encouraging students to learn through and from assessment is the design of tasks which link clearly to the real world. Finally, another approach is to design authentic assessment practices to harness students' personal interests and concerns, for instance, by basing activities in students' everyday lives, to engage, motivate and sustain learning.

This section of the chapter highlights three broad approaches to putting authenticity into practice. These are:

- putting it into practice by enhancing students' perceptions of the meaning and relevance of assessment;
- putting it into practice by drawing on and linking to the real world;
- putting it into practice by developing a sense of personal engagement.

Under each of these broad approaches, we have selected a range of different examples to show some of the diverse ways in which assessment can be engineered to offer a range of authentic experiences to students. These examples, of course, revolve around different concepts of authenticity and complex learning.

Putting it into practice by enhancing students' perceptions of the meaning and relevance of assessment

Using assessment tasks to promote deep approaches to learning

Trowler and Trowler (2010: 14) in a recent Higher Education Academy review, concluded that: 'Individual student engagement in educationally *purposive* activities leads to more favourable educational outcomes' (our emphasis). So far in this chapter we have been suggesting that one way of engaging students in purposeful activity and heightening their appreciation of the need to take a deep approach to learning is to design 'authentic' approaches to assessment. These can help combat damaging attitudes to assessment, such as those displayed by Karl at the start of the chapter. From this perspective, students need to see the value of what they are being asked to do in an assignment and perceive its importance to learning. Above all, they need to be convinced that what they are doing in terms of assessment is worthwhile, even when they find it demanding and challenging.

Students' approaches to learning and, importantly, assessment, are significantly influenced by their perception of the meaning and relevance of the activities they are asked to undertake. Earlier in the chapter, we highlighted the ways in which students like Karl often view exams with high degrees of scepticism. This can happen, too, with traditional essays. Whilst lecturers who set essays typically envisage them as highly complex learning activities, unfortunately some students see them quite differently. The following viewpoint expresses a student perception that we have heard frequently: *"In essays, all you have to do is, basically, go to the library and copy down the information in a different language."* It is important to recognize, though, that in overall terms, the important issue we are addressing here is not what the specific assessment method is, but, most crucially, what the *consequences* of using it in a particular way are in terms of learning.

One problem that frequently occurs with traditional forms of assessment, like the essay, is that students misperceive, undervalue or struggle to address the implied audience of the assessment format. In addition, they often feel when they are writing assignments or exam responses simply for tutors to mark that their work *"just goes into a black hole"*. In interviews, they frequently express the view that *"no one really reads your assignments, only a lecturer"*. In these instances the backwash message is that writing for assessment has little to do with communicating ideas, making connections or developing a voice or a stance in relation to a body of knowledge. Instead it seems a rather pointless, or, worse, painfully repetitive exercise in which students feel forced to demonstrate a restrictive, limited and repetitive set of qualities which keep getting assessed over and over again during their time at university. Some focus on what they regard as skills to the neglect of knowledge or understanding: *"there are people on my course who always do better than me simply because they are better writers – they might not know any more than I do"*.

Furthermore, many inexperienced students adopt surface approaches to learning because they think that is what is required. Deane and Borg (2011: 28) argue, for instance, that students often 'think that academics want them to reproduce – as accurately as possible – what they have learned from their lectures and assigned readings'. Most university marking schemes, however, in fact reflect tutors' desire for an informed contribution that will build on existing knowledge and demonstrate independent thinking. The question is: how can we minimize the gap in perception about what approach to learning is really required?

The simple act of specifying a 'real' audience for assessment can be a powerful way to improve learning, by prompting students to see that they are being asked to develop a stance, communicate and explain ideas and genuinely master subject knowledge, rather than just produce work for someone to mark. If students form a sense of addressing (or even interacting with) a specified audience that they perceive is meaningful, they begin to realize that they need to find a range of relevant sources and throw light on the topic, so they can have something worthwhile to say. It often repositions learners, so that they see themselves as experts in the making and people who get to grips with knowledge and use it, rather than thinking that lecturers do not want to hear their ideas. The following example illustrates this.

Designing leaflets about a complex topic for a lay audience

A social science lecturer was keen to enable her students to enjoy their learning and become enthused and engaged with the material under discussion. Wanting them to learn to communicate and discuss their learning more effectively, she had previously experimented with various group projects to provide a social context in which to communicate ideas, but had struggled to make them work when it came to formal assessment. Instead, she decided to experiment with new assessment formats which maintained an individual focus.

To replace the traditional essay-based assignment, she asked her students to produce leaflets for a lay audience, that is, one with no expertise in the academic area under discussion. She explained that their leaflets needed to convey complex concepts in a clear and accessible manner, but without watering down or mis-representing the challenges underpinning the subject matter. They also needed to highlight the possible implications for the person reading the leaflet, in terms of decisions and action they might take in light of the information and in view of the research findings being presented. The students' leaflets were submitted for grading together with a critique, this time for an academic audience, in which each student was required to explain her/his reasoning for including particular pieces of information.

The lecturer found that the students appeared to tackle the assessment with enthusiasm and read round effectively in order to undertake the task. The leaflets were interesting to mark and the accompanying commentaries gave her useful and revealing insights into the level of complexity with which a student thought about and viewed the material as a whole. Students felt that they had to under-stand the material more fully in order to communicate it clearly. They also commented on the ways in which this way of conveying information was more realistic: they could envisage being asked to produce this kind of work in the future, whereas they felt they were unlikely to be asked to write a formal academic essay in most workplace situations.

Using assessment to position students as active learners

For students to gain a sense of ownership in their learning, assessment needs to position students as active learners (Boud *et al.*, 2010). However, some students can feel very intimidated by the requirement to write in academic styles and formats. It takes time to master the skill of expressing one's ideas in formal academic prose, especially given the use of the passive voice and the air of formal debate that underpin the rhetorical essay (Knights, 2006). Instead of viewing this format as a vehicle for expressing complex learning, as intended, some students 'hide' behind the essay, mimicking academic writing conventions by regurgitating large chunks of reading, loosely strung together.

By contrast, the opportunity to create something 'useful' or 'applicable', especially if it is developed in an ongoing, supportive process, can help stimulate students into developing a position and an understanding which they then seek to express. The following example demonstrates this.

Preparing a glossary

In a module on which undergraduates were conducting observations of practice in social work, students were asked to create a glossary of terms. The glossary became an element of both the students' learning and the module assessment. To compile their glossary students were required individually to select twenty academic terms from a long list provided by the lecturer. For each term the students were asked to provide a brief definition, with the sources clearly identified. In addition, where possible, they were also invited to supply evidence of their personal appreciation of the relevance of each term. This might include examples from observations, examples from reading or notes drawn from dialogue with peers.

This assessment format first encouraged students to research concise, appropriate meanings for the terms listed. This explicitly focused them on comparing different theoretical viewpoints as they investigated possible meanings for each. This helped position them as active interpreters, rather than passive recipients of others' meaning and helped them to pinpoint areas of debate and contestation. Second, the requirement to provide illustrative material helped them make connections between abstract theory and the real world embodied in their observations in practice settings. This encouraged them actively to apply ideas to the complex situations of professional practice.

Students felt that this assessment format encouraged them to read more articles and journals than they usually would. They also talked of engaging more fully in analysing practice in the settings they visited, consciously looking to relate theory to practice. Often they showed their glossaries and illustrative material to other students to gauge if they 'worked'. This, in effect, all helped the students to realize that they were expected to do more than simply summarize, repeat or just quote from other people's definitions. Instead, they needed to engage in active reading and build on academic sources to think critically, consider implications and look for reasons in relation to forms of academic discourse.

Using assessment to emulate complex disciplinary ways of thinking and practising

Authentic assessment tasks which offer students genuine, hands-on experience of participation in the subject, perhaps experiences similar to those of researchers in a discipline, can offer a valuable way of fostering complex learning. Often this can best be achieved if students feel that assessment tasks demand a need to understand material, look for integrating principles and question ideas in an extended fashion over time, rather than respond in a formulaic manner or write to a prescribed recipe at the last minute.

From this viewpoint it is important to design the content and methods of assessment to emphasize authenticity and complexity in an holistic, embedded way. It could involve, for instance, students working, perhaps in groups, on open-ended problems or projects. Here course designs might seek to develop a series of fully integrated authentic formative learning tasks which help students work gradually towards an authentic summative assessment task. One way of doing this might be to set a realistic disciplinary problem which is open-ended and ill-defined, so that it clearly requires students to define the tasks and sub-tasks needed to complete it successfully. According to Herrington, Reeves and Oliver (2002), authentic activities need to allow competing solutions and diversity of outcome. Here it is especially helpful if assessment products are viewed by students as valuable in their own right, such as data to contribute to a wider research programme, rather than simply being viewed as a preparation for something else.

Baxter Magolda (2001) sees involving students in research and research-like activities as supporting them in developing more sophisticated 'ways of knowing' or conceptions of knowledge, which increase their confidence as learners and heighten their capability for independent thinking. As the following examples highlight, in some subject areas assessment can be made more authentic by requiring students to gather and analyse research data that they collect, share and report.

Working with authentic data

In a course on Ecology, second-year undergraduates were involved on a field trip to gather data from a local farm, where they compiled data about the soil animals and then wrote up the details for an individual assessment. A report, collaboratively prepared by staff and students, was also written up for the farm, so that the work had relevance both to the students themselves and the farm.

In another course on community sports development, students were required to participate in 'real-world' action research. They were asked to work, in small groups, with external organizations and agree a project focused on the evaluation of a community support programme in terms of its effectiveness. This was fed back to the organization as well as being written up as an academic assignment.

Designing assessment to promote hands-on experience of study

Arguably it is important that students learn to develop a sense of 'really doing the subject', so that they engage in complex learning, rather than simply (and unthinkingly) performing calculations or other procedures because they have been told to, or because they have been drilled to respond to particular questions in a particular way. Being required to tackle a project for the purposes of assessment can encourage students to actively explore and seek out new evidence for themselves, rather than waiting for the lecturer to provide all their information (Kahn and O'Rourke, 2005).

In this way project work or enquiry-based learning can help students feel that they are immersed in the ways of thinking and practising of a particular discipline. From this perspective, learning can then become based around a series of authentic learning activities which comprise complex formative tasks to be investigated by students over a sustained period of time. These can be engineered to provide the opportunity for students to examine the task from different perspectives, using a variety of resources. Students can also benefit from working together on such tasks, as in the following example, so that they learn to participate in discussions with peers and subject-specialists in disciplinary communities of practice.

Working in teams on real-world scenarios

In one example, engineering students were engaged in authentic tasks in the form of a real-world engineering problem. They worked in groups to discuss high-level issues and ideas relating to the design of communication systems. They were then required to design a particular element of a system, namely a Wi-Fi link, between two buildings of the university. They were asked to cost the project and plan how this communication system would be implemented in the specific context of the university and produce a report that described the system and its implementation.

Students enjoyed being involved in an authentic task, as this helped them see the point of abstract theoretical material by situating it in a context which made sense to them. They also felt that, despite the challenges, working in teams on the project replicated the real-world challenges they were likely to face as engineers of the future.

In subjects that do not have a professional or immediately vocational focus, though, it can be even more challenging to design assessment to promote complex learning and foster a sense of thinking and practising like a disciplinary expert. Because so much assessment in analytic–discursive subject areas involves essay-writing, there are useful possibilities in assessing students in other ways to promote authentic learning, as the following example suggests.

Bringing assessment off the page

An Art History module required students to develop an art exhibition on the Web for summative assessment. It required them to link 'practice' and 'theory' by presenting an interpretation through the medium of an exhibition, which they called a 'virtual gallery'. Students developed their virtual exhibitions with enthusiasm and valued the opportunity to choose an artist, period or style that interested them. They also enjoyed the chance to present their exhibition in their own way, which encouraged them to communicate their learning, adopt an independent stance in relation to the material and develop their analytical (rather than descriptive) abilities. The process of learning and communicating understanding stimulated student learning and engagement. The final submission of the gallery for summative assessment was seen as an opportunity and the whole approach as something 'worthwhile' rather than just a means of accumulating marks.

Putting it into practice by drawing on and linking to the real world

Linking learning to practice: learning in and through communities

Boud (2009) argues that it is useful to use practice from the professional world, to inform the ways we design and organize assessment to make it more authentic. This might require us to redesign assessment tasks so that they more clearly link to practice-like situations. This might, for instance, help focus attention on learning which has a clear point of reference beyond the artefacts of the course. Further, it may mean acknowledging that any decisions that are taken by participants have consequences for others which extend beyond their own individual learning. Boud asserts that it is vital that assessment must move away from an exclusive focus on the individual if it is to prepare students for learning in the longer term, beyond university. Given that practice occurs in a social context, he argues, 'it is necessary that the skill of involving others is an intrinsic part of learning and assessment. Assessment with and for others needs far greater emphasis in courses' (2009: 42).

Indeed, the concept of authentic learning first became popular in learning theories such as situated learning and cognitive apprenticeship (Brown, Collins and Duguid, 1989; Collins, Brown and Newman, 1989) that focus on learning in meaningful contexts in which people learn by working closely together in particular communities. Lave and Wenger (1991) also placed emphasis on learning through participation in authentic activities. This includes the process of 'legitimate peripheral participation', a process whereby a novice's involvement in the activity of a learning community develops their understanding and knowledge and enables them to develop fuller participation and membership. In university programmes assessment can be designed to encourage productive shared participation in authentic tasks, with similar benefits, as the following example suggests.

Students as learning mentors

In this example final-year librarianship students were trained to become learning mentors as part of a module. The training enabled them to offer support and guidance to first-year undergraduate students from a degree programme in a different disciplinary area from their own. Working in a practice-like way with the less experienced students afforded the librarianship students with a real-life experience of providing learner support. It required them to analyse and respond to user needs: aspects which routinely underpin professional practice in their own subject area.

The students were assessed on three elements of the mentorship process. First, they carried out and submitted their user needs analysis of their first-year mentees' requirements. The second part of the assessment took the form of a nine-week mentoring plan. In this students included descriptions and analyses of activities they had devised and implemented during the mentoring process. The final element of the assessment was a personal reflection on the process of acting as a mentor. This allowed students to reflect on the module and on the issues and challenges they faced during their own mentoring activities.

The students valued what they saw as the real-life experience of being mentors. They highly rated the opportunity to actually apply the theories of learning and information use that were examined and investigated throughout the module. Being able to contextualize the theory and discuss what they were doing with their own group of learners provided experiences and insights that deepened their appreciation of what was involved in doing their subject. Lecturers also felt this approach to assessment would help students with building their curriculum vitae, and would stand them in good stead when they eventually entered the workplace.

Interestingly, the librarianship students also commented on the immense satisfaction they felt when their mentees understood something or became confident with their referencing or information search techniques. This afforded students with a different sense of authenticity – a sense of personal satisfaction and the genuine feeling that their work was having some impact and making a positive difference to other people.

Addressing real issues in the workplace to highlight the need to develop long-term dispositions, skills and competences

It is important that students recognize the point of the learning they do while they are in HE. One way of trying to highlight this is to involve practitioners, or other people from beyond the university, in students' learning. For example, visits from employers or practitioners can enhance students' sense of the relevance of what they are learning in university, as the following example illustrates.

Involving employers in assessment episodes

In this example, part-time students on a Business Studies module focused on corporate management were all working in organizations. Assignments were linked to the topic of workplace improvement. Managers from the organizations were invited to come and talk to the students about authentic problems in the workplace. Students were then asked to demonstrate their learning by suggesting possible solutions to the problems and presenting these back to the practising manager. At the end of a module students prepared a poster exhibition and took their posters back to their individual organizations to disseminate their ideas for improvement in the workplace.

The lecturers felt that having staff come in from organizations to talk to students, providing real issues and problems for the students to research and address, drove home the relevance of the module and enhanced the learning experience of the students involved. It meant the students had to self-evaluate and monitor their own learning whilst bearing employers' perspectives in mind, giving a practice-like feel to the content being studied.

Working on authentic cases

Some subject areas lend themselves readily to clear and explicit links to workplace situations. In these contexts, simulations can be employed to drive home to students the relevance of their studies. Indeed, the internet and the growth of technology and simulation technologies have resulted in an interest in and expansion of games and simulations linked to authentic learning activities. Authentic learning environments can therefore be developed in both digital and real-life settings (Lombardi, 2007).

However, authenticity can also be viewed as a student-centred problem-based form of learning, where students 'solve ambiguous problems with real-world significance' (Lombardi, 2007; Maina, 2004; Rule, 2006). Assessments need to be carefully designed to become authentic in relation to this kind of learning. The following example sought, for instance, to stimulate students to create a presentation on 'real' scenarios within a practice context, so learners developed a sense of engagement with the relevant professional community.

Working on real cases

In a Built Environment course, students studying health and safety management were asked to research, prepare and deliver a multimedia presentation based on case study material about a real-life accident that they had pinpointed and researched. Their presentation was expected to refer to relevant regulations, codes of practice and guidance; outline good management practice in relation to their chosen hazard, and formulate a detailed hazard-control risk assessment for what should have been the appropriate management of the accident in their case study.

Students found the assessment challenging but enjoyable. They valued the ways in which they felt the assessment supported their future professional practice in tangible ways. They also felt that this way of learning had been fun, as well as educational. They valued the ability to learn from other students' presentations, which focused on different types of hazard. The lecturer found the work was interesting to mark, as the students came up with diverse cases and a range of ways of presenting the information. He felt, too, that the assessment format focused students' attention on the process, not just the content, of professional practice in valuable and important ways.

Authentic tasks in non-professional courses

We have already observed that most studies of authentic assessment have taken place in the context of professional education. But another challenge lecturers might face is how, in less directly vocational humanities and social science subjects, to design authentic assessments which encourage students to link the subjects they are studying to the real world. This is important, because if students perceive the relevance of the abstract ideas they are studying it can help to enhance their sense of interest and engagement with regard to the subject matter and content of their courses, deepening the quality of learning they aim to achieve and providing a strong sense of motivation.

Davison's research (2011) looked specifically at students' experiences of authenticity in non-vocational subject areas, and found that students' capacity to apply learning to real-world contexts or practices, or the opportunity to learn with real-world contexts or practices, was an important and beneficial dimension of learning. In non-vocational subject areas this could, for instance, involve assessments which enable students to work together in ways which emulate many working practices, rather than always requiring them to perform individually. In the example below, the lecturer designed assessment to offer a more 'realistic' way of working than she felt was normally the case in her subject area: English Literature.

Writing in groups

Literature students studying modern American poetry were invited to compile anthologies as opposed to writing a traditional essay. This assessment aimed to give students an opportunity to work together, rather than working in isolation, as they were traditionally accustomed to doing when preparing academic essays. Students worked in small groups to compile their poetry anthology, which encouraged them to engage in dialogue and negotiate their plans with others.

The first piece of summative assessment was an introduction to the anthology which was written and submitted individually, although it was based on the work undertaken in groups. The introduction served to justify the choices made and to explain the students' own understanding of modern American poetry. The second piece for assessment, again individual, reflected upon the choices made, the necessary omissions and the ways in which the anthology constructed a poetic tradition. While students' group work was not marked, they were asked to work together to produce an artefact within a limited time frame. The lecturer felt this infused the work with a sense of authenticity because it mirrored students' assumptions about the ways they would be required to function in the world of work.

Putting it into practice by developing a sense of personal engagement

Research which focuses on the impact of socio-cultural influences on learner motivation and participation offers another rationale for trying to make assessment practices authentic and meaningful in some way to students, either individually or collectively. Bloomer (1997), for example, argues that dispositions towards learning and achievement are 'socially and culturally grounded' and are profoundly affected by personal identities. Ecclestone (2002) argues that motivation and approaches to learning cannot be isolated from the unstable yet important contexts of learners' own interests. The quality of learning is enhanced when individuals can make a personal connection with the subject matter they are working with (McDowell, 2008). Equally important is the opportunity to talk about their thoughts and interests with peers as this seems to reinforce personal commitment and ownership. Contrast the student who said: *"Me and my friends are doing different subjects but the same kind of big ideas come up and we're always talking about our ideas and our assignments – even down the pub – because it matters"* and a student on the same course: *"I never really spend any time discussing what I'm studying. I'd like to but no one's bothered so I get the feeling it's not that important really seeing as nobody is interested."*

Harnessing learners' everyday experiences

This might, in practice, mean trying to design assessment to enhance students' sense of personal involvement. In one sense, this can be done by explicitly building up opportunities for learners to draw upon their own personal experiences by, for example, basing activities in the context of learners' everyday lives. This can act as a mechanism to engage, motivate and sustain learning. In Davison's (2011) research, authentic learning activities seemed to help learners access the curriculum, gain confidence and maintain motivation.

Students who feel able to follow or develop an individual interest or enthusiasm, rather than simply feel that they are doing whatever everyone else is doing in order to get through an assignment, often feel a genuine sense of involvement in learning. This can lead to a sense of connection with the work, as the following example indicates.

Individual projects

In a History of Design module second-year students were offered the chance to investigate the design and development of a local building of their own choosing. They were supported to research the ways in which decisions had been made about the building, including controversies over changes of use and planning regulations. As they investigated the issues, and, in some cases, interviewed local stakeholders to gain insight into public opinion, students frequently became extremely enthusiastic about the module, as it brought their learning to life. As one said, *"It became a really personal project for me. I really wanted to do it!"*

Designing authentic assessment to bring a 'live' feel to assessment

Another way of engaging students in deep, lasting learning revolves around making sure that students have explicit opportunities to discuss assessment tasks with other people. This might mean, for instance, explicitly building in the requirement for students to explain their ideas and defend the work they produce for assessment purposes. The requirement to explain one's thinking to a 'live' audience, who will ask follow-up questions and probe the rationale for decisions that have been taken, prompts many students to adopt deep approaches to learning in an effort to really understand the material. Peer assessment, which can be formative or summative, can play a part here, as the following example shows.

Running a mini-conference

In a scientific subject area, undergraduates in their final year conducted a capstone project which integrated and built on the learning they had achieved over the whole course. Projects were traditionally simply reported in written format. This year, however, students submitted shorter reports, but also participated in a mini-conference attended by staff and student peers. The conference sought to mirror the style of academic conference which would be typical in the scientific communities of the discipline. Students gave talks or presented posters based on their experimental research work. These were peer assessed as well as being assessed by members of staff.

This enabled students to engage in the type of activity that is practised by 'real' researchers and gave an added sense of purpose to the research tasks they undertook in the course. Making a good presentation, especially in front of other students and local employers as well as staff, challenged students to do their best rather than just meeting the assessment requirements in a strategic or formulaic way. Because the assessment format was interactive, and students clearly felt they were 'on the spot', and were expected to address any questions that might be asked, they tried to genuinely understand the material, rather than 'blag and waffle' as they admitted they might do in a project report which was simply going to be read by an examiner.

Designing assessment to encourage students to focus/reflect on and evaluate their own learning

Authentic assessments may explicitly require students to identify their personal connections with a subject or topic and use that as a basis for assessment. Reflective commentaries, for instance, might be used to this end. Alternatively, students might be encouraged to 'put more of themselves' into their work by being invited to write or talk about the implications of the topic for their own practice. The following example illustrates a student thinking about the personal implications of a topic, which was assessed by an authentic task.

Assessment which encourages personal engagement

On one course, which focused on the theory of Assessment for Learning, students were required to develop a guide to AfL which would be suitable for others. The following student talked of searching for personal meaning while preparing her guide, rather than her usual experience of 'doing assessment', which involved trying to simply produce what she thought someone else was expecting or wanted to hear: *"Normally I don't write it for me. I don't think I write my academic assignments for myself, I'm writing them for the person who is reading them."*

> She saw the guide as offering her the chance to think and reflect about her own experiences, rather than performing a task in an atomistic way, by 'putting in' material that others seemed to demand: *"I used it to think through the things with assessment that had happened to me. It was about me, which my assignments aren't normally. I just normally check what they're asking and put bits in on each criteria."*

Authenticity can also imply assessment tasks which seem authentic in relation to professional contexts, or to other 'real-life' or 'real-world' settings, but which emphasize this at the level of meta-learning rather than the practical skills or knowledge level. For instance, students might be encouraged to develop the qualities and dispositions of self-evaluation or self-regulation by being asked to undertake assignments which clearly highlight these qualities.

Progress and personal development

In another example, still in the context of professional courses, but this time in which students were preparing for the teaching profession, learners were required to compile a training development file of their practice. This focused their attention on an analysis and reflection of their work. It included session planning, reflective logs, appendices in terms of any presentations that had been given, together with feedback they received, and teaching observations. The file was used for summative assessment purposes but, like many of the examples in this chapter, was compiled steadily as the module unfolded and clearly served a strong formative function.

Further, as alternatives to reports and essays, some subject areas encourage students to submit journals, reflective logs or personal accounts about their experiences of the business of learning subject-content. This can help students genuinely connect with, and see the relevance of, their learning, by focusing their attention on the progress they have made, and honing the skills of self-evaluation, rather than placing all their effort into providing a polished performance purely to gain marks.

Reflective writing

In a first-year Humanities module introducing key theoretical concepts, students were required to submit a commentary outlining how far and in what ways their views of particular theoretical standpoints had changed and developed over the course of the module. They did this by building directly upon learning activities, group discussions and short writing tasks built into the module. These gradually moved students from constructing highly personal interpretations of the texts they were studying, towards more complex and theorized accounts of the texts, which were developed via guided reading.

The lecturers felt that this assessment format was useful, because it encouraged students to begin to perceive and explicitly talk about the standards and theoretical level which they should be aiming to achieve. This meant that, if major misunderstandings about the relevance of theory became evident in the commentaries students submitted, tutors were able to offer clear and focused feedback, raising awareness of the complexity of the disciplinary area.

Students can become very engaged in empirical or theoretical enquiries that focus on issues or topics of personal interest where they really want to know what the outcomes will be.

Personal ethnographies

Second-year students on a Social Science programme took an Ethnography module. The theme of the module assignment was simply 'family' giving students considerable scope to select their own focus. The lecturer encouraged them (but did not require them) to gather some ethnographic data first hand in addition to drawing materials from texts. This inspired a high proportion of students to investigate aspects of their own families. For example, one student looked at surviving and prospering as an immigrant family including ethnographic work with her contemporaries, siblings and cousins. Some benefits of this approach were that students felt a real sense of ownership of the assignments that they carried out. They also felt like an 'expert' because they ended up knowing more about the topic than anyone else. The projects led to a lot of discussion at home, for some, *"the first time anyone has been interested in what I actually learn at Uni!"*. Finally, students wanted to understand and explain the contexts they were studying which made them much more keen to examine theoretical texts and apply them to 'real life'.

Voicing the issues revisited: a case study of authentic assessment

Students producing guides to Assessment for Learning

One of the authors of this book decided to create a module which explicitly invited undergraduates to engage with, and contribute their voices to, recent research and development work on assessment and feedback. She did this because, while it was apparent that the CETL offered novice and experienced staff across the university many formal and informal opportunities to learn more about assessment and to engage in scholarly work around their own assessment practice, students were rarely targeted.

The lecturer hoped the students would feel a genuine sense of participation in the CETL AfL activity, so she decided to encourage them to create staff or student development materials which might inform other people's approaches to assessment. To this end, once they had studied the scholarship of assessment (Rust, 2007) and engaged with seminal work being disseminated and debated within the educational development community, the students were invited to develop guides to AfL. Participants were advised that, with their permission and editing, where appropriate, the materials they produced would be used in 'real life', to support staff and student development activities.

The students' guides were, on the whole, collaboratively created and were targeted at lecturers or first-year students. Students came up with a host of creative and imaginative ways of tackling this task. They produced booklets, guides, interactive games, manifestos, workshops, videos and posters. Their ideas were expressed in highly distinctive, engaging ways. Many offered highly accessible and powerful ways of encouraging staff and students to think more deeply about developing their approaches to assessment. Some materials were, indeed, subsequently used to engage lecturers, via, for instance, staff development workshops within and beyond the university. In many instances, these sessions were attended by their student authors, who introduced or co-delivered their materials. Others were adapted for publication within the university staff development publication series. Some were used to engage less experienced students, by being incorporated into Study Skills sessions for first-year students, for instance (see, for example, Storey, 2007; Wake and Watson, 2007).

Students were, on the whole, extremely enthusiastic about producing their guides. Instead of simply producing these assignments because they felt they were compelled to, they talked of really enjoying the experience, because it felt meaningful and relevant in some way. For instance, one explained: *"Normally I'm writing them for that percentage in the box, I suppose we really didn't do that for this one because we had such fun."* Most claimed to especially enjoy working collaboratively, in pairs or small self-selecting groups. They felt this offered a more 'natural' or authentic way of working. The social interaction gave them the chance to debate ideas and develop their thinking:

> *"We definitely discovered working together you're giving so much more. You're pulling things out of each other, you didn't realise you had. I don't class myself as a creative person, but when I looked at that final product it worked really well. Whereas, writing a normal academic assignment, it's very isolating."*

Furthermore, because they had a strong sense of a 'real' audience for their materials, students endeavoured to make points and communicate their ideas effectively. Interestingly, they saw this, too, in stark contrast to the ways in which they approached their 'normal' assignments. One, for instance, claimed she normally handed her essays in with the sense that they were simply being processed: *"Normal assignments have no audience. I don't know what happens when they go in, they get read and they get sent back"*. For many, there was a sense of personal investment in producing the guides which was lacking in the ways in which students undertook routine assignments. As one said: *"Usually there is no obligation, you're writing for a set task and set thing and once it has been achieved then that's it."* Another also claimed that it was important to believe that the guides had a genuine purpose beyond the acquisition of marks, because this helped her focus on trying to communicate complex ideas: *"We were conscious that we wanted to use different ways of getting the point over rather than just a load of writing. . . . The pictures were deliberately chosen to illustrate the point."* Being asked to focus on helping other people to understand key concepts and ideas appeared to foster creativity, rather than make the students feel that they simply needed to comply (Torrance, 2007) with tutors' criteria for a 'good' essay.

> *"The sense that someone would read this – I think that helped us create it, especially after seeing the guides that they handed out as examples and they had said it might [be displayed]. People might pick it up, have a look through it."*

But it also involved a sense of personal investment: *"It is not just a pass or a fail or a number in a box, there's other important things like satisfaction, there's recognition, there's the feeling that it is going to help other people."* This student's feelings of pride and achievement were commonly expressed by others.

Key questions to think about

The following key questions are designed to help course and module teams develop their practice. They could, alternatively, be used for personal reflection.

- **How do your students regard the assessment on your programme: as hoops to jump through or tasks which help them learn?** You and your students are inevitably going to spend a lot of time on assessment activities so it is important to know how your students regard the assessment you design for them. The distinction between 'jumping through hoops' and 'really learning something worthwhile' is a crucial one. You need to find out more about what your students think and you could do this in many ways, such as: staff–student discussion; open-ended questionnaires or feedback sheets; focus groups; use of existing student learning questionnaires which are freely available e.g. Enhancing Teaching–Learning Environments questionnaires (http://www.etl.tla.ed.ac.uk/publications.html) or the Northumbria AfL questionnaire and interview schedules (http://www.northumbria.ac.uk/sd/academic/sches/lt/afl/cetl_afl/research/toolkit/cetl_res_help).

- **Where and how do your assessment tasks encourage students to develop a sense of engaging with meaningful activity in the discipline?** Related to the previous point, you need to know what your students regard as meaningful but you also need to discuss what the teaching team of academics regards as worthwhile and meaningful. In order to move towards disciplinary competence do students need to engage in research and enquiry? Or acquire and apply new analytical tools? Develop new ways of writing or new forms of dialogue? It may be surprising to discover that individuals on the teaching team have widely different views on what is important and meaningful in the subject!

- Can your students be given opportunities for assessment tasks which are more realistic compared to the perceived artificiality of 'normal' exams and assignments? This so-called artificiality is a long-standing student grievance. Do you offer students any alternatives such as writing for different audiences in formats other than the essay? Do some of your exams use different forms such as requiring students to address a case study? How much does working in groups feature?

- How and when do your students have the opportunity to apply what they have learned to solve real-world problems or explore real-world issues? Many teachers want students to engage in learning outside the classroom and most students support this. They find it motivating and hope to develop their skills and employability. If your programme team wants to pursue this it will be important to spend time investigating local resources, organizations, facilities and networks that can provide opportunities beyond the university. You will need to be imaginative and creative and draw on all of your personal and professional connections. Don't forget though the potential of virtual environments and simulations to provide authentic experiences for your students.

- Where on the programme are your students able to make choices about assessment tasks which allow them to develop their own interests? You may allow students to generate their own assignment title or make their own choice of topic but they often find that difficult and are reluctant or cautious. However, when students really engage with something of personal interest the benefits are evident. So you need to think about how you support students to take the initiative. It might be a good idea to take small steps at first, offering students more independence when they are ready to accept it.

Chapter 2

Balancing summative and formative assessment

When it comes to designing effective Assessment for Learning environments, the idea of trying to achieve a better balance between formative and summative elements is a key principle to bear in mind. In this chapter we will explain how useful it is to avoid an over-focus on summative assessment, which can be detrimental to learning.

This chapter covers:

- the power and pervasiveness of summative assessment;
- impacts on students of assessment; the 'backwash' effect and the hidden curriculum;
- learning from summative and formative assessment;
- qualitative differences between learning goals and performance goals;
- strategies to balance summative assessment and formative assessment.

Voicing the issues

Caroline is an experienced lecturer in Politics but she feels that students aren't responding as she expects to her module this year. She spends a lot of time linking the module themes to current events, making sure that her lectures and seminars are up to the minute. This usually gets students engaged in discussion and sharing ideas but when she used this approach in a lecture this semester one of the students asked: *"Could this be in one of the exam questions – because it's not in the module handbook?"*. Caroline explained that this specific example was not absolutely needed for the exam but that it was very useful to apply what they were learning to current examples and it would help them to understand the module. At this point she noticed that quite a few students stopped taking notes, sat back and did not engage in any discussion. Part way through the module Caroline's students chose, from a set list, the essay topics they were going to address as summative coursework. In the lectures after that attendance was poor, sometimes as low as 50 per cent. When Caroline asked one of the regular attenders what was going on he said: *"It happens quite a lot. Once people know what assignment they're doing they only go to the lectures that are relevant to that."*

The example above illustrates one way in which an over-focus on summative assessment can be detrimental to learning. Lecturers may notice that many students are failing to engage in learning activities or formative tasks because they seem willing only to spend time and effort on things that carry marks. Formative assessment may be on offer, but it is not taken up. Some researchers argue that it is the breakdown of programmes into modules, that has led to small segments of programmes, often delivered over one semester, being the subject of discrete assessment and that this has generated an over-focus on frequent summative assessment (Rust, 2000). This type of curriculum delivery structure has indeed generated activity but it may well be activity that is focused on the accumulation of marks within a regime of frequent demands that students are required to manage. When we also consider the imperative on students to obtain good grades and a good class of degree in a competitive employment market, it can be seen that it is no easy task to shift current practices to place less emphasis on summative assessment. However all of the evidence from research and practice tells us that if we wish to promote good learning we need to address the ways in which assessment operates. This chapter particularly focuses on different ways of doing this.

There are substantial learning benefits to be gained by rethinking and redesigning summative assessment tasks and processes. Nevertheless there remains the danger that summative assessment 'takes over' and it is this aspect that we address when attempting to rebalance the assessment environment so that there is also engagement in forma-tive assessment. There are ways of integrating formative and summative assessment activities. For example, the best known and most widespread approach which attempts to do this in Higher Education is the provision of tutor feedback on marked coursework which is intended to be formative in relation to future assignments. Unfortunately, we now know that such feedback *on its own* is rarely very effective. We need to take additional steps to make sure that such feedback has the potential to be useful in a 'feedforward' (Carless, 2007a) way and that students pay attention to it.

Theories and debates

Formative assessment and summative assessment are distinguished by their different purposes. Formative assessment goes hand-in-hand with learning and has an improve-ment focus. It opens up a space where students can try things out, make mistakes and be supported to develop. Summative assessment, on the other hand, leads many students to put on a performance which illustrates that they have met requirements – whether or not their performance is underpinned with genuine understanding or capability.

Summative and formative assessment both have some capacity to promote learning, but it is easy for summative assessment to become the focus for students. After all, as Brown and Knight (1994: 12) have vigorously asserted: 'Assessment defines what students regard as important, how they spend their time and how they come to see themselves as students and graduates'. One of the strongest emerging themes in the literature on assessment is the extent to which different approaches to assessment impact on student learning (Black *et al.*, 2003). The formal assessment tasks that we set send powerful backwash messages to students about the skills and qualities that are being valued in any learning context (Biggs and Tang, 2011). In other words, our assessment tasks send implicit but strong feedback to students, which they interpret to determine what is 'really wanted'. This creates a 'hidden curriculum of assessment' (Sambell and McDowell, 1998) that is always somewhat different from the curriculum that the lecturer intended, being based on students' perceptions of what is required.

Summative assessment is a powerful force. It is a very public element of education and of interest to many different stakeholders. The views of the public, employers and parents are often very traditional with regard to summative assessment and the methods that should be used. In relation to Higher Education the conventional form of closed-book unseen exam is often seen as the benchmark for rigour and standards. Assessment is a high-stakes activity and there are also entrenched ideas about what the outcomes should be like. Implicit expectations are challenged if, for example, 'too many' students attain the highest grades. Shepard (2000) argues that these concerns stem from a period when education's social aim was to select 'the best' to fill high-status jobs, slotting others into roles matching their capacities. Assessment was meant to distinguish between different levels of performance and to be distributed in the population in a pattern that was something like a normal distribution or 'bell curve'.

However, in contemporary knowledge economies, the espoused aims are to develop the capabilities of all and maximize the sum total of capabilities, skills and knowledge available to the economy and society as a whole. Discrimination between different levels of attainment should therefore be less important overall than the imperative to ensure that everyone develops and learns to the extent that they can reach their full potential and make their maximum possible contribution. Unfortunately views of assessment have not necessarily changed to take into account these different and important goals. There has not been enough of a shift in the meaning of summative assessment away from a means of ranking or 'sorting out' to a means of identifying how far individuals have developed and their potential for further learning. The term 'Assessment for Learning' is highly relevant here because AfL means using approaches that help learning to take place as widely and effectively as possible. It does not mean reducing or ignoring the attainment of 'high fliers' but its social aims are for a broad engagement with learning and achievement.

These structural conditions at the societal level can lead to assessment dilemmas such as formative assessment being neglected or 'under constant threat' (Knight and Yorke, 2003: 43). They lead to widely held assumptions that continue to influence the way in which assessment is conducted. For example, there is a view, which we challenge in this book, that summative assessment is required to manage student behaviour and ensure that they engage in their studies. Perhaps twenty-first century students are more utilitarian in their approach to university study but if so we must recognize that this does not stem from some moral deficiency on their part but from the conditions in which they find themselves. Society encourages them to maximize their grades because this will enhance their employability, job opportunities and personal financial gains over a graduate career. Universities are systems with a strong emphasis on summative assessment in their procedures and processes, and in relation to quality assurance and professional body requirements.

We must accept that assessment of the summative kind is a key driver for learning and teaching. In relation to teaching, the term 'teaching to the test' is frequently used to indicate situations where the emphasis is on narrowing the curriculum to exclude anything beyond the test requirements and on coaching or training students to perform well on assessment tasks rather than helping them to develop broader knowledge and skills in the subject. It could be argued that teaching to the test is not a problem if the assessment is well-designed and encompasses all of the desirable learning outcomes. However anything approaching this level of perfection is difficult to achieve in practice and assessment often subverts the real aims of a module or programme. Nevertheless we can use approaches to the design and practice of summative assessment to promote good learning.

Students often look to summative assessment to tell them what it is that they should be learning, especially if there is little in the way of formative assessment to help them. Students adopting a surface approach to learning try to meet module requirements without necessarily acquiring the skills and knowledge as intended. Gibbs calls this 'faking good' (2006: 25). The research on approaches to learning contrasts this with a deep approach where the student *is* aiming to gain understanding and capability. High-performing students are likely to adopt a deep *and* strategic approach, aiming to gain a good understanding but also adapting to the specific assessment requirements (Entwistle, Tait and McCune, 2000).

Learning and teaching that are centred too much around the marks to be gained and lost in summative assessment can lead to poor learning in terms of the desired skills and knowledge and also to damaging effects on individual learners. The work of Dweck (2000) identifies the problems that arise when students are too fixed on the 'performance goals' of achieving marks, and not enough on the learning goals of mastering the subject. Too much focus on performance goals can lead to students being risk-averse, being unwilling to admit to difficulties, covering up problems and regarding other students as competitors. Emphasis on competition rather than collaboration clearly does not promote good learning communities. Learning goals can be encouraged by helping students to understand requirements and to put effort into improving their work. This is best done though guidance and formative assessment. However there is a common view that students 'deserve' or need to be given marks for the activities they undertake as they are going through a module or programme. This embeds summative assessment throughout and it can be reassuring for lecturers and give students a sense of security from having 'marks in the bag'. On the other hand it can mean that the whole experience is dominated by summative assessment which tends to encourage students to focus on performance goals.

In our mass HE system we tend to operate on the basic belief that formative and summative assessment can be combined within the same learning activity or task, e.g. assignment or exam. However, research in assessment generally shows that when summative and formative assessment are combined in the same activity or context, the demands of summative assessment tend to dominate and formative assessment is often subverted (Black and Wiliam, 1998a). Neglecting formative assessment in favour of summative can mean that students may not understand assessment requirements or may be tested whilst they are doing something for the first time before they have had opportunity to develop. Summative assessment in stages throughout a module also presents problems; it may have some formative functions but it may mean that students are graded on achievements too early in the process or as Sadler (2009) notes on 'non-achievement' elements such as attendance.

AfL places considerable importance on formative assessment but encompasses more than that. Our approach to AfL takes into account the whole assessment environment. This holistic version of AfL has much in common with other perspectives on assessment such as 'learning-oriented assessment' (Carless, 2007b). We acknowledge the difficulties of the dominance of summative assessment but provide ideas for ways forward that will harness the potential of formative and summative assessment operating together, the formative value of marks or grades and ways of securing time and space for formative activities. The issues that this chapter addresses are about ways in which we can accommodate summative assessment in AfL practice, ideally using summative assessment to support learning and ensuring that summative does not dominate formative assessment or reduce its effectiveness.

Putting it into practice

There are many ways in which academic teachers have tried to reduce the dominance of summative assessment and improve formative assessment. This may mean developing the formative potential of summative assessment. One way of doing this is to develop assessment tasks that offer students genuine learning opportunities. Marks or grades are an important part of summative assessment and can also be used in ways that promote learning, providing another way of learning through summative assessment. Perhaps the most challenging approach is to address the summative/formative assessment balance directly by rebalancing time, effort and focus towards formative assessment making a quantitative or qualitative change to assessment practices.

This section of the chapter highlights three broad approaches to achieving a better balance between formative and summative assessment in our practice. These are:

- putting it into practice by developing the formative potential of summative assessment;
- putting it into practice by learning through marks and grades;
- putting it into practice by rebalancing time, effort and focus towards formative assessment.

Putting it into practice by developing the formative potential of summative assessment

Enhancing learning through summative assessment tasks

Making summative assessment a valuable learning activity is one of the fundamental ideas of constructive alignment (Biggs and Tang, 2007). The key principle of constructive alignment is that assessment is made productive by the careful integration of learning, teaching and assessment as a system that promotes good student learning and attainment of the intended outcomes. Students should, by carrying out the assessment task, acquire the knowledge and skills that they are intended to learn. What they are supposed to learn is, usually, understanding of relevant subject content and closely associated skills, such as how to write in the discipline or how to undertake a process such as finding and summarizing relevant evidence. If students are going to learn the right kinds of things, the task set must genuinely be aligned, that is, a valid assessment fully representing the knowledge and skills that students are meant to learn. For a task to be *constructively* aligned, that is, based on constructivist learning principles, the course must also use active learning processes that enable students to achieve the desired knowledge, understanding and skills. The emphasis here is on what the student does supported by a framework designed by their teachers. It is a form of 'learning by doing' within a collaborative context.

Research on student learning in Higher Education shows that students do not always go about their learning in the ways that their lecturers expect. Students may adopt a surface approach, such as relying on memorizing subject content to get through an assessment task when in fact a deeper level of understanding was intended. Often students use these strategies because they see little point in assessment tasks other than the need to accumulate marks. Assessment that seems to have no relevance to anything students might need to do in 'real life' is often seen as pointless and unfair. In contrast, if students can see that the assessment task requires real, valuable learning they may also feel that there is something more in it for them than just marks; the opportunity to gain worthwhile knowledge or skills is available. Tasks which students see as meaningful and valuable are more likely to secure appropriate effort so constructive alignment is a useful principle.

However, in practice some students may not understand an assessment task and may be unsure of what they are supposed to do or how to go about it. Learning by doing a task can be very effective for learners who understand what they are being asked to do, are able to direct their own learning, reflect on their progress and plan what to do next. In general, learning by doing an assessed task is a good strategy but, with any diverse group of learners, it is much more effective when the 'doing' is supported by formative assessment such as guidance, review, practice and feedback. As Knight (2006: 441) said, good learning needs ' . . . plenty of good tasks afford[ing] plenty of opportunities for judgment and conversations about judgment'. There are many examples of this principle in many disciplines since actively 'doing the subject' is not only applicable to professional programmes such as those in business, or health but also programmes in academic disciplines such as humanities or 'pure' sciences.

Collaborating to learn professional skills

In a module taken by students in a range of built environment disciplines, students were required to develop and be assessed on a set of practice-related skills in measurement and surveying. The lecturer organized students to work through-out the module in small groups where they practised the skills with lecturer feedback and advice as needed. Summative assessment was conducted on a group basis. Students had to perform the skills in a practical test but only one student from each group, selected at random on the day, was tested. Normally the student did well and the group members passed the assessment; if they did not, the group were allowed to do further work and resubmit for assessment, when a different, or the same, group representative might find themselves selected. The practical form of test was closely aligned with what students needed to learn for this aspect of their professional practice. The group approach taken maximized the learning amongst peers in the preparation for the test and reduced any tendencies for competition amongst individuals.

Learning from guidance on summative assessment

It is widely accepted that students should receive information and guidance about their summative assessment. In practice, students may be given: an assignment brief detailing what they are required to do; marking/grade criteria; recommendations on style of writing, referencing and so on. In relation to exams it is common for students to have access to past question papers to inform them of the requirements. What students learn from this type of guidance is the detail of what they have to do, which may help improve their summative assessment performance. They may also, through the experience of guidance on assignments and exams over time, develop a better understanding of how they need to do things generally in the subject and what counts as 'good work'. In the best circumstances this helps students to develop their competence as learners which is what lecturers intend. It is now generally agreed that these good intentions, while fulfilling the requirements of quality assurance systems, do not go far enough. It is difficult for students to understand what terms such as 'critical analysis' or 'synthesis' actually mean. They may readily understand the words 'Give an explanation of . . .' but still be uncertain about what kind of explanation is required, how detailed it needs to be, or what kind of evidence is needed to 'back up' their explanation. This type of guidance will be much more effective if students do not just receive guidance and information, but are able to discuss it and ask questions. More active engagement with peers and lecturers such as exercises where students apply the assessment criteria they have been given to a sample piece of work rather than just reading a list of criteria is particularly valuable.

Learning from guidance and information about summative assessment should not be a one-off activity related to a single instance of assessment. For it to be effective it needs to be a process that continues throughout a programme of study as students absorb explicit guidance and also acquire the tacit understanding of how things are done in the subject area, the underlying principles and the standards by which academic work is judged (O'Donovan, Price and Rust, 2008). Participation in a relevant learning community with fellow students and lecturers is essential if the exchange and dialogue that goes on around summative assessment is to function as a kind of 'meta' level of formative assessment where students acquire the ways of thinking and practising in the subject (McCune and Hounsell, 2005). The programme team need to consider assessment as a developmental pathway rather than just an assorted collection of module assessments indicating attainment at various points.

Guidance tutor meetings based on assignments

In a modular degree programme students meet four times over the year in progress groups with a guidance tutor. The meetings are scheduled to occur before submission dates for course assignments. Students bring assignment briefs and discuss the approaches they plan to take. The tutor helps students to understand the assessment requirements, in particular the standards that they need to meet. There is also discussion of the place of particular assignments in the programme overall and links are made to programme-level learning outcomes and attainment.

Learning from feedback associated with summative assessment

Feedback on something you have done should be very helpful to further learning. However there are a number of difficulties in the current HE context in trying to provide students with good-quality feedback on their learning. Feedback is frequently regarded as part of summative assessment and routinely viewed as written comments from the marker of an assignment or exam paper. Ideally students use this feedback to derive generic guidance that they then transfer to other academic tasks. In practice many students do not do this. At best they use feedback to identify 'where I went wrong' and at worst they do not read the feedback at all. This is partly due to structural problems in the feedback process which mean that essential features of quality feedback (Boud *et al.*, 2010; Carless, 2011) are not attained. Feedback is not timely, informative, specific and detailed, nor does it afford opportunities for dialogue. In current practice, the summative assessment process is often required to carry too much of the responsibility for providing feedback without sufficient support from good formative assessment processes. In comparison with a good feedback process we often provide feedback that is:

- too late – at least several weeks after the student completed the work;
- too brief – with large classes it is rarely possible for markers to provide extensive feedback and often quicker methods such as checklists are used;
- not specific enough – not related sufficiently to the individual student's needs;
- not generic enough – little guidance is given that actually helps students to see how the feedback could be used generically in future assignments.

If we really want students to learn from summative assessment feedback we have to take different approaches which address some of these structural problems and enable us to give better, more useful feedback.

The use of computer-delivered tests can give students immediate feedback on their performance, and could be used more widely, where the subject matter can be addressed by means of multiple-choice, true–false and similar forms of question. In written assignments, feedback can become more appropriate to individual student needs if they are asked to indicate what types of feedback they would particularly appreciate when they hand in their assignment. Lecturers may give generic but timely information before students complete an assignment by reporting the key feedback points that were given to the previous group of students who undertook the same assignment or the same type of assignment.

Staged tutor feedback

In a science discipline, laboratory reports were handed in every few weeks for marking and feedback, including individual written comments. They were returned to students within five days. With increasing student numbers staff found it difficult to give this timely, good-quality feedback. The solution found was to require students to continue to hand in reports for individual assessment.

However on each occasion comments and marks were given only on one element of the report such as the description of the research method, or the reporting of data, rather than trying to cover the whole report. All specific elements were addressed with rapid and detailed feedback over a semester period. The approach was effective in relation to student performance. Some students also found it useful to focus on single elements of the report and how they needed to improve, rather than having to consider all components at the same time.

Putting it into practice by learning through marks and grades

Marks are often seen as a necessary evil within summative assessment rather than as a positive force for learning. Marks can draw attention away from key features of learning as students focus on how to gain marks, how they are performing in terms of numbers, how they compare with other students and so on. Marks may lead to concerns about very small differences such as the difference between 58 and 62 per cent on an assignment rather than considerations about attainment more broadly. What students normally learn from marks and grades is about their position as an individual, whether they are 'doing well' or 'borderline'. Grades invite comparisons – 'I'm doing about the same as my friends' – and this can lead to competitiveness which is disruptive to the development of learning communities. This is illustrated by the concerns in group work about how marks will be allocated and worries about 'giving away good ideas' which may result in fellow group members improving their marks.

There are popular beliefs that a student who gets a poor mark will be stimulated to do better next time, presumably recognizing what they need to do differently. However the student may not realize what it is that they need to do. Similarly it is assumed that a student receiving a very good mark will gain in confidence and develop further, this is not necessarily, perhaps not often, true. Many students who have received good marks are very uncertain about what they actually did to achieve the mark and how to achieve similar success in future. This uncertainty does not enhance their confidence in facing the next assignment. Grades in themselves do not guide students towards any particular form of action should they want to make a change. Grades can direct students very strongly towards a performance focus which according to Dweck (2000) can lead to concentration on maximizing marks and, if need be, giving only the appearance of understanding. This is in contrast to learning goals which direct students' energies towards mastering the knowledge and skills they are learning and improving their capabilities.

Nevertheless marks can be useful to students as a tangible goal to work towards, a clear, if limited, indicator of achievement and a target that can stimulate students to expend time and effort. Marks in some form are here to stay and it is possible to gain some positive learning from them.

Understanding marks or grades

Marks and grades are a form of feedback and are sometimes the only feedback that students receive or the only feedback to which they pay attention. Marks and grades can have a powerful impact on students but perhaps only in terms of an immediate reaction. A poor mark can be disheartening and a good mark, though initially pleasing, is still of uncertain long-term benefit to a student who does not understand how marks are achieved. As one sociology student said about her essays: *"sometimes I get 62 per cent and sometimes I get 72 per cent and I don't know why"*. Some students adopt marks as a label or even part of their identity – *"I'm a 60 per cent person"* – which again does not give any incentive to try to improve and do better. It has been shown that students tend to simply accept marks that are round about what they usually get and only express concern if they get a substantially lower mark (Flint and Johnson, 2011).

Students need to learn much more about how marks are arrived at, what criteria are used and what they mean, and to understand what makes good work in the subject. They may then begin to realize that it may be possible to change what they do and produce better work rather than being stuck at 60 per cent! When they understand better what is required, students can exercise more control of their own performance and be more effective in self-regulation of their work (Nicol and Macfarlane-Dick, 2006). Despite the negative emphasis in discussions about the impacts of marks on students, there are effective strategies to tip the balance towards more positive effects though they need to be embedded throughout a programme rather than a one-off activity.

Using a model answer to identify strengths and weaknesses

A lecturer in Law used one class session for students to spend time reviewing the work they had handed in by comparing it to a model answer with a marking guide. Students were asked to identify strengths and weaknesses of their own work and consider what mark it merited. After that the tutor handed out her feedback comments and the mark she had awarded. This meant that all students were very interested to look at the tutor feedback and, for many, the mark they had been given was no longer quite such a 'mysterious' judgement. They were also more willing than usual to discuss feedback and marks with the lecturer, showing a higher level of engagement and learning from the marking process. Taras (2010) suggests several variants on this type of approach.

Changing marking scales

There has been some research to suggest that fine-grained marking scales can lead to students concentrating on accumulating 'points' (Dahlgren *et al.*, 2009). At the other end of the spectrum, marking to a threshold of performance on a pass/fail basis may redirect attention towards mastering the knowledge and skills required. This is an under-researched aspect of marking but the limited research conducted is supported by the experience of many lecturers. There is also some logic in the argument that fine-grained scales, such as the percentages used in the UK, open up opportunities for more manipulation and strategic approaches to gathering marks than is the case with simpler qualitative scales such as Distinction/Pass/Fail. Where percentages are involved students can monitor the marks they receive across different modules and calculate what marks they need to achieve a desired overall mark at the end of the year. In relation to a single assignment students are prone to ask where they 'lost' marks: "*What should I have put in to give me the four marks to bring my 56 per cent up to 60 per cent?*". It is difficult to regard categories such as Pass/Distinction in this quantitative manner as they are more clearly qualitative.

Self-testing to reach outcome standards

Staff teaching Economics found that students in the second year did not seem to remember many of the technical terms and procedures that had been addressed in Year One and now needed to be built upon. They found that this happened in most years even though second-year students had passed their Year One exams, some of them with very good marks. A strategy was developed which greatly reduced this problem. The relevant Year One summative exam was redesigned as a set of computer-based tests. Students had to pass each of three tests at a threshold level of 80 per cent. However, by using a question bank which could create different tests from a large pool of questions, students could be given the opportunity of practice tests, taking the test as a summative test when they felt they were ready and retaking it if needed. As a result students engaged more effectively with the material they were learning. They used the questions to test themselves and gain feedback, often working in small collaborative groups. Almost all students passed in the subject and they seemed to retain the knowledge better than had been the case in the past.

Formative marking

When considering formative assessment we often focus on feedback comments or discussion. It may indeed be suggested that we avoid giving marks since they tend to promote performance goals rather than learning goals. However, marks can show students how well they are performing in a concrete way that is meaningful and familiar to them. Comments normally encompass a number of positive commendations and suggestions for improvement in students' work and it is often difficult for a student to put this together and form an impression of the 'level' that they are reaching. Actual or indicative marks can be used to help students to see ways in which they can improve or maintain their performance, rather than regarding marks as definitive statements about their capability or numbers to be banked.

In some cases it is possible to focus marks almost entirely on progress in a way that is self-referenced to the individual student. This can be introduced as part of a first-year undergraduate study where a key aim is to enable students to reach a broad level of attainment, bearing in mind that individuals may vary considerably in their prior knowledge, experience and attainment. Individuals could be offered a choice of pathways with learning outcomes, assignments and feedback/feedforward that are more appropriate to their individual needs (Hughes, 2011: 361)

Self-referenced marks can be used even where verification of standards achieved is the main purpose of summative assessment. One way of doing this is to benchmark student performance against some very clear outcome standards and test students periodically so that they can see how they are progressing towards achieving the final standard level.

Marks to monitor personal progress

In a Medical Education programme one component of the assessment strategy is a test taken twice per year by students at several stages from beginning students to those in later years. The test is in the form of computer-delivered questions (multiple choice, true–false, calculations, etc.) and some short case study questions which require analysis and problem solving. The standard is set at the level of knowledge and comprehension expected of a final-year student of the programme and such students must reach a high score in order to pass. The pass level is lower for students in earlier years. The test enables students to understand what is expected of them and as time goes on they use the results to identify their own strengths and weaknesses and areas where they need to improve. The marks clearly indicate a student's own progress against a fixed standard.

Putting it into practice by rebalancing time, effort and focus towards formative assessment

Summative assessment takes up a lot of staff and student time in contemporary universities. It is particularly noticeable for staff. When there are large class sizes, just carrying out the marking in itself is very time-consuming. Being responsible for a coursework assignment or an exam brings a lot of work with it: quality assurance procedures, marking; double marking and/or moderation; giving feedback to students; keeping and checking records; dealing with requests for extensions or allowance for non-submission; dealing with any suspected academic misconduct; and seeing students who have questions or complaints about the process or results.

Most students study on programmes divided into modules with separate assessment tasks associated with each module. From one viewpoint this can lead to a lot of assessed work to be done and there are often complaints about 'over-assessment'. On the other hand assessment within a module is frequently restricted to one assignment or exam. The assessment then is always high-stakes because as a student said: *"It's one shot and that's your lot!"* There is only one chance to gain a desired grade in a module and whatever the result, it will often carry forward to become one of the marks that are combined together to create degree classifications. From some viewpoints this could be seen as under-assessment.

Some students are highly focused on acquiring marks and the importance they place on any study activity depends on how much it is 'worth', i.e. how much it contributes to overall module or programme grades. Some students may value assignments purely on the basis of how much they 'count'. When asked what they have found interesting in their recent studies, they reply by saying something like: *"Well, it's been the project because it was worth a lot {of marks}."* Perhaps because, as we discussed in the previous chapter, students see many assessment tasks as artificial with no relationship to activities beyond university, the only way that students can find value to give them an interest in the assessment activity is through its worth in terms of marks. We also need to bear in mind that students have a lot of calls upon their time. No matter how committed students are to their subject and to good learning, time spent on activities that 'don't count' comes with an opportunity cost. It may not contribute, or at least not directly, to gaining good marks.

Making a difference to allocation of time and effort

Many staff are concerned that if any study activities are not part of summative assessment then students will not undertake them. The real situation is usually less extreme but summative assessment requirements are likely to affect how students allocate their time and so we need to make a quantitative shift in the time spent on formative activity which is about learning and summative which is, largely, about demonstrating capability. One approach to this is to reduce the time and effort that summative assessment demands from students and staff.

We need to use summative assessment as a 'checkpoint' activity rather than expecting it to do all kinds of other things such as: being the main way in which students are given feedback; motivating students; securing 'time on task'; and constituting the main vehicle through which students acquire skills and knowledge. There is currently (in 2013) a tendency in universities' approaches to assessment to suggest that 'everything' has to be assessed. All defined learning outcomes, and there are often six or more of these in a single module, have to be demonstrated. This has become accepted practice but has developed mainly through the demands of a range of stakeholders – professional bodies wanting to ensure that 'everything' is covered; employers who want to be told exactly what graduates will know and be able to do; quality assurance agencies who want clear and explicit processes described in detail. This approach has not on the whole been developed with the primary goal of promoting good learning and good teaching. Whilst other stakeholders are important, any assurances given to them about the trustworthiness of our assessment systems are only worthwhile if there is a basis of good learning and attainment at the heart of the system.

If we can accept that all assessment is a form of sampling, we can reduce the time taken up by summative assessment by improving and defending our methods of sampling. A good sample would address breadth of learning, such as coverage of subject matter or the range of skills required, and depth, that is use of the higher-level skills needed in the subject such as: analysis, criticality, creativity or independent management of a project. This will work best if summative assessment is designed across the programme or stage of a programme rather than independently for each module. For students, a reduced summative assessment load frees up time and energy for other learning and formative assessment activities that develop students' capabilities but do not at the same time demand that they focus on demonstrating that capability and manage the process of acquiring marks that 'count'. For staff, the workload associated with summative assessment is also reduced again allowing for time to engage with students in more productive ways.

Using oral assessment

Oral forms of assessment tend to capture time for learning, including productive time on task, and have other positive benefits. A lecturer in Environmental Studies replaced a 'normal' written assignment with a class presentation. Students generally spent their time differently than they usually did with a written assignment. There were comments such as: *"You have to spend time really understanding your topic"* and *"I feel I've got to know what I'm talking about because I have to tell other people"*.

Another example of oral assessment is the use of individual ten-minute vivas where the student is asked 'unseen' questions on the module content. Individual vivas may seem to demand a significant amount of staff time but in fact the time spent compares favourably with the time that would be taken up with marking written work.

These approaches then not only have a generally positive effect on learning but make the overall assessment process more concise and so could be regarded as efficient.

Shifting what is seen as valuable and important

We want students to value learning and achievement and for this to be more of a driver for their behaviour than the acquisition of marks. Interesting and authentic tasks are one way of engaging students in learning. Another is participation in activities where they can develop and review knowledge and skills that will be required in summative assessment. The ways in which we guide students and, importantly, give feedback on their work can also make a difference. Feedback which is tied in closely to marks, focusing on a justification of why a particular mark has been awarded or where marks were 'lost', reinforces a focus on performance goals. Instead feedback should focus more on the qualities of the work, what it demonstrates about the student's capability and ideally, acknowledges students' progress and achievements and ways in which they could develop further. Since many universities require anonymous marking the process of awarding marks and the processes of giving feedback may need to be separate processes, as suggested by Whitelegg (2002).

Reducing the number of summative assessment checkpoints as suggested above can also have a qualitative effect on students' efforts. If marks are awarded for a number of elements of 'coursework' as a module goes along this may give students some reassurance that no element will be too high-stakes but it also keeps the idea of working for grades at the forefront throughout the module with the likelihood of a 'tick-and-go' mentality centred on the accumulation of marks rather than on the development of knowledge and skills.

Portfolios for summative assessment

In a History module on research methods students were asked to undertake various tasks and exercises, e.g. undertaking primary document analysis, and document them in a personal portfolio. These pieces of work were not marked although they were discussed in class time with the lecturer and/or fellow students. Towards the end of the module students were asked to submit a concise written summary of the work they had done, and sum up how overall they had met module learning outcomes. This strategy dissociates each small piece of work from summative assessment and provides good opportunities for formative assessment and improvement during the module.

Voicing the issues revisited: a case study of balancing formative and summative assessment

Innovations across the programme in English Literature

Colleagues in a Humanities department engaged with AfL approaches appropriate to their own disciplinary teaching. On the English degree programme ways of improving the balance between summative and formative assessment were tried. The innovations introduced in both the first year and final year of the degree illustrate how some of the ideas and suggestions given in this chapter can be used and how students may respond.

In the first year of the degree, a core module in Literary Theory was redesigned in two main ways using a combination of formative and summative assessment. First, there was much more structured activity in seminar classes, including short writing tasks and presentations given by students in groups. These activities introduced formative assessment into the module. This helped to avoid the situation where students in seminars left most of the talking to the teacher and many did not take on board the expectations of the subject. Some students did not understand why their participation was important. This is typical of students who are focusing on summative assessment by 'getting the notes' only to put them away until assignment submission at the end of the module. In the Literary Theory module one student, whose normal practice was to focus on summative assessment by going to go straight to the assignment title, noted the change in her own approach:

> "It makes you think differently rather than just looking at [the essay title] straight away and reading up on the author blah-de-blah . . . it's about looking at your way of interpreting it."

In this module there had been a single end-point assignment in the form of an essay. This was changed to one essay at the mid-point and one at the end. This meant that students undertook a practice assignment and the lecturer gave detailed feedback on this first assignment. As part of the second assignment students were required to indicate how they had responded to the feedback.

The lecturer felt that the first-year students benefited greatly in terms of confidence particularly from giving class presentations:

> *"These sessions where [students] are taking a lead, you are really getting to see who is doing what, and there are some really interesting things coming out . . . it really shows you and it's showing them more than you telling them, that they can do it."*

The module balanced formative and summative assessment so that there was space for learning, from feedback, guidance and participation whilst there was also enough summative assessment present to ensure that students were engaged and active.

In the final-year module in Modern American Poetry, students worked in groups to develop a poetry anthology aimed at undergraduate students. Although the anthology was agreed collectively, the summative assessment was individual. Each student wrote an introduction to the proposed anthology explaining the choices made and demonstrating their own understanding of Modern American Poetry. A second assignment required students to reflect further on the choices and omissions made and the ways in which their anthology constructed a poetic tradition.

For these students the development of an anthology and undertaking this as a group was an innovative assessment task. This was one of the reasons why they engaged productively with the summative assessment. Students related the experience in the module as having some authenticity in relation to employability. One suggested that the group working and the 'practical' nature of the task were important: *"I think that it's important that they do [this] in the course. It's a big thing to be able to do really. It's an essential sort of skill."* These final-year students were well-practised in the ways to manage assessment demands but in this module it was different. The student quoted below explains her normal approach of homing in on what is needed for the end-point essay compared to looking more broadly and perhaps more deeply in the creation of an anthology:

> *" . . . you do an essay in a normal module and you think – well, I'll do them [sic] two books, or I'll do them for an exam – but with this you have to get a wider knowledge and . . . after we'd written the introductions you knew quite a lot more."*

The lecturer also noted that module attendance was high compared to normal modules where students were quite likely to attend only those sessions that addressed the author or topic on which they wanted to write their essay. In this module they had to look more broadly. It was a requirement but also one that hooked them into fuller engagement across the theme study area.

Key questions to think about

The following key questions are designed to help course and module teams develop their practice. They could, alternatively, be used for personal reflection.

- **How much time do you think your students spend on 'doing assessment' as opposed to 'learning the subject'?** Summative assessment can capture a lot of student time because it is imperative for them to engage with it. You may find that you are requiring students across a programme to undertake a lot of separate pieces of assessed work and spend their time managing competing deadlines and demands. Sometimes, but perhaps not enough of the time, assessment tasks encourage high-quality learning. More often students describe it as 'churning stuff out' or 'just gathering marks'. By looking at the whole picture rather than just building up from module assessments you may be able to reduce the dominance of summative assessment.

- **How do the summative tasks you set help students develop their learning?** There are sure to be examples on your programme where assessment really is a good learning activity and is recognized as such by students. Some assessment may be what we have called in this chapter 'authentic'. If it can work in some parts of your programme you need to explore how that could be extended, perhaps by linking assessment in more than one module so that you can use more substantial tasks with high learning value.

- **To what extent are marks the main incentive for student engagement in your programme?** Are most of your students engaged in real learning as opposed to just accumulating points? If so that is an indicator of good assessment. If you see many examples of disengagement from learning it might be a good idea to look first at your assessment and explore with students how they experience the assessment regime.

- **What kinds of developmental activities are offered in the programme and how is this achieved?** Formative assessment is a key to development because it enables students to try things out, without worrying that their grades will suffer, and it provides them with guidance and feedback. Are there specific formative assessment episodes built into the programme which achieve this? Do students also have opportunities to be active in their learning generating further opportunity for embedded formative assessment?

- **How do your students come to appreciate the standards and qualities which marks signify or represent?** Students need help to understand what makes for good work in their subject. This is not something that should be addressed as part of induction but rather throughout the programme. The ability to judge academic quality is a slowly developed skill requiring ongoing guidance and development. Where in your programme are there opportunities for this?

- **How are students encouraged or helped to monitor their own progress?** If students understand what assessors' comments and the marks awarded mean they can turn that information into feedforward with a formative purpose. Are there any processes in your programme, such as asking students to maintain a progress file, to encourage them to do this systematically?

Chapter 3

Creating opportunities for practice and rehearsal

Giving students extensive opportunities to engage in the sorts of tasks that develop and demonstrate their learning is a useful principle to bear in mind when trying to design effective Assessment for Learning environments. We can design opportunities for formative activities into the student experience. Effective planning and structuring of our teaching sessions, so that students have ample opportunity to build, rehearse and practise important qualities and skills before they 'count', can be particularly helpful here. AfL approaches, then, typically inform the way we teach, as well as the ways in which we assess students.

This chapter covers:

- designing learning and teaching to promote practice and rehearsal;
- course design to promote gradual development;
- learning from active involvement;
- learning from social interaction;
- challenges and issues in creating effective formative assessment environments;
- strategies to promote learning communities.

Voicing the issues

Lucy is an experienced student who is now in her final year. Here she is talking about her experience of doing a module which had been explicitly redesigned to adopt a range of AfL approaches. Lucy felt the 'new' module represented a radical departure from other modules she had been doing, especially in relation to the classroom experience it offered. She explained her reasoning in the following way:

> "In most modules, you've just got to go along and get the notes, basically, and then hope you've got the right idea, to the level they're expecting, when it comes to the assignment. The problem is, you can hand in an assignment thinking that you've got it . . . but sometimes you really haven't! But by then, it's too late!
>
> With this module, it's different. We've done so much more talking. I think that's the difference. You're a part of the discussion, part of what's going on. So you're not just chucked in at the deep end . . . they build you up. It's sort of, try your hand at this. See how you go. Chat it through and listen to classmates, see if you've got it yet. See if you're getting

the right idea . . . You do wonder if you're getting the right idea, so it's much better to have a go before it all counts."

Lucy's remarks suggest that her experience of AfL relates to the whole module. For her, the module designed on AfL principles that she studied stood in stark contrast to the design of other modules which, as she saw it, simply required her to 'go along to get the notes'. In particular, she valued the chance to become directly involved in learning activities and social interactions which helped her to gauge how she was doing and build up her mastery of a field of knowledge steadily, with guidance and feedback provided as she did so. This approach allowed her to practise relevant skills and rehearse subject knowledge before these were summatively assessed. In other words, Lucy placed particular emphasis on the developmental value of the educational environments her teachers created for her, because they fostered her active participation and supported her learning holistically in formative ways.

Lucy's remarks importantly illustrate some of the ways in which students typically experience modules that use AfL approaches. Survey work our CETL researchers carried out (McDowell *et al.*, 2011) found that students reacted more positively to modules where AfL approaches were used in comparison with what they saw as more 'traditional' modules. They saw AfL modules as more engaging, more supportive and more likely to foster and develop their understanding and deep appreciation of the subject matter. There are significant learning benefits, then, to be gained by rethinking and redesigning modules to promote student activity, engagement and participation. So the issues this chapter addresses are about ways in which we can design our teaching, learning and assessment to offer formative opportunities which allow plentiful scope for students to rehearse and practise.

AfL places considerable importance on formative assessment. One common way of implementing formative assessment is by offering students the chance to have a dry run at specific assessment tasks. This is the familiar approach of having 'mock exams' as practice before the real thing. In a similar way, lecturers may build in opportunities for their students to practise giving an oral presentation, perhaps allocating 'indicative' marks even though the marks do not actually count towards module grades. This means that students will have had the experience of giving a presentation, received some feedback and be able to judge from the indicative mark how well they performed before they undertake a presentation that counts for summative assessment. However, as the previous chapter made clear, shifting the balance from summative to formative assessment like this is not without its challenges. In fact, it may have unanticipated and even undesirable side-effects, such as causing students to focus predominantly on chasing marks, rather than genuinely getting involved in valued learning.

However, if we neglect formative assessment it can mean that students may be tested whilst they are doing something for the first time, before they have had opportunity to practise and develop. Students in the first year or in a new subject might well think it is unfair that the first assignment that they write counts for module marks when they have had no opportunity to find out how to do this particular form of assignment. This chapter argues that formative assessment can be much more than giving students the chance to have a dress rehearsal or walk-through of a particular assessed task on a straightforward level. A better approach is to constructively align our courses so that they engage students in appropriate formative tasks *throughout* a course or module, offering students ample opportunities throughout to learn from doing tasks, practising and finding out how they are doing so that they can improve (Black and McCormick, 2010; Hounsell, 2007).

Theories and debates

In practice, most people actually learn by doing (Race, 2005), so learners need opportunities to participate actively in the learning process, with time and space to practise making their own sense of a topic area or concept. Indeed, learning at university is generally a matter of complex sense-making, in which students actively construct (rather than passively receive) meaning. Effective learners generally practise making their *own* sense of subject material by, for instance, organizing it into meaningful concepts, exploring ideas, reflecting, making connections by trying to link new content and associating it with what they already know. They pay lots of attention to making their *own* interpretations, then, which constantly shift and grow as they construct their sense of the material in progressively more complex and informed ways. However, we often assess students too soon (Sadler, 2009), when they have not had time to practise developing, using or consolidating their new knowledge, understanding or skills. They may then fall back on surface learning strategies such as the memorization of the meaning of terms.

Furthermore, while some students appear to realize that worthwhile and complex learning takes time and effort, others do not, or do not know how to go about learning effectively (Haggis, 2006). It can be argued that we can do more, then, to create formative assessment environments which encourage students to appreciate the time and effort that is required on task (Gibbs and Simpson, 2004). In our classrooms, the tasks we set can help students perceive the sorts of things, like reading widely or applying theory, things that experienced learners do 'behind the scenes'. Not only that, they can engage students in actually doing them, and sharing with others their experiences of doing them, rather than simply being told they need to do them.

Formative activity can take place in our everyday classrooms if we plan and structure our teaching to guide students' effort in productive and challenging ways. For instance, we can design students' classroom experiences so that learners are encouraged to become directly involved in meaningful tasks within the subject domain. We can structure activities, so that they help students to see and experience the sort of things they should be practising. We can use our classes to emphasize that only by doing things, rather than waiting to be 'taught', will learners begin to gradually develop a 'feel' for the relevant subject area.

Learners also need time and space to try things out, so that they can see the extent to which they have mastered them. Students benefit from opportunities to practise actually using new terminology, rather than simply reading it or listening to it, as they progress through a module. There is, of course, even more benefit if there is formative assessment providing guidance and feedback on their efforts. This approach, though, does not have to rely exclusively on resource-intensive one-to-one tutor–student interactions: lecture halls can usefully be viewed as formative assessment environments (Black and McCormick, 2010) which allow students to learn from active involvement and trial and error.

From this standpoint, making mistakes or having underdeveloped ideas or misconceptions are not problems, but are to be regarded as helpful, because recognizing mistakes enables students to learn and progress (Black, 2007: 19). However, to learn from trial and error means that students need to feel comfortable enough to 'have a go' and air their thoughts, however tentative or provisional these may be. They need to feel they will not be penalized or made to feel silly if their ideas are wide of the mark. Tolerance, trust and openness are all key to genuine involvement.

This typically means that formative assessment environments need, from students' viewpoints, to be experienced as 'low-stakes' environments (Knight and Yorke, 2003). In other words, they need to be experienced as 'forgiving' spaces, which allow students to learn from taking a risk and getting something wrong, or not quite right. Summative assessment on the other hand is not normally helpful to 'trying things out' in this way, because students will naturally want to gain marks and impress examiners, and this often leads to playing safe rather than having a go, perhaps taking a risk, and seeing how things work out. After all, as one student said: *"Let's face it, when you write an assignment, you're trying to show the assessor that you do understand, not that you don't!"* As this chapter suggests, it is important to remain acutely sensitive to the ways in which students are invited and encouraged to immerse themselves in the learning environments we create.

Furthermore, opportunities for practice and rehearsal are arguably most productive when they involve some form of social exchange (Brown and Adler, 2008). Research has shown that one of the strongest determinants of success in Higher Education is a student's propensity for engaging in dialogue about learning with others (Light, 2001). Social views of learning shift the focus of our attention from the *content* of our subject domains to the *process* of the learning activities and interactions around which the learning is situated.

From this viewpoint, knowledge is socially constructed and learning in a particular subject domain actually entails learning to think and see in the complex and subtle ways that a disciplinary specialist does (Meyer and Land, 2005; Moon, 2005). This involves students gradually developing, via opportunity for practice and rehearsal, a 'feel' for the practices and norms of established practitioners in a given domain. It is important for learners to recognize and practise using the tacit knowledge which implicitly frames the specific expectations, cultural and disciplinary orientations of the lecturers who design courses and assessment tasks (Bloxham, 2009; Lea and Street, 1998; Lillis, 2001). In consequence, mastering a field of knowledge involves not only learning about the subject matter, but also learning, eventually, to become a full participant in the field. Arguably this can only be accomplished gradually, by participating with other people, discussing problems, debating ideas and thinking things through collectively. Here, much like apprentices do in the workplace, students learn by taking on progressively challenging tasks whilst working in interactive social groups in a common space. They also learn from having the sense of genuinely immersing themselves in the practices of the subject, rather than just doing tasks because they are told to.

Putting it into practice

There are many ways in which subject lecturers try to improve the manner in which their students experience the benefits of opportunities to practise. One way of doing this is to redesign 'teaching' to promote active involvement, interaction and student activity.

Our everyday lectures, seminars and associated tasks are an important aspect of AfL and can be used in ways that promote genuine, worthwhile learning. Carefully structured tasks help to scaffold students' approaches, so that they build steadily and gradually through ongoing practice of progressively more challenging activities. Moreover, the development of trust, the confidence to share ideas and take risks are important features of effective environments but these can be difficult to establish in the current context of mass Higher Education. Strategies for fostering a favourable climate for learning, in which mistakes are not experienced as too risky, can help students develop good habits, such as taking up the mantle of responsibility for learning. Finally, strategies which harness the power of social interaction around learning can offer productive ways of putting formative assessment into practice.

This section of the chapter highlights three broad approaches to giving students ample opportunity for practice and rehearsal. These are:

- putting it into practice by planning and structuring courses to maximize active learning and student involvement;
- putting it into practice by creating low-stakes formative environments;
- putting it into practice by creating opportunities for social interaction.

Putting it into practice by planning and structuring courses to maximize active learning and student involvement

Designing learning tasks for students to undertake within lectures

A key principle of AfL is that students should be encouraged to spend time and effort on regular study, distributed across the module (Gibbs and Simpson, 2004). In practice, this means placing considerable emphasis on what learners, rather than their teachers, do. Successful learning emanates from students being involved in tasks and activities which give them lots of chances to practise making sense of the subject so that they achieve appropriate mastery of it (Sadler, 2009).

Viewed like this, the lecturer's role is to carefully consider the tools, resources, activities and affordances which make up students' experience of the learning environment of a module (Beetham, 2007), rather than simply delivering course material. Obviously, in this sense, the term 'learning environment' means much more than just the physical space of the lecture hall, and refers to everything that contributes to the students' capacity to interact with, or make personal sense of, their subject. This includes directed study tasks, projects, data collection and other tasks that are directly associated with the module, as well as whatever goes on in designated teaching sessions. Carefully structured tasks and activities can prompt students to direct their effort in meaningful ways.

In fact, the way that lectures are planned and delivered sends a powerful, often unintentional, message to students about what sort of roles they are expected to occupy. Sometimes the enduring image of a lecture suggests that the student is someone whose role is to passively receive information, rather than someone who actively builds their own sense of the subject matter. As the following undergraduates make clear in a guide to AfL they produced in their second year, too many lectures offer scant opportunity for students to practise honing important skills (Wake and Watson, 2007). Their tongue-in-cheek cartoon of the 'surface learning lecturer' humorously highlights the problems of teacher-dominated transmission models, focused mainly on delivering content and information, where students are positioned as empty vessels into which knowledge is poured, rather than as participants in the learning environment:

Figure 3.1 The Surface Learning Lecturer will always stride to provide ... (adapted from Biggs and Tang, 2007; Ramsden, 2003)

One of the key challenges in today's system of mass Higher Education, with increasing student–staff ratios, large classes, and a diminishing unit of resource, is to find ways of creating interactive and engaging environments for the large numbers of students we often have on our modules. Students soon pick up cues about which courses require engagement, but an ethos of active participation can be particularly hard to achieve in very large lecture halls. One strategy is to design activities for students to undertake in class time. Use can be made, for instance, of interactive technologies to encourage students to practise working in the discipline.

Using personal response systems in large lecture contexts

In an Engineering course the lecturer arranged to issue his students with hand-held voting technologies which could be used by every individual in the class. These personal response systems encouraged learners, anonymously, to attempt a set of questions and problems which the lecturer put to them. The questions were designed to encourage students to use and apply important concepts and algorithms to particular design scenarios.

During the lecture, the lecturer allocated a fixed amount of time for students to work on each problem. After the allocated time, students were asked to use the voting system to submit their responses, which were then displayed to the class in aggregate form. The lecturer then invited students to reflect, in groups, on the reasons that might underpin the incorrect responses: thus encouraging students to learn as much from making mistakes as from getting it right first time, by practising doing certain tasks and then reflecting on the processes of arriving at particular solutions.

By building in learning tasks like this, distributed across the module, lecturers can encourage students to take a deep approach to learning (Marton, Hounsell and Entwistle, 1997). As another example, in some subject areas, short, informal writing tasks can offer opportunities for students to practise putting complex ideas into their own words, thereby encouraging them to construct their own meanings. Many lecturers, however, worry that high student numbers prohibit the setting of formative writing tasks. They fear that this sort of activity will involve them in lots more work: taking student work in, reading it and producing formal feedback comments. However, as the following example highlights, informal writing tasks can actually be interspersed in class time and can even be built into large lecture formats.

Formative tasks in class time

A lecturer was working with over one hundred students. At the end of a brief exposition on a challenging topic the lecturer invited her students to write on blank postcards. She asked them to summarize, in a couple of sentences, the concept she was trying to convey. After students had taken a few minutes to put their own thoughts into words, the lecturer collected the postcards in. Skimming quickly through them during a quick coffee break, she selected a sample of students' responses, which, taking care they were anonymous, she showed to the class on a visualizer, asking for comments about how to improve each one and offering her own views about the extent to which the concept had been grasped by each one. Not only did this approach encourage all students to think about making sense of the lecture, in addition, the lecturer derived valuable feedback on how well her students were doing. She could see if more practice was required before she moved on to cover another topic.

Enhancing learning by designing tasks for students to undertake outside class time

Students may need time to practise consolidating an area before they move on to something more complex. Some subject areas readily lend themselves to the development of online tests which allow students to practise, say, working out solutions or doing complex calculations. These help students work through things in their own time, practising and consolidating what has been learned.

Using online tests

In many health-related courses, the ability to perform accurate drugs calculations is vital and is tested rigorously at key assessment points. Students benefit from the creation of databanks of online formative tests which relate directly to this aspect of their summative assessment. Students can take the objective tests as many times as they wish and no marks are attached. Many take them several times, because doing them allows them to practise and develop their skills before they attempt the summative tests, which require them to achieve 100 per cent.

Carrying out activities with a fixed solution like this may inherently give the learner a good idea about whether they have taken a good approach, simply by seeing if the approach adopted works out in practice. However, the 'right answer' is less obvious in predominantly essay-based subject areas. Here, too, students need to practise the process of actively interpreting information in the relevant subject domain, so that they get ample opportunity to move beyond surface levels of analysis. However, in these types of task it can be difficult for students to see, simply by practising the task per se, how far they have actually mastered the required concepts. They also need to benefit from the chance to share and discuss their responses, so that they have the chance to calibrate their achievements and form a realistic picture of how they are doing.

Here 'thinking–writing' (Mitchell, 2010) tasks, which students practise undertaking outside of class time, but which are systematically built upon in class time, can be extremely valuable.

Designing activities to undertake outside class time

In one module, directed study tasks were regularly set, which allowed students to practise using the ideas and concepts of the discipline. The work students produced became a key focal point for specific activities in large-lecture settings with over seventy students.

For instance, students were asked to come to one lecture prepared to discuss the ideas of a specified seminal theorist. They were advised to make notes on his contributions to the field. This required them to engage in wider reading and controversies about the theorist's work.

In the large lecture format students were given a question to address, which asked them to outline in what ways they thought the theorist's ideas had influenced the field. They tackled this task in small groups, creating a flipchart sheet which summarized the main ideas they had drawn out from their preparatory reading and note-taking. To do this they had to practise summarizing and explaining their reading and, most importantly, think about its significance, drawing out the key points to highlight in order to try and address the question.

The lecturers were reassured to find that the students had undertaken the preparatory reading, despite no marks being attached. On reflection, they felt that this was because they had explained carefully to the students, in the lead-up to the exercise, why practising the process of summarizing reading and making points about it would help them develop their academic writing skills in advance of the summative written assignment.

Designing progressively challenging tasks which gradually build students' capabilities

It is widely accepted that students need time and considerable help to absorb, and be absorbed into, the culture of practice of a discipline or subject area (Elwood and Klenowski, 2002, p. 246). Just as apprentices need hands-on practice to enable them to move gradually towards expertise in a trade, newcomers to university or to a subject area that is 'new' to them, begin as novices who are unfamiliar with the discourses, customs and practices of that community, and need help to practise moving from peripheral involvement towards expertise and full participation. After all, as Ramsden (2003) points out, when academics say someone understands something, what they usually mean is that the person relates to it in the way that a subject expert does. This means learning to think and express oneself, for example, like an historian, or like an engineer. It is unlikely that this level of insight can be developed via teacher exposition. Complex disciplinary understandings take time and effort to develop. To achieve this, students need lots of practice, such that they grapple vigorously with the ideas and concepts at the core of a topic, and gradually come to develop an ear for the culturally specific ways of making meaning within the discipline.

We need to use our experience as subject specialists who are well-versed in our disci-plinary ways of thinking and practising (Meyer and Land, 2005) to generate reasonable challenges and tasks which will help our students to get to grips with our subject areas, so that they grasp what understanding really looks like in particular domains. Presenting our students with a series of appropriate challenges will help them to gradually appreciate the ways in which specific theories might be handled, analysed and applied. This requires a careful balance of judgement on our part, about what is reasonable to expect a 'novice' to know and be able to do at particular stages of learning our subjects, whilst challenging students' thinking and enabling them to participate in 'really doing' the subject. On the one hand, learners should not simply be abandoned to sink or swim. They need structure so that, while they practise, they do not feel they are being pushed in at the deep end and expected to get on with it alone. Students should not be left to flounder and feel lost in the depth of things. By the same token, learners benefit from appropriate academic challenges (Kuh *et al.*, 2005), not from being spoon fed. So according to Nicol (2009b: 6) it is important that lecturers structure the learning environment in ways that encourage regular student engagement both in and out of class. Normally, he argues, 'this is achieved through a sequence of learning tasks that become progressively more challenging'.

One strategy involves setting a series of tasks which gradually enable students to practise writing about a particular subject domain or topic. This might involve regular short writing activities which are structured to engage the student actively in a flow of discourse (Northedge, 2003) such that they steadily build up a collection of evidence which they can be asked to reflect upon in a summative assignment.

Building in frequent short writing tasks

Patchwork text (Winter, 2003) consists of a carefully structured series of short pieces of writing (patches) in a range of styles and genres, which are then reviewed and discussed with other students in small working groups. This approach was used on a Childhood Studies programme, in a module on Child Development. Students were asked to write a patch each week. Each patch was roughly 500 words long and the final patch was a retrospective commentary on the learning that had taken place, which synthesized the students' intellectual journey over the previous ten weeks or so. The students brought their weekly patch into the session for review by their peer group.

In order to ensure that patchwork text supported and enhanced students' learning, the lecturer felt it was important to match each patch to the learning outcomes and to the taught sessions that comprised the module. She felt it was important, too, to ensure variety in the patches. For instance, the patches were designed with the aim of helping students to progress from personal reflection to more analytic topics. At the end of the module the patches were submitted as part of an overall assignment, together with a retrospective commentary on or synthesis of the learning that had taken place.

In professionally oriented courses simulations offer another means of building in opportunities for students to develop professional practice in safe and carefully structured learning environments. They can be designed to help students apply theory, by enabling them to practise exercising the complexity of making professional judgements in contexts which simulate those found in authentic professional settings. They can also be used to help students practise and develop the use of particular skills and competences before they count in the 'real world'.

Using simulations

'Sim Man,' 'METIman' and 'BabySIM' are hi-fidelity mannequins that act as patient simulators and are used in healthcare education. They react realistically to treatment, and produce altered physiology, including heart and lung rhythms, thus inherently giving intrinsic feedback (Laurillard, 2002) to students on the outcomes of their clinical decision-making and the quality of their interventions. Thus students can practise trying out different procedures and can see if they 'work'.

In pre-registration nursing, simulations can be used to offer immediate, hands-on experiences of clinical practice to students. They provide highly realistic patient simulation training experiences so students can practise, say, teamwork, leadership and communication skills. The interactive mannequins are reconfigured by the lecturers to allow students a wide range of scenarios and patient cases. Additionally, the conditions can gradually become more complex and challenging, so that students can practise the skills they will need to successfully meet the learning outcomes of a module.

Putting it into practice by creating low-stakes formative environments

Designing the introductory session to reinforce the need for active participation and practice

According to Tinto (1993) the more students are academically and socially involved, the more likely they are to persist and succeed in their studies. It is worth planning the first few sessions carefully, to set an ethos of active participation. The first meetings, in particular, can establish student expectations in this regard. Much can be done here to demand student interaction and emphasize the importance of trying out ideas, asking questions and contributing to discussions. Starting from students' own personal perspectives, and valuing the knowledge and experience they already bring, can be a powerful way of signalling that their views and perspectives matter and offer a valuable foundation upon which they can build.

Encouraging students to express and build upon what they already know about a topic

In the first lecture session of a module on a Childhood Studies programme, students were invited to jot down the first words that sprang to mind when they thought of 'childhood'. Once students had created their own lists, they pooled their notes within small groups. Finally, students were encouraged to call out their words while the lecturer typed up a Word document which was shown on the screen in class and ultimately could be placed on the e-learning portal. With well over one hundred students in the lecture theatre, a long and diverse list soon emerged, which highlighted how much knowledge and experience the students already had.

However, the lecturers were keen that students moved beyond common-sense ideas about childhood. During the lecture they helped students begin to practise analysing the list, by, for instance, looking for 'positive' and 'negative' words, which were then colour-coded on the Word document. Debates soon arose about this, and this enabled the lecturers to highlight the importance of relativism and thus raise some of the important concepts on the module. The student-generated list could also be used to practise the identification of commonly emerging themes, patterns and issues. Later in the module the list was revisited frequently, as students built up theoretical tools which meant they developed different lenses through which to perceive and explore the initial thought shower. Students engaged enthusiastically with this and interviews showed that they were looking back at the list out of class time to reflect on their emergent theoretical understandings. As one said:

> "And our work went up on BlackBoard, instead of just the lecturers'. It's our thoughts and ideas, so it makes it more personal. So you are more inclined to read it and remember what it meant because you were more involved in making it."

So this strategy not only encouraged students to practise engaging with ideas and concepts, it also underlined the message that the lecturer would value and analyse what views and experiences they brought to the subject domain, rather than casting them in deficit, or as 'empty vessels' into which knowledge is poured. Moreover, it established an ethos of participation which encouraged students to take control of their own learning by practising deeper levels of analysis as the course progressed.

Designing formative activities in which provisional views and mistakes are valued

However, the imperative to participate can, of course, expose misunderstandings and inadequacies, which can, from students' viewpoints, feel extremely uncomfortable and potentially disempowering. Carless (2006) and Handley *et al.* (2007), for instance, found that students often felt student–teacher dialogue was 'unsafe', because they were worried they might expose their inadequacies to an assessor. This made them reluctant to get involved in formative discussions with lecturers about their work. Handley *et al.* suggest 'there is clearly an issue about encouraging students to feel that they are members of an academic community where the norm is to discuss one's work in a relatively open, informed and scholarly manner' (2007: 14).

So while a major goal of AfL is to minimize hierarchical relationships (Broadfoot, 2007), in practice, with certain groups of students, this can very challenging to achieve (Marshall and Drummond, 2006), especially given the power differentials embedded in assessment (Knight, 2006; Orr, 2007).

Moreover, novices' sense-making in a domain which is 'new' to them is likely to be tentative and provisional at first, so students need to be clear that it is acceptable to have a go, make mistakes and learn from them. This all means that seeding communities of learners which are, as far as possible, low-stakes (Knight and Yorke, 2003) and non-threatening, and where the disposition to try things out, rather than only sharing highly polished performances, is valued.

Using a log book to promote seminar discussions

Seminars are, potentially, valuable learning spaces in which students discover a lot from discussing relevant issues in small groups. It can be hard, though, to encourage all students to participate fully, and seminars can become dominated by the voices of a few students, rather than everyone. In this example one teaching team designed a log book which formally required students to undertake a series of short writing tasks. The log book was designed to facilitate discussions in the four seminars which were linked to the rest of the module. Students were asked to complete each task 'in rough' before each small-group seminar. The tasks were not marked, but were used as the basis for seminar-group discussions and activities.

During the seminars, each student was asked to share his or her response with the whole group, in order to gain feedback from peers and the tutor and discuss how it might be further improved. Students generally felt that the small tasks were useful practice in trying out new skills and gaining suggestions which would help them improve before they were required to submit pieces of work to be marked. Most felt they benefited, for instance, from the chance to practise and discuss the ways in which they were using academic writing conventions in the discipline. It is interesting to note the extent to which, from this perspective, getting something 'wrong' and learning from hearing other students' approaches was particularly helpful, as the following student explained:

> *"One thing we learned from doing that {task} was that a lot of us were changing the authors into alphabetical order when they'd written an article. But it was only when we discussed that with each other, and got it wrong, that we really learned it."*

From this perspective, the process of making mistakes was useful, but most students claimed that for this to happen, it was important that the formative tasks were not graded or marked in any way.

Helping students to see the rationale for engaging in practice

According to Nicol (2009b), while lecturers should create academic structures and experiences that involve and engage, it is also important to develop ways of moving the locus of control to students themselves and find ways of encouraging them to take ownership and responsibility for their own learning. One approach is to offer students activities which enable them to practise making judgements for themselves about the relative quality of examples of student work. This can be done in carefully structured ways so that they are guided by their lecturers to hone their capacity to make effective evaluations.

It can be important, though, to spell out to students the thinking behind the tasks you set, so they can fully appreciate the point of the formative activities in relation to their own learning. For example, in the following example, students were asked to work, in class time, on concrete examples of students' work in order to develop a deeper appreciation of the meaning of plagiarism. In the preamble to the activities, the lecturer explained that having direct access to a range of examples of student work, and learning to make qualitative judgements about the degree to which any academic misconduct occurred in each, would be one of the main ways students could learn to avoid plagiarism themselves, by developing a nuanced and in-built feel for what it might look like in practice. Thus she sought to encourage her students to see the importance of learning to evaluate work in low-stakes environments, before it counts.

Enabling students to practise identifying plagiarism

Students can develop a fuller appreciation of what plagiarism means and what it might look like in practice, by practising identifying plagiarism in a range of examples of student writing. This helps them rehearse making decisions for themselves as to whether authentic extracts of student writing should or should not incur penalties. In one Study Skills lecture, delivered to 160 first-year undergraduates, the lecturer issued students with photocopies of brief illustrations of student writing which had been compiled to make specific pedagogic points, together with the original texts which the (imaginary) student authors had accessed. Students were asked to read all the material. Then, in groups, they were asked to discuss and identify which exemplars were copied verbatim; which summarized material with no acknowledgement; which summarized with some acknowledgement, although the student's referencing style was inadequate; and which clearly acknowledged the source material and built independently on the reading the student had done.

Enabling the students to practise in a low-stakes context meant the groups generated concrete examples of 'good' and 'bad' practice which could be discussed in the plenary session with the lecturers. This helped illuminate the dangers of incorrect citation and 'accidental' plagiarism, as well as more blatant, clear-cut examples. Seeing others' mistakes, which commonly occur in novices' academic writing, enabled students to realize, well before they came to prepare and hand in an assignment themselves, how easy it is to believe you have cited someone else's work, when actually you have not employed academic literacy conventions appropriately. It also signalled the limitations of a highly descriptive, 'cut and paste' writing approach which aimed to 'put in', rather than summarize, build on and make links across, other people's work. In this way the activity helped students practise identifying plagiarism and avoid common mistakes and surface approaches to learning, before they prepared their own work for the purposes of grading.

After this, students were offered the opportunity to submit their draft assignments to the internet-based plagiarism detection service, Turnitin. The lecturer activated Turnitin on the e-learning portal, Blackboard, so that students were able to gain an originality report on their assignment before they handed it in for the purposes of grading. This enabled students to check their own work for possible problems, and to make changes, if necessary. It also allowed them to raise any questions, uncertainties or issues with the lecturer, in time to address any misunderstandings. Given the strict penalties that students face if problems are noticed in work that has been submitted for grading, students really valued being able to check their own work before it counts.

Putting it into practice by creating opportunities for social interaction

Enhancing learning by building in carefully designed class discussions

When they come to tackle a new subject area, students often benefit from explicit encouragement to practise expressing and sharing their sense-making. Engineering fruitful situations for focused peer discussion and shared meaning-making is an essential part of designing interactive experiences for our students, both within and beyond our classrooms. Informal interactions with peers are highly important ways of learning (Boud and Middleton, 2003) in universities, because this places an inbuilt emphasis on a process of reflection, peer review and evaluation (Black and McCormick, 2010).

Working together to discuss what individuals feel are the key points within, say, set reading, can expose students to new ways of looking at something and can challenge their thinking. It also can help to build up their confidence and capabilities steadily, especially if the tasks are carefully designed to promote particularly important aspects of a subject domain, rather than simply expecting students to break into small groups and discuss a topic without a specified brief. Furthermore, by hearing what other people think of their ideas, and listening to how others – staff and students alike – express the sense they make of a topic, helps novices realize when they do not fully understand the ideas that emerge from a discussion or shared activity. By sharing their thinking about a topic and practising using subject-specific terms and concepts, students become better able to identify whether they have effectively grasped it or not.

Discussing the outcomes of in-class activities

In a technology-related course one lecturer arranged to issue his students with handheld voting technologies with one handset shared between every pair in the class. These personal response systems encouraged learners to think about, discuss and respond together to a set of questions and problems, which the lecturer set. During the lecture, the lecturer allocated a fixed amount of time for the pairs to work on each problem, which had no single 'right answer' but where some responses were more appropriate or comprehensive than others. He specified that students should negotiate and be able to explain the reasoning behind the answer they decided to give. After the allocated time, students were asked to use the voting system to submit their responses, which were then displayed to the class in aggregate form.

The lecturer highlighted the better responses and then invited pairs to explain the reasoning behind their answer to another pair. The lecturer then provided his own explanation.

This strategy encouraged students to practise explaining their views and reflecting on the processes of arriving at particular solutions. It also prompted them to engage with others' sense-making processes and learn as much from making a case as from getting an answer 'right'.

Furthermore, research has shown that good learning often develops from conversations (Laurillard, 2002; Light, 2001). This is because by talking about their learning, as they are in the process of doing it, students practise actively constructing meaning and rehearse the process of sense-making within their subjects in an ongoing and developmental way. When they are confronted with new experiences, or ideas, students often benefit from talking about them and actively using them within the subject area. For one thing, trying to articulate their own viewpoint to others helps them ascertain whether they are genuinely in a position to apply and use the knowledge productively. For another, trying to explain something to others helps them to *do* something with the material they have read, for example, so that they see whether they are able to field questions on it, or express something in their own words (Race, 2007). This all helps them to 'own' the ideas and perceive how far they genuinely understand something. In addition, hearing how other students express ideas can also be very helpful in developing an individual's understanding. By negotiating meaning with peers, students may discover other ways of approaching a topic, but also find their own thinking challenged and re-examined through the collective discussions of the group.

Staging a classroom debate

In discursive subject areas the process of staging debates and playing 'devil's advocate' often encourages learners to achieve a better understanding by juggling information; struggling to make sense; playing with different options; making decisions and linking information. For example, an English lecturer used a seminar to stage a debate about a particular literary genre. The group of sixteen students divided into two. One half of the group defended, whilst the other attacked, a particular type of contemporary fiction they were studying. To help students prepare for the discussion, the lecturer made various resources available, including press reviews, articles in newspapers and more considered academic criticism in scholarly journals. She offered students preparatory questions, prompting them to look for arguments others were making on aesthetic and ethical grounds, in order to prepare them to make a case for or against the genre.

In the seminar, role play was used, in which learners adopted different professional standpoints within each interest group. Students enjoyed the debate, which brought out the views of some people who had hitherto been fairly quiet in the larger group. In addition, giving students the chance to play an expert (for example, a university professor), also seemed empowering and brought out new theorizations and viewpoints which were not readily articulated in ordinary class discussions. The formative task encouraged students to engage enthusiastically with the subject (Mayes and de Freitas, 2004), so they were involved in spending their time on meaningful and productive activities. As one said: "... it was eye-opening and made me think. My analytical ability has improved because of this way of working."

Enhancing learning by encouraging students to form their own study groups

Nicol (2009b: 6) suggests that learning designs which trigger productive social relationships are important, because they can influence the identities that students form and their sense of belonging within academic structures. Cultivating supportive social relationships, where students have time and opportunity to interact and practise discussing material, can be challenging, given the relatively short periods of time when students are on campus and the competing demands on their time, which can make it hard for them to physically meet. One approach is to use online learning environments to offer formative experiences.

Encouraging students to discuss ideas online

In one module traditional face-to-face sessions were interspersed with web-based sessions, in order to help students understand and begin to share their reflections on the themes of the module. Activities were carefully designed in the online sessions, with students undertaking specific tasks. These involved them in locating information (in this case, about particular educational interventions) and then engaged them in discussions about what they found, in relation to a core concept (in this case, inclusive practice). Guided by key prompt questions, students were expected to research the issue for the online session by looking for information on the web, and posting their reflections on the topic, including reference to their reading, on a discussion board. The submissions were read by the tutor, but she took no active role in the discussions.

The web-based postings helped students to practise formulating their thoughts and communicating them to others. Some said it helped them begin to look at topics in greater depth, taking the time to clarify what they really felt, thought and wanted to say about the issue. Others felt it was helpful to have time and space to genuinely consider their views, and how to express them, which the 'live' nature of face-to-face discussion did not always allow time for. Some admitted that knowing other students would read the work meant that they read more thoroughly than they normally would, whilst others felt it was helpful to be able to read other students' attempts and ways of interpreting the tasks, which, in turn, broadened and deepened their own understanding.

Dialogue can mean more than just discussion, though. It can involve a sense of shared enterprise and social connection which can have a positive backwash effect on academic learning.

Enhancing learning by encouraging students to work in groups to collaboratively produce an agreed output

Boud (2009) argues that it is important that students learn to work in a social context. Most professional practice that they will encounter in their future lives will draw upon the skills of involving others. Like anything else, this takes practice. It can be helpful to design open-ended formative activities which require students to participate socially and intellectually to co-produce a specified output. This need not be formal, in fact, it can become part of collaborative in-class activities, as the following example illustrates. The social interactions can scaffold the skills of individual students while they practise sharing their ideas with others, and provide positive social support.

Engaging students in design activities

The lecturers invited students, in groups of four, to design different schools according to particular theoretical perspectives on childhood. A thumbnail sketch of each perspective was provided as a learning resource.

This activity helped students to step outside their personal views and opinions, compelling them to articulate, discuss and apply theoretical perspectives outside of their own personal frame of reference. The school designs could then be compared and contrasted, with students being asked to make notes on the similarities and differences, and to discuss the thinking behind each design feature. Two students from each group circulated around other posters, asking questions, while two people stayed to field questions about the rationale for their group's design. The lecturers' time was spent listening to the discussions, and helping students to ask more probing and pertinent questions. Students found the discussions challenging, but useful: *"Listening to the views of others allowed me to see how varied our responses to the data were . . . and made me start to think . . . It's not just cut-and-dried and there isn't just one way."* Many claimed they felt proud of what they had managed to achieve collectively and surprised by the level of intellectual sophistication they were able to manage, even at this early stage of the course.

Students can also be asked to work collaboratively to produce summatively assessed work. Working on a group project can encourage students to practise constructing and negotiating subject material together.

Collaboratively produced assignments

In one module students were required to produce guides to the topic which would be suitable for first-year undergraduates. Learners could decide to work alone, or with others, to produce these materials. Most students chose to develop their materials in small self-selecting groups or pairs. They claimed this offered them a more 'natural' way of working, in which ideas were shared and co-produced in a constructive process of dialogue, negotiation and peer review:

> *"Working on the same thing together is kind of helpful with this. Because we both have a working knowledge of the topic, we could actually say, 'No, I don't think that's right. Does this mean this? Should we put it this way?'"*

Hounsell (2007) argues that collaborative assignments like this can help foster connoisseurship and a fuller appreciation of academic standards amongst students, as students can learn from co-generation and co-writing as they practise using and applying subject material together.

Voicing the issues revisited: a case study of rehearsal and practice

Redesigning the whole module to inspire students to practise developing the skills and qualities of an emergent researcher

Two colleagues teaching on a Social Science degree used research-informed teaching (Brew, 2006) approaches to redesign a whole year-long first-year module to encourage students' practice and rehearsal. The student responses to the developments were explored. This illustrates how some of the suggestions given in this chapter can be used and how students may respond.

The lecturers introduced enquiry-based learning (EBL) to replace more traditional modes of teaching the introductory theoretical material. Baxter Magolda (2001) sees involving students in research and research-like activities as supporting them in developing more sophisticated 'ways of knowing' or conceptions of knowledge, which increase their confidence as learners and heighten learners' capability for independent thinking. Her findings suggested that students' development of complex assumptions of knowledge stemmed from participating and practising in a mentored, but independent research experience.

In this module, throughout the year, students were required to conduct a project. The teachers carefully designed a series of structured activities which supported learners to carry out a series of authentic small-scale enquiries which built students' confidence, skills and understandings up steadily (Sambell, 2009). These tasks involved students in the following ways:

- working in research teams;
- gathering, disseminating and analysing data from the field;
- sharing their interim findings as 'work-in-progress' reports;
- becoming involved in peer communities via a student conference.

The project work was broken up into three key stages in order to scaffold the students' experiences.

- Stage 1 involved students in gathering images. Here students were encouraged to act as research assistants, gathering and analysing data, by capturing digital images of literal signage they found in their local environment and gathering and analysing artefacts and documentary evidence about a specified topic from the physical public environment. Using such sources helped students practise identifying, selecting and analysing 'real-world' data by gradually using and applying diverse theoretical perspectives to the varied material they had gathered.
- Stage 2 involved students sharing and discussing their findings. The students' signs were produced as thumbnails on a 'Researchers' Forum' discussion board on the e-learning environment, so learners practised writing informally about their discoveries in the virtual environment. When they made a post, for instance, they were asked to comment on:

- their reasons for choosing a particular sign to display to others;
- comparisons about the potential meanings of different signs;
- observations about common themes and emergent patterns;
- interpretations of the signs' meanings in relation to theoretical perspectives and constructs studied on the course.

Class time was devoted to the discussion of emergent themes and links were made to the literature.

In interviews with our researchers, students noted, importantly, that the module was 'very different' from other lectures. They valued the ways in which the approach helped them practise generating tentative theories, informally, before their ideas 'counted' in terms of marks.

Here, the experience of working together with peers seemed crucial. They commonly felt that "*the conversations really do help*", and offered the following explanation:

> "*It's actually starting to formulate it in a way that makes sense and in a fun way and in a small group way that you feel comfortable with. And then you'll find that different people will take it in different directions.*"

Sharing ideas and feeding back on their research activity became centrally important from this perspective: "*Hearing everybody's answers you could see how differently people saw them [the ideas]. It was really interesting, and we don't do that in any other lecture.*" In this way the module's approach activated students as instructional resources for each other and as owners of their own learning (Black and Wiliam, 2009). This theme will now be specifically taken up and further developed in the following two chapters on feedback.

Key questions to think about

The following key questions are designed to help course and module teams develop their practice. They could, alternatively, be used for personal reflection.

- **How do you design your teaching (lectures, seminars, tutorials) so that students are active and participate fully, rather than just listen?** The contact time that students have is an important resource in their learning. You will want to use the time in high-value activities that enable tutors to interact with students and also use the social resource of everyone in the classroom. When discussing or planning module delivery it is easy to think about what each lecturer will deliver in terms of subject content. It is equally important to share the processes to be used amongst the teaching team to ensure that opportunities for participation offered to students are comprehensive and coherent.

- **Do you do anything to prompt your students to meet and discuss work or participate actively in other ways outside formal class hours?** After the class sessions are students simply referred to recommended reading or, in some technology-based subjects, given problem sheets to work through? Are students recommended or even required to undertake other specific study activities that continue the kinds of activities started in the classroom and which may include collaboration with other students? Student contact outside of the classroom is now greatly facilitated by online communication.

- **How do you create a climate for learning and discussion which makes students feel comfortable enough to have a go?** Activities which are part of summative assessment are inevitably high-stakes for students. They think about how their marks will be affected and, often, are concerned about the impression that they may make on a lecturer/assessor. Are there spaces in your modules which students accept as purely formative so that it is really worth having a go? If formative spaces are built into the programme on an ongoing basis the accepted culture of teacher–student interaction can change.

- **Where, and how, is your course built so that students can learn from making mistakes?** Even where students understand that they are not risking marks by 'having a go' they, like many of us, may feel uncomfortable to be seen by their teachers or fellow students as getting things wrong. However, valuable and useful learning rarely proceeds without some mistakes and misunderstandings. Covering these up and ignoring them is not helpful whereas trying to resolve them is. Do any members of the teaching team talk to students about what makes good learning and the role of 'mistakes'? How is that reinforced in actual classroom practice?

- **Where and how do your students have opportunity to practise summative assessment tasks?** Mostly we have emphasized the general idea of 'practice' in relation to subject knowledge, skills and understanding. However summative assessment is an important and high-stakes activity. It is vital that students are given guidance on summative tasks and where possible given the opportunity for some focused practice. If, for good reasons, you are using a range of different assessment methods on your course it is particularly important for students to have a dry run of any unfamiliar ones. This will vary from subject to subject but in some subjects students may never have been assessed by an oral presentation, or a portfolio or an open-book exam. A systematic look at the types of assessment in use and how students are prepared for them is essential.

Chapter 4

Designing formal feedback to improve learning

This aspect of AfL focuses on offering students learning environments that are rich in formal feedback aiming to support and accelerate learning. The chapter suggests that formal feedback can include, but also, importantly, take many more forms than tutor-written comments on summatively assessed work. Effective feedback can come from a wide range of different sources, and in different forms.

This chapter covers:

- problems and limitations with 'official' university feedback procedures;
- rethinking dominant conceptualizations of feedback;
- course design to provide more timely and usable feedback;
- involving students in producing feedback;
- engaging students with feedback;
- developing students' understanding of the role of feedback in relation to learning; enhancing students' feedback literacy.

Voicing the issues

Paul is a lecturer at the end of his first year of teaching Literature. He wants to help his students succeed and each term he takes immense care in writing his feedback comments on students' essays. During the university's two main assessment periods he blocks out his diary to attend to his marking and finds himself staying up into the early morning filling in the feedback forms and annotating the scripts with helpful suggestions. He thinks carefully about how students might respond to what he writes, and is careful to make positive as well as critical comments. He points out which aspects of a student's essay work well and offers constructive suggestions for elements which could have been developed to make the work even better. He links his comments to future assignments that the students may tackle, in an effort to help students take his suggestions on board next time round.

Paul feels rather surprised to receive an email from the Assignment Office, asking him to come and check that he's happy for the administrative team to dispose of a large volume of students' scripts. It turns out that nearly a third of Paul's students haven't called in to collect his feedback comments. Despite all his hard work crafting written feedback comments, many of them are actually thrown away, unread, at the end of the academic year. He is even more taken aback when he attends the Student Forum, where he discovers that the Student Representatives are mounting a Feedback Campaign, asking for more feedback. Paul is already feeling overwhelmed by the amount of work he is expected to invest in providing feedback, and when he reports the uncollected feedback to the rest of the staff team, several of his colleagues complain that even when students do collect the feedback, they don't seem to act on the advice they've been given.

AfL places considerable importance on formative assessment and feedback. However, Paul's experience illustrates one way in which the official university systems and procedures for providing feedback are limited and problematic, unless they are combined with other, arguably more important strategies to support learning. Lecturers like Paul may notice that, paradoxically, many students are failing to engage with this 'official' type of feedback, whilst at the same time appearing to demand more and more of it (Hounsell, 2003). One of the solutions often proposed is to provide more rapid feedback, or more high-quality feedback on summatively assessed work. While this may help, up to a point, it doesn't, on its own, really get to the heart of the matter because it still tends to regard feedback as a *product* which is associated with summative assessment rather than a *process* which is associated with improvement and development. If we wish to promote good learning we need to rethink and redesign feedback in a much more holistic and complex way.

However, Paul's experiences importantly illustrate the shortcomings of the limited and perhaps flawed model of our 'normal' views of feedback in university education – as the simple delivery of information about a student's performance. As Paul discovered, feedback on its own, no matter how good, is rarely effective. It is especially problematic if it is predominantly associated with summative work. For one thing, the 'official' model of providing feedback at the point of marking and grading is costly and time-intensive, especially as student numbers grow. For another, as we will argue, it is often ineffective in terms of improving students' learning. This means that we need to find ways to augment the dominant model of 'official feedback' which is actually part of summative assessment.

Theories and debates

Hounsell (2003: 67) argues that:

> it has long been recognised, by researchers and practitioners alike, that feedback plays a decisive role in learning and development, within and beyond formal educational settings. We learn faster, and much more effectively, when we have a clear sense of how well we are doing and what we might need to do in order to improve.

Wide-ranging research reviews (Hattie, Biggs and Purdie, 1996; Black and Wiliam, 1998a) have revealed that pedagogical interventions based on formative assessment and feedback have frequently been positive and impressive in relation to improving learning. On the basis of this evidence it is widely recognized that formative assessment is highly effective in improving student learning.

So it is now commonly accepted in Higher Education that the provision of high-quality feedback – information which helps learners form a realistic picture of how they are doing and what they might do to improve their current approach – is a crucial means of improving student learning (for example, Brown, Bull and Pendlebury, 1997; Gibbs and Simpson, 2004). Furthermore, the importance of feedback is duly acknowledged, for instance, in policy and enshrined in our codes of practice. The Quality Assurance Agency, for example, endorses the role of feedback and states that feedback should be 'sufficient, constructive and timely' (2006: 21). In particular, the effective use of staff time is emphasized and may entail: providing feedback at an early stage; different forms of feedback; encouraging student reflection; feedback to groups; and 'the effective use of comments on returned work, including relating feedback to intended learning outcomes and assessment criteria' (QAA, 2006: 21).

This chapter, and the ones which follow, seek to address some important issues surrounding feedback. In university education we need, urgently, to take a deeper, more careful look at how we design our feedback practices, and how students might experience them, because there is arguably plenty of scope for improvement. For example, Rust (2007: 231) asserts that while assessment practice in HE is generally deficient, 'the evidence is that it is in the area of feedback that we are possibly worst of all'.

Debatably there is room for development of feedback because in HE we have generally become more focused on the *provision* of feedback than on its context, quality and thus its effectiveness. In other words, all too often, feedback is conceptualized simply as the provision of information. But, as Paul's experience of feedback suggests, while on one level things may appear to be working well, beneath the surface they are not. There may actually be a large gap between staff's and students' viewpoints, for instance, which our attempts to survey the quality of learning and teaching (and feedback) may reveal as a difficulty, but do not illuminate in sufficient depth.

Crook, Gross and Dymott (2006) suggest that the quality assurance procedures which university staff use to monitor their assessment practices are largely paper-based, and may mask some difficulties. Their studies revealed that staff and students operated in different spaces. While staff felt confident that their assessment processes were working well, students were less convinced. For instance, from a student perspective, there were problems with insufficient guidance being provided before the assignment which meant that the feedback revealed too late what they should have done. To students it seemed that tutors were just providing feedback routinely – because they were obliged to – which made feedback feel impersonal, as if the marker did not know who they were, or didn't care. For Crook *et al.*, this meant, in practice, that our current assessment processes represent 'an enforced distancing of the principal participants, tutor and student' (2006: 11).

One of the problems with our attempts to meet students' apparently insatiable desire for more feedback (Hyland, 2000; McDowell *et al.*, 2008; O'Donovan, Price, and Rust, 2008) is that the most dominant way of 'doing feedback' in universities has become associated almost exclusively with the comments that tutors write on individual students' work. In fact, in everyday university discourse the term 'feedback' is usually taken to mean the written comments that lecturers like Paul provide on student work that has been submitted for marking. Here feedback becomes associated with the mandated university systems for the provision of feedback. For instance, many universities have introduced a policy to provide feedback on summative exams, in an effort to improve feedback. This usually means that students receive written comments on their performance in the exam (as opposed to simply receiving a mark, which used to be traditionally the case). While this is a step forward it still tends to position feedback as inert information which is provided, often retrospectively, and often with little obvious opportunity to discuss it.

As Paul's case showed, much staff time and effort is taken up producing written feedback on students' assessed work in this way (Nicol, 2010a; Price *et al.*, 2010). In one sense, this chapter opens up our debate about improving feedback by focusing on ways of beginning to remedy some of the shortcomings of this particularly limited model of 'official' feedback. There is widespread dissatisfaction with the current state of affairs. It has a number of problems beyond the ones already mentioned. For one thing, this kind of feedback is extremely costly, because the economies of scale which are achieved by teaching large classes are not matched when it comes to marking work and providing feedback for large groups (Gibbs, 2010: 8). So the provision of feedback has now become something of a flashpoint, especially in light of the pressures of widespread student dissatisfaction with feedback, which National Student Surveys (NSS) (e.g. HEFCE, 2011) routinely reveal. Given the importance attached to the findings of such surveys this dissatisfaction is prompting universities to respond in arguably technicist or managerial terms, rather than educationally driven ways. The imperative to turn around marking more rapidly, and provide more written feedback at this stage, is starting to exert immense pressure on staff workloads.

There are issues, too, about the timeliness of feedback. In practice, it often comes too late to enable students to improve their performance (Higgins, Hartley and Skelton, 2002), especially if students fail to see the relevance of feedback comments for work they may do in future. One possible reason for Paul's experience, when students didn't even go to collect and read their feedback, is that they felt that the 'bit' of learning was over and done with, so there was little point in worrying about how to improve it. Laurillard (2002) makes a useful distinction here between 'extrinsic' feedback, that constitutes a commentary subsequent to the action, and 'intrinsic' feedback, which takes place within the context of the action. It stands to reason that the latter seems more valuable in terms of enabling change and influencing a learner's future action, but most formal feedback sheets are given to students at (as they may see it) the end of a module or a unit of learning, when they've moved on to new topics and modules. Furthermore, by offering a summary judgement (such as a mark or grade), traditional feedback forms tend to position this kind of 'official' feedback strongly within a measurement rather than a learning paradigm. This might distract a student from engaging with any developmental function the feedback has been designed to offer (Black and Wiliam, 1998a).

Another possible reason that so many of Paul's comments were left unread was that he did his best, from his point of view, to refer in detail to the specifics of the particular assignment, and show his students ways of improving in relation to the concepts and issues of that precise task. Bloxham (2009) has pointed out how the traditional university feedback form is, from the lecturer's perspective, inevitably often linked to accountability and quality assurance, which might mean the feedback-giver actually has as much of an eye on the external examiner and a perceived need to defend and justify the grade awarded (Price, Handley and Millar, 2011), as on the student for whom the feedback is, ostensibly, crafted. After all, feedback forms are often the main source of tangible evidence that appropriate feedback mechanisms are in place on our courses. This might mean that the feedback comments tend to look back at what was done well and less well, rather than forward to future work. Consequently, students often feel unable to transfer the guidance to other pieces of work, which may seem to the student to be quite different.

Research has found, too, that feedback in this format is difficult for students to understand. This may be partly to do with the language in which the tutors' feedback messages are couched (Chanock, 2000; Lillis and Turner, 2001; Price *et al.*, 2010). Phrases which make perfect sense to an academic, like 'develop your argument' or 'probe the ideas further', may not help a student to make sense of what they actually need to do next, how they might adjust their approach, or what that might look like in actual student productions. Whilst the issue of language could be addressed on a straightforward level, it remains the case that many of the concepts that are applied to academic work are, at deeper levels, very difficult to understand. This is especially true for those who are, by dint of limited experience, on the 'outside' of the conventions and ways of seeing, thinking and practising that seem commonplace to the expert community (Haggis, 2006; Lea and Street, 1998).

But arguably the most important limitation is if this kind of feedback is regarded, on its own, by staff or students, as being the main means by which students can find out how they are doing and what they need to do to improve their work. In its extreme form, this view of feedback can become equated in people's minds with a linear model in which tutors are the sole providers of advice and guidance. Here the student's role is to simply wait to receive feedback, as it is only after this 'gift' has been given that they can move forward in their learning. This 'transmission' model, or feedback-as-telling, relies exclusively on the tutor dispensing advice, or, perhaps, instructing the student what to do. From this perspective, feedback is conceptualized merely as a *product* which is delivered (or withheld) by staff, rather than a *process* within which staff and students are 'jointly and severally liable' (Black and Wiliam, 2009: 7). In other words, it positions the student in a passive, dependent mode of reliance on their teachers.

Furthermore, there are plenty of indications that students themselves possess limited or unhelpful models of feedback (Ecclestone, 2002; Glover, 2006), which potentially prevent them from making the most of its benefits. They may, for instance, have come to university having experienced a model of feedback in school which has been dominated by submitting coursework, and receiving teacher comments on drafts, which are actually about being 'told' what to put in, and what to leave out of, an essay (Sambell, 2011). We may need to work hard to encourage students with these sorts of experiences of feedback, to begin to see feedback through a new lens, or see how it might be used. They need to see, too, the active part they need to play within the feedback (and learning) process.

There are clearly substantial learning benefits to be gained by rethinking our overall approaches to the provision of feedback (Nicol, 2009b). It is important to recognize that unless students actually engage with feedback information and use it to adjust their learning it will fail to have any of its intended regulatory or transformational effects. In other words, to actually 'count' as feedback, any information which emanates from an evaluation of a student's performance must actually modify learning activity in some way (Black and Wiliam, 1998a). In this sense students' active involvement with, or *reaction* to, feedback must be emphasized in our feedback designs, otherwise feedback will not contribute to learning. It is this aspect that we address when attempting to improve and enhance feedback practices in this chapter.

One of the strongest emerging themes from developments in research and policy is to question both the way in which the feedback process itself is conceptualized and the role of the student in that process (Boud and Falchikov, 2007; Elwood and Klenowski, 2002; Nicol and Macfarlane-Dick, 2006; Sadler, 1998; van de Ridder *et al.*, 2008). These new perspectives are in line with the social views of learning we have discussed in earlier chapters of this book. The premise is that, just as learning does not occur through the mere transmission of information, nor does feedback delivery, on its own, necessarily lead to learning improvement. From these perspectives, to ensure that feedback is effective, we must do much more than construct better feedback messages after the event, or provide extra written feedback in a traditional sense. Learning can be improved by offering more plentiful and richer opportunities for students to *engage* actively with formal feedback, and by embedding feedback in learning communities. To be truly effective this would mean that we reconceptualize feedback as a cycle, which importantly includes information and reaction (van de Ridder *et al.*, 2008; Nicol, 2010a), with the possibility for exchange and dialogue. This recasts feedback as an important aspect of a process which is threaded throughout a student's learning journey, based on a clear vision of AfL. Feedback in any form needs to go hand-in-hand with learning and have an improvement focus. Feedback has the capacity to promote learning but to do so it must be embedded, and learners must see the point of it, reflect on it, and comprehend how they can use it to help them. Above all, students must actively use feedback, and the giver of the feedback ideally needs to see what the impact has been.

This chapter argues, then, that formal feedback is an essential component of formative assessment, but it can take many forms. Formal feedback can be much more than providing students with written comments on university feedback forms. Other approaches are possible, and, we would argue, desirable, to augment and complement this commonplace and main way of providing feedback in Higher Education. Perhaps above all we need to design strategies which help students see and experience feedback in a complex way as a process that can support learning, with students actively engaged with feedback during the act of learning itself. It is important to remember that the actual effects of feedback in any specific case will be influenced by contextual features. Nevertheless, the quality of feedback and the context within which it occurs are vital to the success or otherwise of feedback. It is this issue that this chapter focuses upon and as Nicol and Macfarlane-Dick (2006) argue, two important principles of good feedback include teachers designing opportunities to:

- deliver high-quality information to students about their learning which helps them to correct their own work;
- provide opportunities for students to act on feedback, enabling them to close any gap between current and desired performance.

From our perspective, there are a range of ways in which teacher feedback can be constructed, delivered, communicated and so on. It can be infused throughout the curriculum, for instance, and occur more often. In addition, feedback can emanate from a range of sources, not just teachers. Peers and employers, amongst others, can also help to provide a rich array of timely, usable feedback. But for feedback to be effective, students must 'own', internalize, understand, reflect and act upon it, so that they can use it to close any gap between their current performance and the standard of performance that is required in any given context (Price *et al.*, 2010). This actually entails assisting students to come to appreciate, and realize for themselves, what counts as high-quality work in the subject area and enabling them to use a range of feedback to regulate their own work, during the course of actually producing it. This is the particular focus of the next two chapters. But first, to pave the way for students to work like this, there are substantial benefits in students coming to understand the role that formal feedback plays in relation to learning, and the part that they play in relation to it. This means that tutors might productively design activities which prompt students to engage actively with the formal feedback they receive and, better still, take high levels of responsibility for understanding the feedback process and for playing a participative and generative role within it.

Putting it into practice

There are many ways in which subject lecturers have tried to improve the manner in which their students experience the benefits of formative assessment by carefully designing their courses to offer their students enhanced feedback opportunities. One way of doing this is to ensure that students regularly receive high-quality information which indicates how well they are currently performing with their work and how such work might be improved (Nicol and Macfarlane-Dick, 2006). A teacher providing rich, ample, timely and targeted feedback on draft or provisional work is one way of achieving this, with the aim of showing students what has been done well, and what has not, and how their work could be better. Second, peers and others can be deployed to provide more formal feedback. Finally, strategies which help raise students' awareness of the role of formal feedback in relation to learning, and their part in that process, can help students to be in a better position to recognize, use and seek feedback. This begins to develop their feedback literacy.

This section of the chapter highlights three broad approaches to putting formal feedback into practice. These are:

- putting it into practice by enhancing tutor feedback to make it work better;
- putting it into practice by deploying others to provide feedback;
- putting it into practice by focusing student attention on feedback.

Putting it into practice by enhancing tutor feedback to make it work better

It is widely accepted that a key principle of AfL is that students require access to specific and detailed information which helps them see how well they are doing and focuses upon ways to improve. In practice, this means providing them with feedback-rich teaching and learning environments in which they are not only actively involved in undertaking formative tasks and activities, but also gain lots of feedback on the degree to which they are mastering the subject appropriately and on what they need to achieve. Viewed like this, the lecturer's role is to carefully consider the ways in which rich, timely feedback can be provided on episodes of transacted work, at formative and summative stages.

Enhancing learning by providing comments on work while students are producing it

Gibbs and Simpson (2004: 230) identified a range of features of assessment that support learning. Seven of the eleven features which they noted specifically concerned the provision of feedback. For example, their work drew attention to the need for students to receive sufficient feedback, in the sense that feedback was given both often enough and in adequate detail. They also emphasized the need for feedback to be timely in that it is received by students while it still matters to them and in time for them to pay attention to further learning or receive further assistance. In addition, their research suggested that, to be really meaningful, feedback should be appropriate to the purpose of the particular assignment and related to its criteria for success. Feedback must be appropriate in relation to students' understanding of what they are supposed to be doing.

Many of Gibbs and Simpson's principles emphasize the desirability of trying to ensure that feedback provision moves away from being exclusively provided on students' assessed work 'at the end'. Instead, end-point feedback is supplemented by earlier forms of feedback, so that formal feedback is available to students in time for them to act upon it. This may entail, for example, trying to build opportunities for formal feedback to be offered iteratively, in loops which become threaded throughout a module.

From these standpoints, students will benefit, for instance, from feedback which their teachers provide *before* their work is submitted for summative assessment. One way of achieving this is to build in opportunities for students to receive feedback on draft work which doesn't 'count' in terms of marks, but has high learning value because it has consciously been designed to operate in iterative cycles within a module. This process allows students to gradually hone and develop their performance over a period of time, supported by feedback which clearly shows students what has been done well, what has not, and how their work could be improved (Boud *et al.*, 2010: 2).

In the following example, the effects of providing students with teacher feedback about the quality of their work and what next steps they could take in relation to their draft assignment-work was amplified by enabling students to listen to the comments that were given by the teacher to fellow students in their group.

Providing teacher feedback on students' draft work

Towards the end of the second semester, Biology students submitted drafts of their final essay three weeks prior to the submission date. They received written tutor feedback in the form of annotated notes on their script, which the lecturer used to try and point out what had been achieved well, and offer pointers for further development.

In addition to providing these tutor comments, the lecturer asked his students to come along to discuss their feedback in group tutorials. This allowed students to discuss anything they were unsure about and ask any questions on issues on which they wanted further clarification. If, for example, a student did not understand a feedback comment, or what they were meant to do to improve their work, they had the opportunity to talk about it. They also had the chance to listen to the comments that were made about other students' work, and questions asked by other students in the group, which helped some become clearer about what was being required.

The tutorials were well attended, because most students felt it was extremely helpful to be offered the chance to hear the lecturer's views about the quality and standard of their work, before they were required to hand it in. Moreover, the students were keen to find out what constituted good work, so they developed a better picture of what they were aiming to achieve. The tutorial discussions of the feedback began to open up discussions of 'better' and 'less effective' work which started to help students to learn to appreciate what the criteria for success actually meant in this particular assignment.

For some lecturers, especially those working with relatively large groups of students, providing more written feedback, as outlined in the example above, is simply not feasible. Another approach, however, involves offering students choice about *when* to receive their written feedback. This approach entailed the lecturer getting prior agreement from the department to 'shift' the time she would normally spend writing feedback on students' scripts. In effect, she offered her students the choice of receiving lengthy written comments *either* on their summative essays, *or* on draft work. (She needed to be careful to negotiate this in advance with departmental colleagues as it did not sit readily with the normal quality assurance mechanisms nor the workload model.)

Giving students the choice of when to receive feedback

First-year Language students on one particular module were asked at the beginning of the second semester whether they would prefer to receive 'traditional' written feedback on their essay after the module was over or whether they would rather receive this detailed feedback three weeks before the submission date and have the opportunity to redraft their essay. The tutor said that for reasons of her workload they could only have one or the other and if they chose the detailed feedback at the earlier stage they would only receive a mark written on their final feedback sheet. The students all agreed that they preferred to have feedback prior to submission when they would have time to use the feedback given in improving the quality of their work.

Thus, students were asked to submit a draft of their summative essay on the last day before the Easter break in the second semester. The tutor was firm about submission and stipulated that the drafts had to be submitted at an agreed time and no late submissions could be accepted. The tutor then prepared her feedback on the essays and, in the first week back after the break, lectures and seminars were given over to feedback sessions where students received oral and written feedback (in the form of comments on their scripts) in group tutorials. In these small groups of five or six students the tutor talked about individual essays while all the students listened. This gave all the students in the small group tutorial an opportunity to learn from the issues raised in others' work. Once students had had the chance to ask questions and talk about their drafts in these tutorials they still had three weeks in which to improve their submission before finally submitting it to be graded.

At the end of the module the tutor wrote only a percentage grade on the feedback sheet, thus avoiding time-consuming provision of written feedback on module sheets that students may not be able to use in the context in which it was given. The tutor felt that this approach helped to recast students' views of feedback as formative activity rather than as an '*add-on*' to teaching and learning activities (Orrell, 2006).

Over the three years when this method was used in the module, nearly every student engaged with the process. For instance, in one academic year only four of the seventy students did not take up the chance to submit a draft of their final summative assessment to receive formative tutor feedback before the completion date. As one student said:

> "... *when you got it handed back to you, you found out if your style worked, or how you could do it. It helped all round really, because with not having any assignments handed in and given back with any feedback since May in the year before our A-levels, it was nice and helpful.*"

Setting short tasks which allow students to gain formative feedback

Carless (2007a) argues that for assessment to promote learning, students need to receive appropriate feedback which they can use to 'feedforward' into future work. From this viewpoint effective feedback should be timely and forward-looking so as to support both current and future student learning. However, as we noticed with Paul's example at the start of the chapter, modularization all too easily encourages staff and students alike to adopt a view of formal teacher feedback coming at the very end of a unit of learning, so it becomes associated almost entirely with the summative assessment. One counteractive strategy is to ensure that students undertake lots of short formative tutor-marked tasks early on in a module, so that they gain rapid and plentiful feedback, such that they can subsequently take forward any advice into future summatively assessed work.

Feedback on short tasks

In Psychology scientific report writing plays a major role, so students need to learn how to write reports effectively. Given the resources and large classes, however, one teaching team was finding that it was becoming impossible to set a number of full reports which allowed their first-year students to practise, and gain feedback on, their report writing skills over the course of the year. Convinced that it was important to provide students with feedback on their achievements, however, the team decided, instead, to give rapid feedback on a series of much shorter pieces of work. Instead of trying to formatively assess and provide feedback on complete reports they decided to break the tasks down. In week one they asked the students to write a results section; in week two they were required to write their method; in week three, their abstract, and so on. This meant that students received a good amount of teacher-written feedback throughout the first semester. It also provided a framework for them to write a full report in the second semester. As in the earlier examples, seminars and tutorials were used, on occasion, to discuss students' feedback with them on a personal level. This was further augmented by tutors discussing aspects that students had generally undertaken well, and points which generally needed development, with the entire group during lecture time.

Helping students learn from feedback associated with staged summative tasks

Hounsell (2007) suggests it can be useful to aim to provide prognostic 'feedforward' rather than retrospective feedback, in order to promote a cycle of learning and development that looks towards future activity instead of encouraging students to concentrate on past errors. One way of accomplishing this might involve breaking down a module assignment into smaller steps which, while still 'counting' in terms of marks, demonstrably link together and explicitly build on one another.

As the following example illustrates, this approach can be used to engage students with feedback generated from the interlinked summatively assessed tasks which are staged over the year.

Breaking an overall summative assessment down into smaller linked components

In an introductory English module the tutors felt worried that students often seemed to 'miss the point' of the critical theory which was the cornerstone of the module, so that they failed to apply it to their close reading of specific texts when it came to the summative assignment. Lecturers felt that an increase in formal feedback during the module itself might help to direct students' attention to their expectations and requirements. They decided to divide the original single sum-mative assessment they habitually set into two linked components. The first part was to be submitted early on in the semester and the second part was to be submitted at the end.

In practice, this meant that students became engaged in writing for assessment at a much earlier stage than would otherwise have been the case and this enabled tutors to provide them with written feedback that they could use in the second part of the assessment. The tutors made sure, in their comments, to focus on forward-looking points which encouraged the students to think about how to close the gap between their current performance and the standard they would be expected to meet by the end of the year.

In addition to this, when the students submitted the second task, they were asked to write a reflective response to the feedback the tutors had provided on the first task. They were required to submit this as a compulsory component of their second summative piece. The tutors felt this helped encourage students to actively engage with the formal feedback given by the tutor and encouraged the tutors themselves to think about assessment and feedback as a cycle.

Whilst the tutors in the above example believed that it had been useful to break the assignment down into components to enrich the formal feedback opportunities on offer, they were also concerned that, if over-used as a strategy, it may result in students feeling that they were constantly being 'tested'. They worried that this could result in students 'playing safe' rather than taking the sorts of risks and experimental approaches to essay-writing that the tutors believed were necessary to hone the skills and qualities that underpin high-quality work within the subject area. In this instance, they felt the pay-offs outweighed the disadvantages but, as we noted in Chapter 2, it can be tricky to achieve an appropriate balance between formative and summative assessment.

Enhancing learning by offering teacher feedback in alternative formats

The provision of written tutor comments on draft work, on 'practice' formative tasks or on smaller staged tasks, however, is a very resource-intensive means of providing feedback. But formal feedback which is a planned part of any module or programme can take different, arguably less time-intensive, formats. Tutors may, for instance, give students formative feedback on oral presentations or progress reports by using feedback grids composed of general points they know, from experience, students commonly need to pay attention to in work of a particular kind (Bloxham and Boyd, 2007: 108). Ticking or highlighting commonly occurring feedback statements is not only quicker than writing the comments by hand each time, but also lets students see the sorts of advice tutors often find themselves offering, so they can begin to perceive what aspects of the work really matter to an assessor.

Using checklists to provide feedback

In Mechanical Engineering, second-year students were required to work on a design-and-build project. The tutor was keen to provide students with feedback at interim stages of the work, but was concerned that he simply did not have sufficient time to take in, read, and write comments on students' progress reports on an individual basis.

Instead, at key points through the project, the tutor required his students to present their ideas about their project developments to him and the rest of the group. He structured the presentations to focus on particular stages of the design process, so that students would gain vital feedback on their plans in time to alter them, if necessary, to improve their final outcomes.

At each progress report session, the tutor used a checklist of assessment criteria against which to structure the students' feedback. This involved giving the students an indication of whether their work was unsatisfactory, satisfactory or outstanding in relation to the module learning outcomes, with the tutor circling one of these statements in relation to each criterion. This feedback gave students a broad sense of how they were doing. To enrich this, the tutor wrote a few overall comments about strengths of the current work and areas to improve.

The tutor was pleased with the approach, as it meant he did not have to spend lots of time taking in and reading through student work, but could focus his attention, instead, on interacting with the students and discussing their work, whilst simultaneously offering targeted feedback comments and ensuring that students realized whether they were on the right lines.

Improving the accessibility of teacher feedback

There are other ways of providing feedback which also might be less time-intensive than providing written comments on students' work. For instance, some lecturers have found that providing audio-feedback or podcasts, in which they record their comments as they read a student script as opposed to producing written comments, can allow them to offer much more feedback than might otherwise be the case.

There is also the added benefit of this kind of feedback being a much more intimate and personal form of communication, which some students appreciate because they find it speaks to them on a deeper level and is easier to understand than conventional tutor-written comments (Merry and Orsmond, 2008). There is a good deal of evidence in the research literature (Chanock, 2000; Hyland, 2000) that students do not understand the written feedback comments they are given, which limits their ability to use the feedback productively. For instance, the student may be advised their essay is 'insufficiently analytical' but have little idea what to actually do to make the essay 'more analytical'. Alternative feedback formats can give lecturers space to talk in more detail about ways of improving work. 'Talking aloud' rather than laboriously writing comments can also allow lecturers to express and flesh out complex ideas in different ways. This can help us offer better, more useful comments for some students.

Providing feedback via audio files

In a third-year Environmental Studies module, students were offered the opportunity to submit the introductory chapter of their final-year dissertation as a formative exercise half-way through the second semester. After reading the students' work, the tutor recorded his spoken feedback onto his desktop PC using freely available software. The recorded files were then converted to mp3 format, which were subsequently forwarded to the students as email attachments.

Students were very positive about receiving feedback in this format. They felt the tutor's comments focused more clearly on areas they needed to work on further. They appreciated the ability to listen to the tone of the teacher's voice, and the emphasis he placed on certain aspects, which didn't always come across to them in his written feedback. This helped the students to develop a better appreciation of the ways in which the tutor thought about the features of 'good' dissertations.

Overall, the tutor felt the quality of the feedback he had managed to produce was of a higher standard than might have been the case with written comments. However, there were a few technical issues which meant that, in practice, little time was actually saved.

Giving feedback to groups

When considering their feedback designs lecturers often think of feedback as necessarily being something that has to be individualized. They may believe that students can only use feedback that has been tailored intimately to their own personal response to a task. However, feeding back to whole groups in general terms, after their work has been marked, can help students learn from listening to the feedback on the mistakes or inadequacies of other students' approaches and from hearing the feedback on what constituted a 'good' attempt (Race, 2001). The effects can be multiplied by using the production of a class report on a task as a starting point for discussion and dialogue during a whole-class debriefing session.

Whole-group feedback on exam performance

As we observed earlier, universities are often looking for feasible ways of enhancing feedback provision on students' examination performances, where traditionally students often only receive a mark, rather than any meaningful qualitative feedback comments.

On an Accounting programme, the course team agreed to offer students a 'feedback lecture' at the end of any module which contained an examination. The team felt that the provision of generic feedback to the whole group would be a time-efficient way to approach the university requirement to improve feedback practice on examinations. Oral feedback was given by the module leader to the whole group during the feedback lecture. This focused on generic issues and collated the markers' overviews of things that many students did well, and things they commonly did wrong or made mistakes with. The module tutor delivering the feedback made it clear to students that this was an important part of the feedback process, because it would help them identify not only where many people made mistakes, but also would involve the lecturers' explanations about why those mistakes were likely to have been made and how they should have been tackled.

The lecturers involved in this initiative felt it was useful for all the markers of an exam to come together to discuss and agree the general feedback comments which would be drawn out by the module tutor who delivered the feedback lecture. This process enabled them to think about the broad areas in which students were performing effectively, and the areas they needed more work on and help with. As teaching teams, they were able to take this forward in two ways. First, they put strategies in place to help this particular cohort of students with areas many found particularly challenging. This was important, not just for those students required to do resits, but for those doing future work which built on the conceptual areas covered by a particular module. Second, module tutors were able to use the general feedback comments with the next cohort of students to take the module. They used the comments to alert the new group of students, well in advance, to some common mistakes that novices often make when they are studying a particular area, and why. In this way the teacher feedback on exams could act as 'pre-emptive formative assessment' (Carless, 2007a), helping students to see common misconceptions so they were forewarned and could take action to address these before they caused them difficulties in the summative assessment.

Putting it into practice by deploying others to provide feedback

We noticed earlier that many students think of teachers as the sole providers of feedback, and can become very dependent on their lecturers to give them feedback which improves their summative performance on a particular assignment (Sambell, 2011). Arguably, though, feedback should also develop students' understandings of how they need to do things more generally in the subject, and what counts as 'good work'. In an ideal scenario, feedback should help guide students to develop their overall competence as learners, and this is often what lecturers intend. It may be, though, that on its own, the provision of teacher feedback does not go far enough, not least because it risks implying that feedback is simply about tutors teaching learners to jump artificially through some assessment hoops (Torrance, 2007) rather than learning to become genuinely involved with feedback as part of the overall process of learning.

The research literature in Higher Education offers ample evidence of the benefits of providing students with opportunities to give and receive feedback from their fellow students because it encourages and supports them to think more deeply about material, become more critically aware about what counts as quality work, learn more about a topic and gain in confidence (see Boud, Cohen and Sampson, 1999; Falchikov, 2001, 2005a; Nicol, 2009a; Orsmond, Merry and Reiling, 1996, 2002). Hounsell, Hounsell and Tai (2010) note that the introduction of peer feedback has spread rapidly, and many examples can be found across a range of subjects. It is now generally accepted that it is valuable to design structured opportunities for feedback which draw students' attention to the range of people, not just tutors, who can offer them useful feedback.

Using peers to provide feedback

One pragmatic reason for designing-in peer feedback opportunities is that it enables students to receive more feedback more quickly than when academics alone are providing comments. However, the benefits exceed this. Liu and Carless (2006) have called peer feedback 'the learning element of peer assessment'. They note that deploying peers to provide formative feedback does not usually carry the levels of anxiety or concern – on the part of students as well as staff – that can be associated with the kinds of peer assessment that result in the award of a mark or grade, so peer feedback can act as an important means of helping students begin to develop important skills for lifelong learning, such as self-evaluation and justifying one's judgement. They argue that 'with increasing resource constraints and decreasing capacity of academics to provide sufficient feedback, peer feedback can become a central part of the learning process, rather than an occasional option' (2006: 281).

Peer review can valuably be used as a means of enabling students to receive feedback on draft work which they subsequently rework and improve for a final submission. Suitably organized by the teacher, the process of student involvement in generating feedback for peers can also begin to draw students' attention to the goals and standards of the subject, which is a precondition of taking responsibility for their own work.

Involving peers to provide comments on drafts

In Business Studies the lecturer wanted to flag up to her students the importance of attending to broad theoretical issues. She was particularly concerned that, on her third-year module, students often tended to focus on acquiring content knowledge but the learning outcomes also required them to use critical reflection to improve their learning.

Well in advance of the hand-in date, she asked her students to bring a 1,000 word draft of their module assignment to a session. They then peer-reviewed the drafts in groups of three. It was stressed that participation in this formative exercise would help students directly with their final assignment submission because it would allow them to gain feedback on their performance in relation to the module's goals. For the peer review, students were supplied with guidance on giving constructive feedback and were issued with a peer review sheet. At the start of the session the lecturer facilitated a class discussion about her view of the most important assessment criteria on the sheet. She hoped this would help her students discern that she wanted them to make meaning, rather than simply reproduce material on the topic. She encouraged students to focus their feedback comments on the theoretical depth of the draft (for instance, how well points were supported by evidence and how far possible viewpoints on the topic were compared and contrasted), in addition to presentational matters, such as style and format.

Students reported finding the peer comments very helpful, often because they seemed more accessible than the tutors' comments. Coming from a student perspective, the feedback tended to be communicated in a way that made sense to other students.

Peer feedback to support self-regulation

Peer feedback can valuably be offered in purely formative contexts, with comments provided on tasks which are set with the exclusive purpose of providing students with feedback on 'how they are doing', rather than being specifically focused on 'getting higher marks'. Feedback with this clear purpose, which is actually dissociated from a summative task, can help students to see the longer-term benefits of learning to generate, seek and use feedback in their learning. After all, in future professional life, students will be expected to attend to feedback from a range of stakeholders, so it is educationally useful to switch students' attention away from lecturers as the customary providers of feedback, towards peers, more experienced students, employers and other stakeholders as the creators and communicators of useful feedback.

For instance, many students are required to develop high-level presentation skills, and peers can usefully be deployed to provide feedback about this, to help scaffold the development of learner self-regulation, as the following example depicts.

Peer feedback on student presentations

In Psychology it is important that students focus on developing their presentation skills. On a second-year module, the tutor wanted students to become more aware of how far they were developing their skills, and what they needed to work on to improve. She invited her students to prepare and deliver group presentations on a relevant topic, and arranged to have each presentation video-recorded.

Over three sessions, working in groups, students chose a topic and presented a very brief paper on that topic. They were encouraged to try out various techniques during their presentations to see what worked best. The activity was entirely voluntary and carried no marks. Out of seventy-five students, seventy-two chose to take part. While the groups presented, students in the audience filled in feedback checklists, where they rated individuals against specific criteria on a five-point scale. The criteria included aspects like 'effective use of visual aids', 'clarity of information', 'audibility', 'engages audience', and so on.

The videoed presentations were saved to CD. These were distributed, with each group being given a CD of their own group presenting. Group members were subsequently asked to watch the CD and fill in more detailed peer review sheets, using the same criteria, which required them to give each other qualitative peer feedback comments which offered one positive comment and one suggestion for improvement against each. Having a CD to keep meant the students could go back and refer to the presentation again at a later date. Students said that they learned more doing this activity than they had in any written feedback they had received on presentations.

Using technology to enhance feedback provision

Technology can be used to play a key part in enhancing feedback provision (Nicol and Milligan, 2006). Online management systems can speed up the processing and distribution of feedback to large groups of students (Denton, 2001), perhaps by allowing the feedback provider to select commonly used feedback comments from a drop-down menu. Computer-aided assessment tasks can provide instant feedback to learners as they work, say, on objective tests (Bull and McKenna, 2004). But technology can also enhance the opportunities for learners to discuss and interact with feedback, as well as receive more of it. For instance, online interaction, via forums, blogs, email and voice boards can enrich feedback by involving a host of others, without the constraints of being required to physically meet up to comment on each others' work.

Formative peer review to generate feedback in online communities

In Sports Science, students were established in study syndicates via the university's e-learning portal. At specific points during a module, one student became a blog writer who provided a commentary on selected set reading, while the rest of the students offered feedback on the blog writer's analysis – helping them perceive omissions, misunderstandings, or challenge their prejudices. Students received considerably more feedback than they otherwise could have expected from a tutor by using this method. But students also liked the asynchronous nature of this form of communication, which allowed them to post comments and read the comments whenever they liked. Further, they liked the capacity to see a range of feedback comments about someone's work, and valued the ability to go back and read the range of feedback comments about their own work at various points, so they could gauge for themselves whether they had addressed any issues that were raised.

Providing authentic feedback

To be effective, feedback must be offered in a form that the learner perceives as useful and that they are likely to use. Rather than being inherently 'good' or 'poor', any feedback that is provided actually has a relational dimension, whereby students' interpretations of, and responses to any given feedback partly depend on the relationship that the students believe exist between themselves and the feedback provider. Students need, for example, to trust the authority and credibility of the feedback provider before they are willing to take on board their advice (Chinn and Brewer, 1993).

One way of making feedback more authentic is to invite external agents, for example, from the world of work, to provide feedback to students. This can lend a sense of authenticity to the feedback process, as it comes from someone whose opinion is regarded as important and typically highly valued by students.

In the following examples, stakeholders from outside the university were invited to offer feedback, which the students took very seriously indeed.

Using employers and service users to provide feedback

In Design, managers from mobile telephone companies were invited to provide feedback on the strengths of students' projects. They became involved at an early stage in the students' work, identifying improvements and providing direction to students.

In Social Work a group of service users were recruited and consulted about giving students feedback on a client interview. The service users agreed to be interviewed by a student about their specific needs, to emulate a common scenario in the student's future practice. The interview was video-taped and played back as the focus of a feedback meeting between tutor, student and the service user.

In both cases, the comments offered by the employers and the service users encouraged the students to engage very seriously with the feedback and offered them new insights into the ways in which they needed to adjust their approaches to similar scenarios in the future.

It is also important to consider the relational dimension of feedback with regard to peer feedback. On the one hand, unless students have been well prepared and trained to undertake peer review, peers may believe that other students' comments are not worth listening to, or worry that they might offer 'wrong' advice. On the other hand, peer feedback may be deemed more potent, because the recipient of the feedback believes it is coming from someone who is more authentically in touch with the subject from the point of view of a student, rather than 'going over your head' which often happens with a member of staff. In practice, of course, this means that one-size feedback will not fit all. Further, it means it is difficult to evaluate whether any particular feedback strategy actually 'works'.

Putting it into practice by focusing student attention on feedback

No matter how much formal feedback is provided and delivered, students still have to pay attention to it, process it and turn it into actions that improve subsequent work. Unless they do this, feedback has no effect and staff time is wasted (Nicol, in Handley, Price and Millar, 2008: 3). Gibbs and Simpson (2004: 20) have noted that unfortunately 'it is not inevitable that students will read and pay attention to feedback even when that feedback is lovingly crafted and provided promptly'. This state of affairs is potentially frustrating and unproductive for staff and students alike (Hounsell, 2003). Arguably we need to do much more work to try and ensure that the potential for feedback to enhance student learning is developed as fully as possible.

Students' engagement – or, more worryingly, lack of engagement – with feedback may occur for a whole host of reasons. In this chapter we have been focusing so far on issues which surround the ways in which it is provided: how far it is aligned with our learning, teaching and assessment strategies; when it is offered; how transparent and meaningful it seems and so on. However, there is a strong case for focusing, too, on strategies which aim to cultivate and develop the ways in which students become aware of the role and purpose of feedback in the overall learning process (Handley *et al.*, 2008). According to Hounsell (2003), there is evidence to suggest that students do not necessarily recognize feedback in the forms we provide it. This is hardly surprising, as feedback practices vary widely between sectors, across subject areas and so on.

Managing students' expectations of feedback

Students actually interpret the purpose of formal feedback against the backdrop of their own experiences, values and assumptions. Some students may be highly focused on acquiring marks, and the 'worth' they place on feedback purely relates to the extent to which it helps them do this. This is not just a problem when they come to undertake satisfaction surveys, like the NSS. In addition, and arguably more importantly, it is likely to set up resistances and barriers to students' capacity to engage with broader views of feedback as helping to develop longer-term learning or to illuminate deep-level perceptions of what actually counts as quality.

Furthermore, students nowadays often come to university with unhelpfully restrictive or dependent models of feedback in their minds. We may need to work hard to challenge these kinds of general assumptions about the role of feedback in learning if they are to make the most of the formal feedback opportunities on offer on our courses as we intend. The following student's experience of getting feedback on draft work in school, for instance, is not uncommon:

> "For coursework, it was very 'teacher help', if you know what I mean. We would write the essays, hand them in, they would mark it and they would, not make you change it all but like, it was basically the teacher wrote it, if you know what I mean. Like, you would say your view and the teacher would turn it around to try and make it more suitable."

It seems important to carefully manage this student's expectations about feedback, so that her beliefs about the value and purpose of feedback become more closely aligned with the shared values, attitudes and assumptions of the course team (ASKe, 2007).

Carless (2006) found that student and staff views about feedback diverged markedly. There was little agreement between these two groups about the amount and detail; usefulness; the purpose; and the fairness of feedback provision.

Ways forward might include, for example, simply briefing students about the ways in which feedback will be made available (for example, via oral feedback in classes, group feedback, peer feedback and written comments). Alternatively, useful strategies might include explaining to students how lecturers hope their annotations will be used and what commonly used feedback statements mean (Carless, 2006). But they might also involve finding tactics which encourage students to understand, trust and even have some input into deciding upon the formal feedback strategies they will encounter during the course.

Consulting students about feedback provision

In Modern Languages, experienced final-year students were engaged in a consultation exercise about feedback. The results of the exercise fed into the induction programme for new students. It included clear guidelines which set out where, when and how students would receive feedback. This highlighted the diverse range of feedback strategies on the course, and allowed staff and experienced students to explain and discuss their views of the benefits and limitations of specific feedback formats with the new learners.

The third-year students were keen to get involved in feedback workshops for first-year students. In these, they showed the first-years concrete examples of their work, especially draft essay plans which gradually evolved in response to feedback, so that they could see, at first hand, how to build on feedback throughout the programme.

Preparing students for feedback

In practice, feedback actually performs a number of potential functions (Askew and Lodge, 2000). Sometimes these are contradictory. Depending on the nature of the assessment and the level of the student, from the staff point of view the main purpose of feedback may be to correct errors, to explain to students why their work is falling short of the expected standard, to stimulate self-regulation, to motivate, to provide developmental guidance, and to highlight further resources which might help. These very different functions imply a need to adopt different approaches to providing feedback at different times. However, it is important that students appreciate the philosophy behind any of the approaches we develop and become sensitive to the important contextual factors we have in mind when giving feedback. Without it, students can, quite legitimately, become confused about what feedback is really for. This also presents unnecessary barriers to its productive uptake.

Once more, writing down our intentions does not always neatly equate with transparency. Arguably there is no substitute for opening up dialogue in an attempt to communicate and share the 'subtext' about the intended purpose of our feedback provision.

A strategy of 'showing' rather than 'telling' may be a good place to start to open up assessment dialogues (Carless, 2006), so that students learn to think critically about and discuss with us, and each other, the possible purposes of feedback.

Using exemplars to help students understand feedback comments

In Physics, students were given access, via the e-learning portal, to three examples of tutor-marked 500-word explanations of an important concept. The exemplars had been specially prepared by the module tutor to illustrate some of the typical ways students tackle this type of task. The scripts were annotated with tutor comments and students could read the feedback proforma for each one, although these were not attached to the relevant script.

In the lecture, students were asked, in groups, to 'match' each feedback proforma to the appropriate script. This process, and the meanings of the annotations, were then discussed in full. The tutor then initiated discussion about the ways in which each 'student writer' could usefully act upon the feedback in order to improve their work. Finally, he asked students, in groups, to explain another key concept. He made clear the work should include a section explaining how they had used the feedback from the workshop to construct a good response.

Students valued seeing concrete examples of student work, because it helped them to contextualize the teacher's feedback comments and see what was intended by them. They also saw how to take the feedback comments forward to other work of a similar nature.

Designing assessment methods to engage students in the feedback process

To engage in feedback means that staff and students become active participants in an interactive process. In order to use feedback, students actively construct their own interpretation of the 'meaning' of any feedback they receive. Their interpretations are based upon their own experience and beliefs and do not simply refer to the subject-matter the feedback comments upon, but also to their understandings of the feedback process on a more general level.

In research into students' responses to written feedback, Orsmond and Merry (2009) found that not all students responded to written tutor feedback in the same way. The lower-achieving students appeared to be more dependent on tutor feedback than their high-achieving counterparts and focused on the detail and 'surface features' of feedback messages. Lower-achieving students generally accepted everything the tutor suggested and felt that provision of (more) tutor feedback was crucial to their success (Orsmond and Merry, 2009). However, they claimed to experience difficulty in relating teachers' comments to their work, were unsure how to act on the feedback and were confused by feedback that suggested a range of different approaches. By contrast, higher-achieving students saw feedback differently. They tried to understand the general essence of the feedback being given, did not accept all feedback at face value, and were prone to think about some aspects of it, rather than just 'do what it told them'.

Arguably findings like these are a cause for concern as they suggest that the more we simply provide students with direct tutor feedback, the more likely it is that lower-achieving students (that is, those who arguably need it most) will remain dependent on its provision. Orsmond and Merry thus note that it is crucial that students, especially some students, are encouraged to think differently about feedback.

> Changing the perception of tutor feedback in non-high achieving students could have a major impact on their learning. This cannot be done through tutors writing more detailed feedback, or even in tutors and students discussing feedback that has been given.
>
> (Orsmond and Merry, 2009)

One strategy for achieving this might be to design assessment tasks in such a way that students are explicitly required to seek, generate and respond to feedback from a range of sources. By participating explicitly as partners in the feedback process, for example via personal development planning activities, students can be encouraged to formulate their own learning goals, and engage in actions to achieve those goals in a continuous reflexive process (Nicol and Macfarlane-Dick, 2006).

Recording a range of feedback as a basis for self-review and action planning

A Study Skills module was designed for Health students in their first semester of university study. At particular stages in the module students worked with their guidance tutor in seminar groups of about twelve students. To facilitate the seminars and link them to the rest of the module the teaching team designed a log book which formally required students to undertake self-review using a range of feedback. The log book was handed in as an element of the summative assessment.

The log book incorporated four small-scale tasks. Students were asked to complete each task 'in rough', and to take it to their seminar. The tasks were not marked, but each student was asked to share his or her response with the group, in order to get verbal feedback from peers and the tutor and discuss how it might be further improved. The log book was designed so that at the end of each seminar, students were formally required to summarize the feedback comments they had received on each task. This could be feedback they had received directly from others, or feedback information they had gleaned from discussing other students' work. Students were then supported to use this feedback to write a self-review and develop an action plan, which they also documented in relevant sections of the log book. The action plans were then used as the basis for discussions at the beginning of the following seminar, with students explaining how they had put their action plans into use, and any issues or challenges they had encountered in doing so.

Enhancing engagement with feedback

Due to the contextual and relational nature of feedback, which makes it difficult to interpret and fully understand, it is generally regarded as beneficial to open up some form of discussion about the meanings of feedback (Nicol, 2010a). This is important because according to Boud *et al.* (2010) 'true' feedback requires completion of a 'feedback loop'. Without some form of interaction, it can be hard for the feedback provider to know whether their feedback has been successful in influencing the student.

In practice, this means devising strategies which not only provide information, but seek to focus attention on how it is being used and applied. Students might be formally required to reflect upon, discuss and apply feedback information. This might entail, for instance, inviting students to discuss all the feedback they have received on different modules with a Guidance Tutor, to identify common patterns and emergent themes in a co-ordinated review of progress. Or it might involve the formal requirement for students to explain how they have used feedback on later parts of a phased assignment.

Some students, however, appear to resist or even deliberately avoid genuinely entering into dialogue with staff about assessment matters. They need to believe it is safe to do so. Handley *et al.* (2008: 27) noted that even when lecturers offered opportunities for students to discuss their work, many students failed to take up the opportunity for fear of exposing their own shortcomings, or because they didn't want to be a nuisance when staff were patently busy, or because they did not feel sufficiently confident to ask sensible questions. Resistances like these can take considerable planning and patience to address and rely on the creation of learning communities which reduce the 'gap' between staff and students.

One useful place to start might be to consider strategies which encourage students to actively engage with feedback comments in some way. Research has shown that students pay more attention to written feedback comments when they are not accompanied by marks (Black and Wiliam, 1998a). So comment-only marking can encourage students to reflect on feedback, discuss it and attend to it, perhaps by undertaking self-review after tutor marking of an assignment, helping ensure that students engage with feedback (Taras, 2001).

Comment-only marking

In Information Sciences, students' grades were not released immediately after their work has been marked. Instead, students were initially asked to collect their written feedback and reflect on it. They were asked to assess, in the light of the tutor comments, the grade they thought their work had been awarded.

Students were then asked to attend a tutorial where their self-assessment was discussed and the teacher disclosed the actual grade. Any discrepancies between the students' evaluation and the teacher grade helped illuminate misunderstandings about the significance of feedback which could then be addressed.

Voicing the issues revisited: a case study of formal feedback

Integrating feedback throughout the first year of study

Frequent oral feedback, with ample opportunity for dialogue, are important features in helping students to understand the standards which epitomize good work in a subject domain (Gibbs and Dunbar-Goddet, 2007). Without a full and realistic view of standards, students can make little sense of feedback which aims to help them move their work in a desirable direction. Similarly, Bloxham and West's study (2007) identified dialogue with tutors as a key mechanism which helped students understand what tutors were really looking for and, hence, enabled them to make better sense of their written feedback. Nicol (2010a) argues that, when it comes to feedback, students require more dialogue, not more monologue. This is difficult to achieve given some of the factors we have already mentioned in this chapter. In particular, resourcing meaningful dialogue has become a significant issue with large classes, meaning that we need to think about strategies which help build meaningful conversations into our overall learning, teaching and assessment designs.

In an Early Years programme, lecturers were particularly keen to try to shift the balance of responsibility for feedback from the tutor towards the student. To do this the course team decided to redesign the feedback coversheets to include a section in which students could request feedback on specific areas of their summatively assessed work. The idea was that when writing their feedback comments, tutors aimed to address any aspects that the student raised. The course team was disappointed, however, that scarcely any students took up the opportunity to request particular feedback. So, in response, the team began to pay more attention to the ways in which they prepared students to take a more active role in the assessment and feedback process.

The course team designed a range of assessment and feedback workshops which became integrated throughout the first year of study. The workshops were intended to encourage students to perceive themselves as having an active part to play in the feedback process, but in a 'safe' environment, which was purely formative. They involved students working on, for example, the giving and receiving of feedback, and group tasks in which students collaboratively interpreted, and ultimately produced, feedback on exemplars of student work. In this way students gradually explored and developed their skills of asking questions which would elicit helpful information from feedback providers.

Interviews with the students revealed that the preparatory feedback workshops were highly valued by students mainly because they helped to establish a more open climate, which cemented relationships between the Guidance Tutor (who ran the workshops) and the students for whom the tutor was responsible. The workshops, which placed a premium on student activity, discussion and involvement, seemed to legitimize staff–student dialogue. For instance, one student claimed the seminars had boosted his confidence to interact with staff. He had assumed he would simply be expected to sit silently in lessons, with no chance to ask if he was unsure. By contrast, the initiative made him feel happy to approach staff, in the dedicated sessions, to actively seek out and discuss feedback, sooner rather than later: *"If we weren't certain about anything that had been said, or what they expected of us, we knew we could bring that up in the tutorials, to clear it up there and then."* Students also started to discuss the formal feedback they received with one another:

"What I liked about it was that it drew in a lot of people. Not just the lecturers, other people too. So you get their views, their way of explaining it." Students also found that thinking about feedback from the feedback givers' point of view was very helpful. This helped them think about, and discuss, the meanings of common feedback comments, such as 'develop your argument': *"I think about having an argument differently now – I think of it more as having something to say, and different viewpoints, rather than getting at someone, trying to shoot them down."* It also focused some on the deeper-related features of complex academic writing, rather than the surface-level or purely technical features of an assignment:

"We discussed the feedback people had got on their work. After that, I greatly increased my academic reading. I decided to read more of the books, journals and articles on the reading list. It all started to make me reconsider how I describe my own ideas."

Key questions to think about

The following key questions are designed to help course and module teams develop their practice. They could, alternatively, be used for personal reflection.

- **Do your students know when and how they will receive feedback, what form it will take, and what you hope they will do with it?** It will be helpful if this guidance is provided to students at a programme level with details filled out on a module basis. Do you have a clear agreement on what information will be provided to students and when? Students can be surprisingly confused about feedback. We recently heard of a student who complained that she had not received any feedback. Further discussion showed that she had not yet been required to submit any assessed work and that written tutor comments on marked work were the only type of feedback that she recognized! Do your students realize that feedback can be more than tutor-written comments?

- **Do students get tutor feedback soon enough to do something about it?** Has the programme team discussed what is 'soon enough' in terms of feedback from the student point of view? If your programme is based around modules where all the learning, teaching and assessment is completed within one semester, students may ignore feedback believing that it is too late to be useful. However you may be able to introduce other means of feedback which can help students whilst they are still learning on the module. The ways of doing this will depend on subject and context but there are many ideas within this book that could be considered.

- **What sources of feedback (other than from tutors) are available to your students?** We have suggested various alternative sources of feedback such as feedback from fellow students, or feedback obtained through self-testing using online questions. Are you missing any opportunities by not taking advantage of these alternatives? Is there an overall feedback plan so that different forms of feedback are used throughout the year and no methods are over-used?

- How do you encourage students to engage with the feedback provided? Where in your programme does anyone discuss with students what they should do with feedback to make it a useful learning tool? Do other tutors reinforce this message? Is the use of feedback ever part of an in-class or online activity so that a tutor can actually work with students on the process of using feedback – rather than just telling them that they should use it? Do you have any learning outcomes and assessment tasks requiring students to demonstrate their use of feedback, e.g. the production of a progress file, or a requirement to explain how prior feedback has been used when an assignment is submitted?

Chapter 5

Designing opportunities for informal feedback

There is another way of looking at feedback, which builds on dialogue and discussion as a support for learning. Shared experiences strengthen and enhance students' academic experiences as they gain 'feedback-like effects' via involvement and interaction by testing out their developing understanding together.

This chapter covers:

- the value of participation and social interaction in generating a continual flow of information on 'how you are doing';
- the importance of students' internalizing and processing feedback via participation in disciplinary practices;
- the benefits of establishing effective classroom dialogue to improve student learning;
- supporting students to work collaboratively to ensure they have chance to engage with an ongoing flow of informal feedback;
- learning which happens beyond the formal curriculum.

Voicing the issues

Gillian is a Sociology student who is coming towards the end of her first year. She believes that she learns much better on modules where there is good opportunity built in for working together and discussing things with her fellow students. But she often feels that, at least in some modules, she is just left on her own, to get on with it, working pretty much in isolation, unless she takes the initiative to set up meetings to discuss work with other people on her course.

Gillian's sense of isolation is partly due to her course having a large number of 'day' students, who live at home, rather than on campus. As she puts it:

> "Some people come to university, go to the lectures, go to the library, pick up their books and go home. Doing that, some people just don't feel like they actually belong. But I find I can learn a lot from explaining my ideas to other people – that helps me learn, you know? So I desperately try and get groups going. Otherwise, there's no feedback, and I think, especially on your first assignments, you need reassurance. That's something I really need, because you haven't got it at home, so that's what I want from coming to campus. I miss out academically if I can't get support from other students. Because talking with my friends

and classmates about my work also helps me suss out how I am getting on: whether I
understand something fully enough. Some modules are set up like that and some aren't.
With some modules, there's lots of chance for us to do the talking, and I find – for me at
least – that's much better. It's a sort of 'run an idea up the flagpole and see what other
people think' situation. Like, a sounding board for your ideas while the ideas are gradually
coming out of the mist, so to speak, in your head."

In the previous chapter we looked at a range of ways of giving students more feedback on their work, and ways of improving the feedback that students get by, for example, making it more timely. The basic underlying model of feedback in most university systems is that students produce a response to a task requirement and then, usually at some later point, tutors produce a commentary and some suggestions about what the student has done. Seen like this, the feedback is therefore often detached from the presentation of the student work and from the activity and process that went into producing the work.

In our model we have termed this 'formal' feedback because it is built into the formal delivery of courses and modules. From this point of view, the provision of feedback is part of our quality assurance systems and the feedback methods and timings for the delivery of feedback information are likely to appear within the formal documents describing a module. As we suggested in the previous chapter, the profile of feedback has been raised by the outcome of the National Student Survey (see HEFCE, 2011) where results indicate that assessment and feedback is the area which students find least satisfactory. This has led many universities to offer their students a type of feedback 'contract' which indicates the maximum length of time that they will have to wait for feedback. It may also include other features. For example, the contract may guarantee the use of a standard checklist of criteria or a minimum word limit or other minimum standards (like word-processed rather than hand-written comments) for written feedback.

However, one potential problem is that the underlying approach to feedback (in the sense of providing information to the student that she or he can use productively) is not challenged or, at least, it is not sufficiently developed. While the situation can be improved, there are limits to the extent that the conventional approach to feedback can be stretched in this way, and without being supplemented by other approaches, it is unlikely to be able to produce a genuine transformation in feedback practice which actually serves the intended purpose: to improve student learning.

There are however other ways in which feedback can operate in educational systems. This is feedback that is produced and received within the process of learning and teaching itself, almost as a coincidental by-product of students' engagement with the course. To many people who associate feedback with assessment comments, this does not seem like feedback at all. If anything, they see it as 'just part of teaching'. In one sense, that is quite a good place to start because the informal feedback that we are going to address in this chapter is deeply embedded in activity and participation. It is the kind of informal feedback that all of us have been learning from throughout our lives, in educational contexts and more generally. It is the kind of feedback that Gillian, the student at the start of the chapter, is looking for, because it really helps her learn. It is also the kind of feedback that is becoming more widely acknowledged by education-alists from a range of different perspectives.

Theories and debates

This chapter emphasizes how there are ways of enhancing the student experience of feedback which move well beyond seeking to improve the quality and rapidity of the 'normal' type of 'feedback' which tends to be privileged in Higher Education. It will draw attention to the ways in which, as Boud *et al.* (2010) note, 'everyday learning activities as well as special tasks and tests provide opportunities for the provision of feedback'. Above all, the chapter argues that activities which make feedback infor-mation available to students need not be formal, but might usefully be conceived as the strategies a teacher uses to establish a climate for student discussion and participation in productive formative learning activity. As Gillian's comments at the start of the chapter suggest, such activities help informal discussions and tentative musings to thrive, so that students can judge, for themselves, how they are progressing with the topics being studied, as they actively immerse themselves, with others, within a particular subject area.

Sadler (2010: 547) argues, in Higher Education, we often find that: *'Too much attention has been paid at the micro level within the traditional model: what the teacher can do to construct more effective feedback, and what the learner should do to make more use of the feedback provided'* (our emphasis). It is our contention, then, that we need to consider other complementary ways of thinking about feedback, which can help us move towards a more dialogic approach (Price, Handley and Millar, 2011) in the context of an overall model of Assessment for Learning.

Black and McCormick (2010) also assert that the preconception with feedback conceived of as formal written comment on students' work is a limitation to improving learning in HE. They suggest that there is a wider repertoire of feedback practice in schools and other settings which university educators could profitably draw upon to inform their practice. Providing written feedback on students' work is only one of four approaches that they identify. Other, arguably more important ones, are: oral dialogue in the classroom, student dialogue in group work, and peer and self-assessment. Thus, Black and McCormick suggest that more consideration should be given to oral dialogue in the lecture hall if we wish to improve feedback in universities. They also recommend that training and practice in collaborative dialogue will be needed by students (and perhaps lecturers) if it is to be really effective. From this perspective, lecturers would need to take responsibility '. . . not merely as a facilitator, but to engineer opportunities for students . . . to learn' (2010: 495). These are issues that will be raised in this chapter, and strategies for putting this approach into practice in the HE context will be discussed.

Researchers and teachers who are interested in this kind of approach often refer to Laurillard (2002) and the conversational model of pedagogy (see, for example, Nicol, 2010a). Laurillard terms her approach to Higher Education pedagogy a 'conversa-tional framework'. She is particularly interested in the use of educational technologies, although her model applies equally to person-to-person teaching contexts. Laurillard argues that 'action without feedback is completely unproductive for the learner' (2002: 55) but the kind of feedback process that she describes is very different to that which is widely used in Higher Education. Laurillard's Conversational Framework is built on a process of interaction or dialogue between students and teachers. The framework is based on an iterative cycle where teachers provide teaching and guidance, so students have opportunities to try out and display the knowledge or skills that they are aiming to achieve and very promptly receive feedback and guidance adapted to their level of attainment. The cycles can operate in a very short time frame: say within one class session, or over a longer period of learning. Additions to the teacher role include peer feedback or adaptive learning technologies, where a task environment is set up to provide immediate feedback to students on their actions. For example, a lecturer may set up an online simulation exercise which enables students to realize immediately what consequences their actions have had by seeing whether their intentions 'work out' effectively or not. Depending on the focus and timing of the simulation exercise, this provides learners with immediate insight into how well, say, they are mastering a skill, or grasping complex principles.

Laurillard identifies two types of feedback using the terms 'intrinsic' and 'extrinsic'. Intrinsic feedback is an embedded and unavoidable outcome of many actions in the physical and social world. This sort of feedback can, importantly, emanate quite naturally from contact with other people who are also working in a given area. For example we learn how to behave in specific social settings on the basis of the 'guidance' that inherently comes from seeing what other people do and the responses from them to our own actions. It is common, of course, in everyday professional practice, where practitioners gauge what they need to do next by constantly interpreting and adjusting to the rich array of intrinsic feedback that is in play within a particular setting. It also underpins the way in which academic researchers learn from engaging in, say, reading within the field of enquiry and interacting socially in a disciplinary community (Brew, 2006). This kind of feedback can also operate in short cycles within a learning context.

Laurillard argues that whilst intrinsic feedback is an inevitable outcome of action, extrinsic feedback comes in the form of a commentary on action or on a display of understanding. Here, the messages we pick up from being part of a social context may be supplemented. Someone might provide us with written guidance about how to behave in, say, an important business meeting, or comment on 'how we did' after the event. Tutor-written comment on student work is a form of extrinsic feedback although unfortunately it tends to be part of a process that is rather long and drawn out. More effective extrinsic feedback might arise in, say, a design studio, where the lecturer may visit to see and discuss the student's work in progress. It is important to stress, though, that we are not making a case for intrinsic feedback being good and extrinsic feedback being bad. Ideally both are needed. The student may realize from intrinsic feedback that something is not right, for example, but may need comments from someone with more expertise or simply a different point of view to help them to understand more clearly what is wrong and why, and what might be done to improve.

Laurillard's approach suggests that the teacher's role in informal feedback is to:

- set up learning activities where intrinsic feedback can arise as a by-product of doing the tasks
- engage in conversations with individuals or groups of learners, helping them to learn through a staged process of scaffolding and drawing on the resources of informal feedback amongst peers

- encourage students to actively seek conversations in support of learning, beyond the immediate lecture room and curriculum.

Our perspective on informal feedback is supported by Laurillard's approach but more broadly by a range of perspectives on learning, assessment and pedagogy. A frequently cited resource in this area is the work of Lave and Wenger (1991), who adopt a socio-cultural perspective on learning. They propose that good learning environments provide learners with opportunities for action – so that people learn from doing learning tasks, typically in 'communities of practice' which are focused around some sort of common agenda. From this perspective, learning occurs through participation but also through feedback, from and to fellow learners, or more advanced and highly expert colleagues. Lave and Wenger's view suggests that we should set up learning environments so that intrinsic and extrinsic feedback is embedded within them.

Some researchers such as Kvale (2008) argue that it is beneficial to take account of modes of assessment that facilitate learning in the workplace, where Assessment for Learning approaches have been operating as key aspects of apprentice training for years. For instance, Kvale suggests that journeymen and master-craftsmen embody in their work the standards and values of the craft that the apprentices identify with and aspire to join. Learning occurs via daily participation in work produced in the craft shop, where apprentices naturally compare their own work with that of more accomplished others. In this way, apprentices regulate their own work, so that learning and assessment are very much left to the initiative of the apprenticed. Thus the process of assessment is placed at the very heart of the work setting, making it possible for learners to test their own performances at any time, as they feel ready, and until a satisfactory quality has been achieved. Good apprentices, then, purposefully seek lots of occasions for learning and being tested in their daily practice in increasingly demanding tasks.

Claxton (2010) suggests that it is useful to see learning in HE along these lines, as 'epistemic apprenticeship', with students as 'newcomers' and lecturers as experienced 'old-timers' who induct students into the love and craft of scholarship in their disciplinary area. From his point of view, students require different forms of engagement which help them to get in contact with the different kinds of learning that are valued in our own academic practices. These will, on an obvious level, include developing domain-specific skills and theories. But also, less evidently but arguably just as importantly, the development of values, attitudes and identities which underpin academic ways of thinking and practising. This presents a challenge, because some of these things are harder than others to communicate. In practice, much of a lecturer's subject 'know how' is carried at a tacit, rather than explicit level, and can only be learned via engaging in repeated exchanges which, as in the apprenticeship model, enable gradual movement from peripheral to more legitimate roles within the subject community. From this viewpoint, the overall aim is for students to learn to see, think and become able to act like, say, an engineer, or an historian, rather than simply possess subject knowledge.

Lave and Wenger (1991), amongst others, are mainly concerned with learning in workplace environments but many similar ideas about the social nature of learning are proposed and used in the form of 'classroom assessment'. Black and McCormick (2010) suggest that practices which emphasize formative assessment and feedback within active classrooms, with considerable peer dialogue and collaboration, are very useful. These types of classroom assessment are clearly much less in evidence in Higher Education, at least in the UK and Europe, but this is a well-known approach to Assessment for Learning activity in the USA (Angelo and Cross, 1993). As Assessment for Learning has developed in theory and practice, the importance of informal feedback is gaining wider recognition. Wiliam (2011) proposes that we should view peers as instructional resources for each other in formative learning environments. He makes a strong claim for the value of fostering peer dialogue and feedback in classroom settings:

> while peers may lack the training and experience of teachers, they have unique insights into learning, and because the power relationships between peers are different from those between teachers and students, there will be some instructional strategies open to them that would not be open, or would be less effective, when used by teachers.
>
> (2011: 12)

Effective classrooms make ample opportunity for informal self- and peer assessment processes to occur, then, embedded in students' ongoing engagement with material.

Putting it into practice

Dialogue and discussion as a support for learning are essential for informal feedback. Rather than giving feedback per se, the teacher's role is to create effective conditions for learning by placing student involvement, effort and activity at the heart of the learning and teaching environment, such that students find out how they are doing by participating in activities and from social interaction within a learning community. Shared experiences strengthen and enhance students' academic experiences as they gain 'feedback-like effects' via involvement and interaction by testing out their developing understanding together. This kind of feedback is not usually planned in detail, but relies instead on teachers designing a climate that encourages dialogue, collaboration amongst students and interaction about subject-related tasks between teachers and students. Then, useful feedback can occur informally, as part of the normal flow of teaching and learning, almost as a by-product. It can also occur in situations beyond the classroom.

This section of the chapter highlights three broad approaches to stimulating informal feedback. These are:

- putting it into practice by enhancing learning through classroom dialogue
- putting it into practice by encouraging students to work collaboratively
- putting it into practice by seeding activity and dialogue beyond the classroom.

Under each of these broad approaches, we have selected a range of different examples to show some of the diverse ways in which informal feedback can be promoted.

Putting it into practice by enhancing learning through classroom dialogue

Designing appropriate tasks to enhance classroom activity and peer interaction

Working in the Higher Education context, Nicol and Macfarlane-Dick (2006) developed a set of principles for effective feedback and assessment practice. They reinterpreted the body of research on formative assessment and feedback and positioned it within a model of self-regulated learning. These have been widely espoused and offer a useful means of guiding staff to design activities that would encourage learners to regulate their own learning. They include teachers designing learning opportunities which encourage teacher–student and student–student dialogue around learning and which facilitate the development of reflection and self-evaluation in learning.

One way of putting these principles into practice is through the design of learning tasks which promote active learning and ongoing interaction and discussions in the classroom. For a start, good tasks enable students to gain intrinsic feedback, so that they learn by seeing if they can work out a problem or respond to a question. The very act of doing the task may instantly enable them to discover if they are able to achieve the desired outcome. The teachers' question-setting skills are vital here, where the challenge is to emulate the 'use-assessment' (Kvale, 2008) of apprentices in workplace training, in which 'the proof of the pudding is in the eating'. Students in many engineering disciplines learn in this way, for example, by working through 'problem sheets'. These contain analytical, mathematically based problems and the students need to become fluent in these procedures and applications. Working through the problems often provides intrinsic feedback – it becomes obvious if something is not going to 'work out' and the student needs to find out what has gone wrong. In this sense the task prompts students to ask themselves pertinent self-evaluation questions. Has he made a mistake in calculations? Has she been mistaken in her assumptions?

Students in these situations often take the initiative to find more feedback to help them in this task by forming informal study groups. The students may not use that term. They may simply say they have been working with a few friends. Some study groups are ad hoc and ephemeral; others last throughout the degree and develop productive strategies and ways of working over time. Our research on how students study has shown that this is not about just 'getting the answers' or 'copying' from someone else (Tudor, Penlington and McDowell, 2010). Each student knows that they have to understand and be able to solve typical problems for themselves. But they are also extremely aware of the value of collaboration and the feedback that colleagues can give.

Some of the benefits include bringing a new way of looking at their own work, which enables students to see where and why mistakes have occurred: *"When you look through and can't see your mistake usually someone else can point it out. Then you know and you won't make that mistake again."* Being able to 'thrash through' ideas together is also commonly cited by students as a useful activity:

> *"At first we didn't know where to start but then we put our heads together. After a bit, most of us went home but through the evening we were on Facebook discussing it and between us we worked it out."*

Furthermore, students frequently realize that they learn from explaining ideas to others, as well as from receiving feedback. The process of 'coaching' someone else (Nicol, 2011; Race, 2005) helps develop and cement their own appreciation of an area, because it essentially involves meaning-making and knowledge construction. So, as the following student quote indicates, relationships in the learning community become reciprocal in a number of ways: *"I don't mind if people ask {me for help} because when you have to explain it to them you sort of understand it better. Then another time you benefit from their ideas."* Black (2007) suggests that if they want to improve the student experience of feedback along these lines in the classroom environment, some teachers may need to rethink their roles in relation to the purpose of promoting their students' learning. For instance, Black insists that it is crucial that teachers realize that student talk is not just for social and affective purposes, but acts as an important thinking tool. Cognitively productive talk needs careful engineering, though. Black argues that the teacher's role is to provide and specify sufficiently challenging formative tasks which stretch students, while, by the same token, are not too daunting for novices to tackle. The overall aim is to engage students in productive activity and discussion, with clear goals and aims, rather than just allow students to chat.

Black and McCormick (2010) suggest we could do more to build the benefits of collaborative discussion with peers into the student experience of being in our lectures and seminars. This means spending time and energy on designing good tasks and activities for students to work on together in lectures, rather than spending most of our time preparing content or information to deliver. From this perspective, 'good teaching' – which is likely to give students access to useful informal feedback – involves the teacher carefully choosing and specifying targets which the students discuss. In lectures, for instance, carefully planned tasks might be threaded through the lecture, where students have a go at doing something and discuss the work together. This approach can help scaffold students' approaches, so they build steadily through ongoing practice of progressively more challenging activities. This can be difficult, but not impossible, to establish in the current context of mass HE, even with extremely large groups.

Providing well-thought-out classroom tasks and structuring students' discussions

In Film Studies, the lecturer set up a screening for over one hundred Combined Honours students. Often students' screening notes were superficial, and failed to engage in sufficient depth with the theoretical concepts being introduced on the module, which included the male gaze and feminist theory. To help his students developer deeper insights into the film, he provided his students with a set of questions. These gave them elements to look out for during the screening, so helped to focus their attention in productive ways.

Once the screening was finished, the lecturer provided another set of questions, which he asked students to work on in groups. The questions were designed to help structure their conversations so that students identified their viewpoints on the film from different theoretical standpoints. The first discussion task involved students preparing a diagram of all the different ways in which they had noted that women were represented in the film, accompanied by illustrative evidence taken from the screening notes that they had made. This task encouraged students to express a whole range of viewpoints and approaches, rather than feeling they were expected to converge on one 'correct response' or come up with the 'answer' in the tutor's head. Once students had prepared their diagrams, which depicted a rich array of different interpretations of the film in relation to the question, the tutor asked each group to prepare a prototype essay title on the theme of representations of women in the film. He called on different groups to read out their titles, which he typed onto a document and displayed on the screen. He then encouraged a whole-group discussion of each one, asking students to ask questions about the theoretical material which could be drawn upon to develop the ideas further, and the kinds of evidence that 'good' screening notes would help them draw upon. In this way, the lecturer ensured that students gained informal feedback: from their peers, from participating in meaning-making, and from his own responses to the suggested titles, where he was able to link the students' suggestions to the lectures he had given and the reading he had suggested on the relevant theory.

When the lecturer marked the students' essays that term, he was pleased to find that the students had produced more insightful, closely argued and analysed essays than had been the case in previous years, when they had tended to be too general in focus and had described, rather than applied, appropriate cinematic theory.

Establishing a conducive climate for dialogue

Additionally, Black (2007) argues that the ways in which a teacher interacts with a group of students also requires skilled and responsive handling, to ensure that, as far as possible, students are encouraged to talk in order to learn. This means a teacher's role is to establish situations in which students feel it is useful and safe to reveal their thinking (and their mistakes). Teachers' questions should open up dialogue, and time must be given for students to discuss issues with one another, and report back to the whole class. The teacher's role is then to listen, and to respond constructively in the light of whatever issues have emerged. When this works well, students will gain informal feedback which will help them appreciate, on a deep-seated level, how experts respond to their tentative ideas. Black claims that what is of paramount importance, though, is that students feel that the teacher is genuinely interested in what they think, rather than whether they can provide the right answer. Due to the power issues noted above, this kind of responsive, 'forgiving' climate for student–teacher dialogue can be quite challenging to achieve with some students. It is also especially difficult in large groups, where students (and staff) can feel that their performances are 'on show'.

This is why discussion in peer groups offers such a useful way forward, in which students practise formulating, expressing and exchanging ideas in less threatening situations before they are expected to discuss a topic with a tutor. One way to achieve this is illustrated in the next example, in which the lecturers structured their teaching around a series of enquiry-based learning tasks.

Asking good questions

Two Childhood Studies lecturers required their students to work independently each week on a series of progressively challenging tasks. They asked students to gather material for analysis and discussion as part of a semester-long project which they would write up for their assignment. For example, at one point in the semester, individual students were asked to gather data, in the form of literal signs and leaflets they could find in public spaces, about a relevant topic. Before the lecture, students were asked to post examples of the data they had gathered to the e-learning portal. They were also asked to write a paragraph analysing their data using particular theoretical lenses, which they also posted to the e-learning portal. Everyone on the module could view the posts.

Before the lecture, the two tutors skimmed the posts that students had made. They selected one or two effective responses and one or two less effective responses and planned the lecture session, with over one hundred students, around discussions on these. In the lecture, the selected images were shown and students were asked to analyse them in small groups. The two lecturers then opened up a class discussion of these examples, in the process highlighting how each could be further developed.

Students found this process useful, even when their own data was not focused upon, because the lecturers used the discussion to pose questions (rather than provide information) which would help students develop the work further. This helped students learn to regulate their own work, by comparison, as the following student implies:

> "We got feedback in class on our {data}. The lecturers picked out some and we all talked about what was good and stuff. I found that was really useful. Someone had said children were oppressed, which I'd said in my writing. . . . And they said, 'Yes, fine, that's one way of looking at it. But how else could you look at it?' So they weren't saying it was wrong, but that if you add to it, or do it this way, you know, look at it from another point of view, then that would be even better. So that gave me the next sort of step on the road."

It is important to note, then, that students saw this kind of teacher dialogue as useful questioning which offered them insights and guidance about possible future strategies they could take, rather than telling them what to do next, or what was done wrong. One student, for instance, explained the experience as follows: *"You do something, then they keep getting you to go further into it."* Interestingly, students talked about this classroom dialogue as 'feedback':

> "I like the way the module is set out. It's broken down into tasks and they give you feedback. So what you can do is alter or change. Because you get feedback off each session. So if there are areas you need to develop, you can do it."

Using peer discussion to help students appreciate a variety of approaches to tackling work

Hounsell (2007) suggests that effective learning environments offer students ample opportunity to see others' work 'on display', which usefully provides 'feedback-like effects'. The products actually placed 'on display' can, of course, be tentative and provisional, and can include outputs by members of staff, or more experienced students, as well as peers. By working together with academics on a piece of work, students might gain insights into what experts notice, and what they tend to disregard, or what they do when a piece of information doesn't seem to 'fit' their conceptual models, or what they do when they get 'stuck' or can't do something (Claxton, 2010), in ways which reveal an academic's approaches more profoundly than simply looking at the polished output they produce 'at the end'.

However, unless students work together many will find it difficult to move beyond their own frame of reference. Working with others can help them envisage different ways of accomplishing a task. Collaborative work can, in short, expose students to a range of standards and approaches which might otherwise remain invisible to them. This can help them calibrate their own approaches.

Displays of student work

In a course on Children's Literature with over fifty students, a series of three two-hour lectures were given over to small-group production of posters. The teacher structured the group work so that students steadily built a graphic display of their interpretations of a chosen children's text. In week one they analysed the book cover from their personal perspectives, in week two they brought reviews of the book which they had been asked to locate on public internet sites, and in the third week they annotated their group poster with papers which they had been asked to source in authoritative academic journals. Each week, students were asked to build another layer on the poster, by sharing the material they had individually gathered with their group, and then negotiating which items would be selected to add to the poster.

This process helped scaffold students' responses to their chosen text, and helped them see how their colleagues approached the analysis, using a range of sources. As one said:

> *"It was good because you got to learn from other people's work, people's interpretations. You can only learn so much reading academic books and being told what the theory is about, but with this there were a lot of interpretations."*

At the end of each session, students had the chance to pin their posters on the wall and move around the room to look at other posters. They were asked to report back to the whole group, highlighting one thing they had learned from looking at other posters, and one question they now wished to ask the lecturers. The lecturers' responses to these issues, which often focused on which approach was 'best', were then shared with the whole group.

Developing a deeper sense of course requirements

Students can only steer their own work appropriately if they can see it in the light of the intended learning goals, so they must genuinely come to appreciate what the target means and have some idea of what it might actually look like, in a concrete, rather than an abstract sense (Sadler, 1989). Without this appreciation, students will be unable to develop the capacity to audit – and therefore adapt and improve – their own work. So students need informal feedback which helps them to work out what is really expected and required in a given context. It is important to recognize, though, that judgements about the worth of work, or what is expected, do not take place in a vacuum. In practice, the act of assessment is a deeply interpretive process, not a fixed or absolute one (Bloxham, 2009). Lecturers' views about a 'good' essay, for instance, do not exclusively rely on a student's capacity to produce a good essay in a generalized sense (Elton, 2010), but also take into account a student's capacity to work with knowledge within the specific 'voice' and ways of 'thinking and practising' (Meyer and Land, 2005) of the discipline, or even the subject-team who constructed the assignment in the first place (Bloxham, 2009).

Students who do not recognize the 'take' or stance a course encourages them to adopt will probably find their marks suffer (Lea and Street, 1998); no matter how good their general 'essay-writing' skills are. If they do not answer the question their teachers had in mind, or fail to clearly address the task specified, or remain oblivious to their lecturers' requirements, they hand something in that misses the point or wanders off at a tangent. In fact, this appears to happen quite frequently for relatively large numbers of students (Sadler, 2009).

It is, though, far easier said than done to help students genuinely grasp what is required, so that they learn to act in accordance with their lecturers' basic specifications. This is because much of a lecturer's knowledge about what counts as 'quality' is tacitly, rather than consciously, held (Bloxham and West, 2007; Rust, O'Donovan and Price, 2005). Tacit assumptions are mainly learned via experience and become like 'second-nature', so they are largely invisible to outsiders, and even to the people who hold them. They are, also, almost impossible to explicate or put into words. This means that it is much easier said than done to help students to even *recognize*, never mind *understand* and be able to *use*, the aspects that lecturers are really looking for in a high-quality response within a subject domain.

The subtle nuances of specific disciplinary ways of expressing ideas and so on might best emanate from informal feedback in classroom contexts. Students need to learn them through *experience* and *participation* in relevant, highly contextualized communities of practice (O'Donovan, Price and Rust, 2004), rather than from simply being told what they are.

Appreciating quality in the context of the module material

Art History students had been working informally in small groups on collaborative peer discussion activities, which the tutors dropped in on. These focused on the collective analysis of disciplinary material. The following student found this kind of activity challenging, but felt it helped her to gauge whether, as she put it, she was 'on the right tracks':

> *"It's not comfortable to speak out in front of people with your opinion in case you're out on a limb and it's not right. But it helps so much when you do because you're getting that positive feedback: 'yes, it's right. Or if it's not: 'you're not really on the right tracks – this is how it is'. If you don't do that that's when you end up in a position where you don't know what you're doing. You get to assignment time and you're on the wrong track."*

From this point of view she felt that participation in classroom discussions, embedded in disciplinary material, helped her to perceive where she was, where she should be, and how to bridge the gap. She linked this to the lecturers' informal feedback on the students' discussions. In one sense, this was about her teachers verifying that she was on the right lines: *"All you need is an occasional nod from the lecturer. Yes, that's good. Why not try this a bit more?"* As the lecturers moved around the groups, though, pushing students to justify their ideas, validating useful approaches and prompting them to consider others, where necessary, the student realized what her lecturers really valued and how they conceptualized the issues, which she gauged by the nature of the questions they asked and the issues they raised or found interesting. *"It's knowing what questions to ask, which somebody who knows the subject knows. I didn't know the questions {how to approach it} like."* This, of course, showed she was beginning to realize that lecturers' expectations are, in effect, deeply embedded in the specific ways of thinking and practising of the subject community, which tends to 'see' material and talk about issues in highly specific, specialized ways.

What this student needed to know was how to define the boundaries of a subject area which was 'new' to her, so that she did not inadvertently move beyond the scope of the subject itself. Yet many lecturers are scarcely even aware of the values, attitudes and assumptions they bring to bear on their appraisals of 'appropriate' student writing in their specific domain. Because academics have typically been immersed in the specific knowledge-constructing enterprise of their own subject domain for so long, acceptable ways of securing meanings within the domain have become taken for granted and 'invisible', even to themselves. Understandings of quality are carried, then, by an almost intuitive sense of the knowledge, rules and procedures of their specific disciplines. This understanding is not something that is simply acquired in a straightforward way, so is not really accessible by simple advice or instruction. Instead, it is gradually developed by being involved in participatory relationships and extended dialogue with know-ledgeable others in the relevant research community. From this viewpoint social interaction with peers and teachers and participation with the subject matter are a vital means to gain an appreciation of the learning goals. In other words, developing a sense of social-relatedness is absolutely germane to effective self-evaluation. From this perspective active engagement in dialogic learning and teaching, as well as explicit assessment workshops, are crucial elements if we wish to empower students to take informed decisions about their learning for themselves.

Putting it into practice by encouraging students to work collaboratively

Using summative assessment to foster collaborative working

Appropriately designed summative tasks can exert a powerful positive backwash effect (Watkins, Dahlin and Eckholm, 2005) on learning, and they can also be used to foster informal feedback. One important way of achieving this is to design opportunities for students to work together on challenging and authentic summative tasks, rather than always forcing them to work in isolation on privately contracted assessment tasks. The challenge here, though, is how to enable students to work collaboratively as teams, so the learning benefits of working together accrue, rather than competitively in teams, where the main focus is on an instrumental hunt for marks.

Producing assignments collaboratively

On one module, instead of writing an essay, History students were required to produce guides to a topic which would be suitable for first-year undergraduates. Learners could decide to work alone, or with others, to produce these materials. Most students chose to develop their materials in small self-selecting groups or pairs. They found this offered them a more 'natural' way of working, in which ideas were shared and co-produced in a constructive process of dialogue, negotiation and peer review:

> "Working on the same thing together is kind of helpful with this. Because we both have a working knowledge of the topic, we could actually say, 'No, I don't think that's right. Does this mean this? Should we put it this way?'"

Hounsell (2007) argues that collaborative assignments like this can help foster connoisseurship and a fuller appreciation of academic standards amongst students, as students can learn from co-generation and co-writing as they work together on subject material.

The lecturer was pleased with the results, as she found that the work was of a much higher quality than she expected of students at this level of study. She felt the way in which she had organized the marking had helped students to approach the task collaboratively, rather than competing with each other over marks, which, past experience had suggested, often disrupted teamwork. She had made it clear that, where students submitted a jointly produced guide, their reflective commentary, which theorized the rationale for the guide, must be individually produced. This allowed her to allocate an individual overall mark for each student, and avoided students worrying that their grade would be adversely affected by peers' efforts, or conversely, feeling that they could 'free-load' on others' work.

Enhancing informal feedback by setting authentic, practice-like tasks

Boud (2009) suggests that using professional practice or workplace-like approaches as a key organizer for summative assessment helps learners become future-focused, so they see the point of the learning they do in the university and can see how it can be used. Further, he asserts that building assessment which more closely emulates the models of assessment found in the workplace can help 'build the capacity of students to learn and assess for themselves when they are out of our hands' (2009: 42).

Involving students in practice

In another example, second- and third-year students studying Guidance and Counselling as a topic for academic enquiry were invited to become involved in designing authentic mentoring experiences for first-year students. The 'live' and unpredictable meetings with the first-year mentees meant that the mentors carefully thought through the implications of different stances they could adopt. They discussed these at length in their groups:

> *"Each member of the group had an entirely different and very strong opinion on the mentoring role and how the candidates should be approached. And we spent an awful lot of time debating, a long, long time, prior to the actual day of the mentoring, debating how you should do it, what we should do."*

In this way, working together to design their mentoring session engaged students in deep discussion of the subject and its standards, affording students a great deal of informal feedback on their views of subject terminology and debate about appropriate theoretical approaches.

Preparing students for group work

While group work, on one level, is relatively common in Higher Education, especially in some subject areas, it is important to consider what is actually going on when students are asked to work together. Arguably it is the quality, not the mere existence of group work that determines the help it affords to students' learning on an individual level. Black (2007) suggests that, in schools, pupils are often seen working *in* groups but not working *as* groups. He draws attention to work by Dawes, Mercer and Wegerif (2004) which explored the training that pupils need in order to work creatively together. These include the skills of critical questioning, sharing information and negotiating a decision. The aim was to raise pupils' awareness of how talk could be used for working together and to discuss and establish with each class a set of ground rules for discussion, which would generate talk of an exploratory kind. These included, for instance, the principles that all must participate, that all contributions must be treated with respect, that a group must achieve consensus, and above all, that all claims must be supported by reasons. According to Black, research studies showed that these led to improved attainment, suggesting that teachers might usefully provide guidance which helps their students learn to share ideas, make joint decisions, enquire and reason, as well as provide guidance on the content of the subject area. Black asserts:

A meta-analysis of numerous studies . . . has shown that groups in which learners collaborate yield big learning gains over either individual study or work where there is competition within each group. Groups where there is such internal competition produce almost no learning advantage over individual learning.

(2007: 20)

Introducing group work in engineering

In a postgraduate Mechanical Engineering module a tutor had noted that students were having difficulties in using research data and literature in their discussions and judgements. He decided to address this using an informal learning task in which students would work in groups. Students were split into groups of three in the class and each group was given two research papers (relating to the modelling of a manufacturing process such as bulge-forming, tube-drawing or rolling). The students were asked to play the role of consultants who provide modelling services for industry. They had to use only the information in their given papers to consider a decision regarding the viability of tendering to model that process.

Before the group task started, however, the lecturer spent another session preparing students for peer learning. He offered them a clear rationale and alerted students to views of 'what was in it for them'. He discussed the ways in which engineers frequently need to work in research teams, and gave examples of the ways in which he had personally benefited from discussing ideas with colleagues. He also asked along some students from the year above, who had been very enthusiastic about peer learning, to offer their advice and talk about their views of the benefits. He drew out stories about situations (positive and negative) that commonly arise, together with strategies for dealing with them. He briefly outlined a model about how groups form, outlining the stages of forming, storming, norming and performing (Tuckman and Jenson, 1977). Finally, he included the students in negotiating some ground rules for working in groups.

When the students were asked to start working together on the consultancy task, the lecturer tried to be explicit about what students were expected to do and what might constitute an effective discussion of the particular papers. He gave them pointers, advising them to identify particular key factors such as appropriate techniques, process data availability, customer expectations, project deliverables and so on. Each group was given forty minutes in the class to reach a point where they were required to give a brief (approximately eight-minute) verbal summary of their discussion to the rest of the class. In this way the lecturer encouraged his students to grapple together with authentic and relevant tasks so that they could see for themselves the extent to which they and others were able to draw upon literature to make informed engineering decisions. Whilst students were working he was able to spend time dropping in on discussions and prompting students to consider new angles in their discussions. The lecturer felt that his students' discussions achieved a deeper level than they would have had he simply told them to 'talk together' to decide a tender.

Putting it into practice by seeding activity and dialogue beyond the classroom

It is important to recognize that informal feedback can profitably stem from a range of diverse sources. As Boud and Falchikov (2006: 404) suggest: 'we must not make the mistake of attributing all the benefits of education to those aspects under the direct control of teachers or the curriculum'. Indeed, one strong finding to emerge from our CETL research programme was the value many students placed on the importance of feedback embedded within informal learning communities to enhance their academic experience. This is also in line with Nicol's (2009b) findings from a large-scale project which sought to re-engineer assessment practices to promote learning. This also found that students placed heavy emphasis on the value of the social–academic sphere in helping them learn.

Many of the classroom-based AfL activities, for example, spurred students to form their own informal feedback-rich or feedback-seeking communities beyond the classroom. Sometimes this focused on students explicitly creating extra opportunities to discuss their approaches with peers, as Gillian's example at the start of the chapter illustrated. These took the form of fairly focused 'study groups' at one end of the spectrum through to 'self-help' groups (where students discussed assignment requirements and shared resources) right through to 'chats over coffee' at the other extreme. The conversations within these communities served wider purposes such as reinforcing the importance and worth of the discipline or profession being studied, building a sense of community or belonging within the university and developing disciplinary identities.

Students often discussed their assignment beyond the classroom. For instance, second-year Biology students were required to produce a report on a problem-based practical class. They found that it was valuable to discuss the report with other students for a variety of reasons. For one thing, peers could share specific resources which would help students tackle the assignment: *"We just helped each other with the research, so if we got a journal article then we all got the information out of it."* But students also found that discussing the assignment task enabled them to become clearer about what was really required:

> *"I did it with a group of friends . . . we read it {the assignment brief} and we just, we didn't know what it was talking about, {we} were very confused, and once we sat down and shared ideas we got there in the end."*

Stimulating students to engage in peer discussion beyond the classroom

In practice, whilst lecturers can't control, steer or oversee this kind of informal feedback they can, nevertheless, stimulate and encourage it. For instance, our research found that some students found that AfL approaches in the classroom, especially ones which raised their awareness of the value of peers as useful sources of formal feedback, usefully 'seeded' informal study groups. In the following example, for instance, students who were explicitly encouraged, by activities set up in class, to engage in peer review then began to meet regularly outside of class time to discuss their approaches to work.

Seeding peer learning communities

In a Study Skills module in Health Studies, students were required to complete a Personal Development Plan. This involved them meeting in tutor-led groups on a fortnightly basis, where they discussed short written tasks that had been set. The seminars involved a process of peer review, with students providing formal feedback on each other's work.

Interviews with the students revealed that some had, in consequence, begun to meet up outside of class time to talk about their work.

"We've actually started meeting up even though we've got different assignments. Reading parts of our work to each other. Because we have previously worked in isolation. Before I tended to take it off to a corner and just do it and it stands alone. And if it's good, it's good and if it's rubbish, it's rubbish. We do work in isolation but we have started to work more together on academic stuff, now. That's really helped, because you get an idea about what people think you're trying to say. Even if it's not their area, you can sort of see what sense they're making of it, whether you could be clearer."

However, our research also found that many students consciously set out to explain their courses, and their growing perceptions of topic areas, with partners, friends or family members who were not directly involved in their university experience. Often students did this to gauge for themselves how far they were grasping a topic, by seeing if they could explain it to an outsider. For instance, the following student explained why she talked to her boyfriend about her learning. She wanted to see for herself whether she had developed the more complex ways of thinking about and seeing the subject matter that she realized were important:

"I'm just checking. . . . I'm kind of . . . confirming that some people don't actually get it. Because . . . when you get somebody who's completely . . . detached from it they are a better sounding post. And that, kind of, reaffirmed that maybe I was seeing what I was supposed to be seeing."

This could also help reinforce a student's sense of becoming part of the relevant community of practice. In another example, a Biology student commented on how pleased she felt when a 'nature programme' was on television and her housemates asked her questions, recognizing her expertise.

"I love it when people are watching a programme and they're {saying} . . . oh I wonder why that's like that? And I can tell them and I know the answer . . . it's good to know that you can tell people stuff."

In a research study of final-year Social Sciences students these kinds of issues were seen as significant by students. Sarah was one student who had recognized the importance of 'being part of something'. In an interview in her final year she said:

> *"I've found among friends, people have started talking about the subject in their free time and exchanging ideas . . . in a pub context sometimes, even, people will be talking about the work and someone might have come across something that would be useful to someone else and there's a sort of exchange network going . . . people are actually talking about their subject in their spare time just because it's actually come to affect their lives."*

Stuart, a student who took some of the same modules as Sarah had found it more difficult to talk about his interests. He had recently been studying a module on Middle Eastern Politics which was, as is often the case, very much in the news but he said:

> *"People do ask me about it {when they find out} but I don't think that people really want to listen and the major problem is trying to explain in ten minutes . . . so I just kind of end up asking them what they think and nodding."*

Designing in authentic experiences beyond the formal curriculum

Opportunities for field trips and visits beyond the university also provided rich contexts for informal feedback. While these sorts of activities are commonplace in some subject areas, in others, like history or criminology, they may seem more novel. Students' perceptions of the benefits included the opportunity to see their course in a new light, for example, by realizing how useful employers found the skills and qualities they had developed, or how the issues they had covered in an abstract sense related to the 'real world'.

Students often benefit from getting involved, perhaps on a voluntary basis, in additional activities which enable them to gain different perspectives on the formal curriculum, for example, by working directly on community-based projects. One example is an English student working with refugees and asylum seekers to engage them in creative writing. Other examples include peer-tutoring or student-led mentoring schemes, which enable students to work across levels, rather than always working with same-level students (Falchikov, 2001). Student engagement in this kind of civic, community-based voluntary activity may or may not be activity which is directly related to their subject area but there is emerging evidence to suggest that this activity can promote development of critical analysis, social and political literacy and participation in important peer networks (Brooks, 2005).

Setting up a staff–student research group

In Sociolinguistics, a lecturer established a research group. It involved students in a 'live' research project where they discussed issues, collaborated on data collection and met once a fortnight outside of class time. Students formed a research group with their tutor but then independently began research, pooled examples, gathered data in the community and then brought it back to the group. This was a valuable environment for informal feedback.

One student noted:

> *"Working with a group of students who were also using other methods but conducting similar research was valuable. It is easy, when looking at something in depth, to get completely blinded by your own work and the support of the students and staff at the bi-weekly meetings helped to gain fresh ideas and inspiration. It was also useful, working in a group situation, to feed off each other's results and support each other whilst writing the final assignment."*

Voicing the issues revisited: a case study on informal feedback

Collaborative work in Performing Arts

In Performing Arts, a set of final-year compulsory linked modules were based around students working in small groups to develop and deliver performances or workshops in real community settings. In the first of the linked modules, the students had to make contacts, familiarize themselves with the setting, negotiate and develop proposals for performance-based activity. Other elements of the module were designed to extend the opportunities for students to work with external professionals who came in to talk to and work with the students as they developed their proposals and performances. In addition, visits to community-based organizations were arranged. There was also a lot of student-led unstructured activity, interaction and feedback in the module, as students developed their group activities and made external contacts. Groups were routinely encouraged to share what they were developing in class with each other. The module required students to be active and engage with fellow students, visiting professionals and the staff and clients of external organizations.

Students commented on the opportunities to develop their skills and receive feedback by working in community-based activity and from working closely with visiting professionals, where they felt they were finding out what really went on and how things were done in a professional context:

> *"It's been a really good module and I think that's especially thanks to the outside practitioners coming in. I think that's where I've learnt the most because we got to observe different practice and methodologies that really informed our own practice."*

The explicit feedback and guidance from the visiting professionals and their implicit communication of how things might be done and the standards that students should aspire to were a highly valued form of feedback. Practitioner feedback was not referenced so much to the educational setting as to the real-world setting where students were eager to learn and achieve, and it mainly came in the form of tacit feedback by example rather than by instruction. The feedback from 'real' people in the community settings where students worked was also highly valued: *"Going in and doing a workshop . . . it definitely helped . . . doing it in front of people and getting the feedback is just a lot easier and a better way of learning."*

Working with other students in the class sessions was deemed useful, too, because it enabled students to see diverse ways of approaching the topics addressed, providing informal feedback which helped them reflect on and gauge their own tactics more effectively: *"I've really, really enjoyed viewing everybody's work because it just gives you an insight . . . it helps you, influences your own work."* The module is an example of learning through participation an approach which generated considerable feedback, much of it implicit, some explicit (especially from lecturers) and considerable peer feedback. Although the module had been carefully designed, planned and organized by the staff team, the details of the learning environments, the communication with people external to the university and the specific activities undertaken by students were not in their direct control and there were aspects that students found challenging. However, setting up an appropriate environment and then 'standing back' whilst of course being there when needed or to deal with any problems, is probably required if students are to benefit from participation in broader learning communities than can be provided within their academic programme. Mostly students found that the participative approach was positive although it could be challenging.

The high value of embedded informal feedback is shown by its enhancement of students' sense of the worth of the work they were undertaking This helped to develop their sense of commitment and identity as a practitioner which was noticed by one of the tutors who commented after a visit to a community theatre:

> *"I got a sense of . . . light bulbs going off. Several students actually changed their project tack after that visit . . . they should be able to answer the question, 'Why do you want to do this work in this context?' and not just say, 'Oh well, it just seemed interesting'."*

This type of personal commitment was also noted by some students who found that they became clearer about their personal goals developing a view of *"what you want and you can be if you're an artist or facilitator – and what you don't want to be"*.

Key questions to think about

The following key questions are designed to help course and module teams develop their practice. They could, alternatively, be used for personal reflection.

- **How far do your teaching and assessment strategies encourage students to learn together?** We have suggested that a dialogic or conversational context is a valuable way for students to learn some very important aspects of their subject. Purposeful conversations can give students new perspectives, but other pressures, perhaps lack of time or lack of space or even concerns about collusion in learning, can mean that we discourage collaborative activity. What are the barriers to a conversational classroom in your context and how can you redesign your learning environments to promote it?

- **What kinds of productive discussion emerge from students and staff working in collaboration?** The intrinsic feedback derived from collaboration, especially where students and staff are engaged on open-ended tasks with no defined 'right answer' can be invaluable in helping students to see how questions and problems are addressed in the subject. In addition to the usual goals of improving students' subject knowledge, understanding and skills, collaboration can prompt learning in the affective domain helping students see the worth of their learning and start to develop a disciplinary or professional identity.

- **How do you enable students to appreciate disciplinary expectations and develop a connoisseur-like view of the subject?** Understanding what a discipline is really about, what questions are addressed and what count as good answers and high-quality work, is something which develops over time. Where do you promote and encourage and where do you evaluate this kind of 'slow learning'? This is likely to need attention at the programme level rather than just in individual modules.

- **How do you enable your students to test out their learning in contexts beyond the classroom?** Students have other lives and participate in many different contexts beyond the university. Are there places in your programme where you are flexible and open enough to allow students to learn and be assessed on work that happens in their own external contexts? Are there also places where learning is organized by staff to allow students to take advantage of the learning resources in external contexts for specific purposes? The aim could be for students to apply disciplinary knowledge to real settings, to participate in learning communities or to gain confidence and commitment from being able to contribute their expertise beyond the university.

Chapter 6

Developing students as self-assessors and effective lifelong learners

In overall terms, Assessment for Learning is about developing the student's capacity as a lifelong learner. This includes the ability to monitor their own work, rather than relying on someone else to do that for them. This relates to the discussions in previous chapters, but in this chapter we will focus particularly on strategies we might use to explicitly develop students' capacities for self-assessment.

This chapter covers:

- perspectives on the importance and value of self-assessment in terms of supporting learning;
- inducting students into the processes of self-assessment, and the value derived from fostering the skills of self-critique, the capacity for independent judgement and the development of a reflective, critical habit of mind;
- designing and developing strategies which involve and encourage students to become active participants in assessment processes;
- developing students' assessment literacy, by enabling them to better appreciate the standards, goals and criteria required to evaluate outputs within a specific disciplinary context.

Voicing the issues

Gordon is a third-year student who has just come back to the university after a very successful placement. He enjoyed being on placement, because it gave him responsibility for his own work. He found he had to manage his own progress. He developed strategies for actively seeking feedback from others. He also set himself targets, and monitored how he was doing as he progressed towards meeting them. Gordon now wants to apply this to his work at university.

> "Before, I used to get the assignment briefs, and go through the criteria, with a view to making sure that I had all the relevant information. I didn't really think too deeply about what they were really expecting me to be able to know and do. I now see how important it is, because it's what you have to do in the workplace."

Contemporary society clearly demands more than passive graduates who have complied with a fixed assessment regime (Boud, 2006). For graduates, researchers and professionals the capacity to evaluate one's own work, during the course of actually undertaking it, is vital to success. Boud and Falchikov (2006) contend, therefore, that Higher Education should involve students in gradually learning to become effective assessors and self-assessors. In their eyes, enabling students to make complex judgements about their own and others' work prepares them to make decisions in the unpredictable and complex professional and social contexts they are likely to meet in the future (2006: 402). In other words, self-evaluation underpins an individual's capacity for independent, reflective thinking and the aptitude to take responsibility for one's own actions. These are features which employers expect of a graduate workforce (Knight and Yorke, 2003) and the capacity to monitor one's own work is typically seen as a graduate attribute (Barrie, 2007; Cleary *et al.*, 2007).

This chapter emphasizes the ways in which students should be supported to monitor and manage their own learning by developing the ability to evaluate their own work, and that of others, effectively. The focus is particularly on the ways in which we might deliberately engineer opportunities which enable and support our students to learn to make and express effective and informed judgements about the quality of work. The chapter suggests that AfL approaches give considerable attention to the ways in which students are actively and explicitly inducted into assessment cultures which promote independence, personal responsibility and critical thinking abilities. It pays particular attention to the ways in which our assessment processes in Higher Education might expressly be designed and managed to foster the vital capacity for self-regulation.

Theories and debates

Formative and summative self-evaluation activities, and the closely related activities of peer assessment or reciprocal peer feedback, are increasingly being promoted in Higher Education (see, for example, Boud, 1995; Boud *et al.*, 2010; Bloxham and Boyd, 2007; Brown, Bull and Pendlebury, 1997; Nicol, 2010b; Segers, Docher and Cascaller, 2003). Peer and self-evaluation are often considered to be valuable activities that develop students' abilities to become realistic judges of their own and others' performance, enabling them to monitor their own learning effectively, rather than relying on their teachers to fulfil this role for them. As such, they can be regarded as important tools for learning. Viewed from this perspective, student involvement in assessment processes is frequently linked to the notion of promoting, practising and developing learner autonomy (Boud, 1995; Hinett and Thomas, 1999; Knight and Yorke, 2003).

The principle of developing self-assessment in Higher Education can be viewed as a matter of raising a student's consciousness of crucial metacognitive processes and learning-to-learn skills. From this standpoint, involving students actively in the process of making judgements about the quality of work is important, because if learners come to rely exclusively on their teachers to tell them when things need to be improved, or when something they are doing is satisfactory, this will leave many students unprepared for life beyond the university. While some students appear to realize this and engage in evaluation naturally, many benefit from having it brought to their attention and require explicit assistance in learning to develop the skills and dispositions required.

AfL places considerable emphasis on developing students' capacities for self-assessment. One common way of doing this is to mobilize the resources of self- and peer assessment, so that students are positioned as active assessors, rather than as passive victims in the assessment process. Students may be required, for instance, to mark peers' work or to fill in forms which identify the strengths and weaknesses of assignments they are submitting. However, as previous chapters have made clear, shifting the balance of power and control from lecturer to student is not without its challenges, especially in the context of 'high-stakes' assessment, where the drive to gain marks and grades is sharply felt. In fact, within these contexts students may resist becoming involved in the assessment process, or self-assessment may have some undesirable side-effects. Research has shown, for instance, that some activities which are undertaken in the name of self-assessment may actually be used by staff as a means of controlling and disciplining their students' behaviour, rather than empowering them to take control of their own learning processes (Tan, 2004).

However, if we neglect self-assessment altogether it can mean that students leave our modules, and even university itself, having learned to rely almost exclusively on *others* to make judgements and evaluations of work on their behalf. The chapter argues that self-assessment can and should be much more than simply allocating marks or filling in forms with little sense of why or how the reflective or evaluative comments being required are of any value. A better approach is to engage students systematically, in a planned and sustained manner, in assessment practice and reflective discussions about assessment. This entails engaging students actively in thinking about and debating the means by which judgements are made in our disciplines and/or professions, so that students are gradually inducted into the process and supported to develop effective evaluation skills in order to monitor their own learning, rather than relying on others to perform evaluative judgements for them.

This chapter argues, then, that there are significant short- and long-term learning benefits to be gained by rethinking and redesigning our modules and programmes. We take the view that empowering students to be able to discriminate, say, between 'good' and less effective work is not simply a case of helping them get the best grades they can during their university careers, important as that may be. Being empowered to make realistic judgements about their own achievements, during the process of actually learning something, is fundamental to their learning for the longer term, too. Because of this, the chapter aims to propose strategies that can be used in university education which help promote the relevant skills, dispositions and attitudes our students need in order to become effective autonomous learners, both now and in the future.

With these sorts of issues in mind, a significant body of research literature has argued that Assessment for Learning is not just about providing timely feedback and improving student learning *within* the university, but also encompasses assessment practices that prepare students to become effective 'assessors' of their own learning after university and throughout the life course (Boud, 2000; Carless, Joughin and Mok, 2006). In an important sense, if we wish to support this longer-term agenda, universities have an essential part to play in carefully managing students' expectations and fostering positive attitudes towards the roles they need to assume in exercising judgement and controlling their own learning.

Knapper (1990) argues that the ability to exercise learner autonomy depends crucially upon certain prerequisites that surround one's attitudes, values and self-image as a learner. These include one's outlook on learning itself, one's attitudes to specific conditions and contexts (such as views of a teacher's role, or views of the purpose of assessment) and attitudes to oneself as a learner (confidence or sense of power and effectiveness). To possess these attitudes learners need to be able to see the relevance and worthwhile nature of their learning (rather than regarding learning as an arbitrary or meaningless task) and genuinely believe they can achieve success. These dispositions are all underpinned by the principles we have outlined in previous chapters. Fostering such dispositions means endeavouring to create challenging but congenial learning environments and communities which can engage our students.

In addition to developing a positive general stance in relation to learning, Knapper and Cropley (2000) argue that certain skills are also required. Successful autonomous learners need to:

• be able to work independently without direct supervision;
• know how to find information and use resources without guidance;
• know how to set appropriate goals and how to devise strategies for achieving them;
• monitor the extent to which these goals have been achieved and know how to design alternative ways of achieving them.

This is to regard self-monitoring itself as an important tool for empowering learners. Boud (1995) also claims that self-assessment has the capacity to develop students' abilities to plan and organize their own learning, to become proactive in their own learning, and to develop the capability of monitoring what they do and modifying their learning strategies accordingly. He persuasively argues that: 'The ability to self assess is a key foundation to a career as a lifelong learner who can continue their education after formal education has ended' (1995: 14). However, it is increasingly the case that not all learners enter university with the preparedness and understanding that this involves (Boud et al., 2010). It can be argued that we need to do much more to consciously induct students into becoming effective self-assessors. This is an issue that this chapter particularly addresses.

Recent research in assessment has placed considerable emphasis on promoting and developing strategies which consciously foreground the students' role as active participants in the assessment process itself. According to Nicol and Macfarlane-Dick (2006), for instance, self-regulation relates to the extent to which students can monitor and evaluate aspects of their learning behaviours, process a variety of information (or feedback) which has a bearing on the tasks in which they are engaged, and then act upon it to improve their learning. Hounsell (2007) argues that learners can use a diverse range of 'feedback-like effects' throughout the learning cycle to inform their own decision-making process about what is required, what is already mastered, what needs to be done next and so on. For learners to make productive use of this information, though, means that they need to be encouraged and supported to assume responsibility. This is vital, because feedback information can only be of any real use (in terms of having an impact on the actual actions a learner may decide to take to improve their learning) if learners themselves actively *do something* with feedback, in the sense of acting upon it. As we have stressed, this generally means rethinking what we, and our students, assume 'feedback' is.

From our viewpoint, then, we must help our students to become actively engaged in the process of *generating* as well as *processing* feedback (Nicol, 2009a), in addition to simply receiving feedback from a range of sources. Engaging in an evaluation process, through, for example, making judgements about peers' work, helps reposition learners as informed 'insiders', rather than passive victims of the assessment process. Liu and Carless (2006) argue that giving peer feedback is the learning element of peer assessment. In other words, and arguably above all, students need to become actively involved *as assessors* – people who make evaluative judgements about the worth of work – rather than seeing themselves as somehow separate from the evaluative processes that their lecturers undertake (Bloxham, 2008). So, just as they need support and encouragement to take deep and active approaches to learning, students also require support and encouragement to take deep and active approaches to engage with assessment judgements. In short, students need to learn to become members of our *assessment* communities, as well as our subject-related learning communities.

The definition of high-quality formative assessment practice proposed by Sadler (1989) is widely used and accepted as a basis of the links between autonomy and self- and peer assessment in Higher Education. Sadler suggests that effective formative assessment environments must:

1   enable students to understand the goals or standards to be achieved;
2   help students to effectively gauge their own current level of performance; and
3   allow them to have access to strategies for closing any gap they identify.

Black and Wiliam (1998b), two highly influential exponents of AfL in the compulsory education sector have put it in a different way:

> . . . self-assessment by pupils, far from being a luxury, is in fact *an essential component of formative assessment*. When anyone is trying to learn, feedback about the effort has three elements: redefinition of the *desired goal*, evidence about *present position*, and some understanding of a *way to close the gap between the two*. All three must be understood to some degree by anyone before he or she can take action to improve learning.
>
> (Black and Wiliam, 1998b: 143, emphasis in the original)

Black and Wiliam's definition usefully indicates that 'self-assessment' does not inevitably refer to self-*marking* (with students awarding grades or scores), although it may do. Instead, it refers more broadly to a *process* which, in effect, requires students to develop evaluative expertise in order to make effective judgements about their own performance, so that they learn to appraise their own work during the very course of its production. In a nutshell, this is to place emphasis on self-assessment within the context of learning and pedagogic processes, rather than seeing it from the viewpoint of an assessment culture focused on audit or measurement (Gielen, Dochy and Dierick, 2003).

Sadler (2010) suggests that students' evaluative skills can be purposefully developed by creating 'authentic evaluative experiences' for them. From this perspective the objective is to induct students into an ability to recognize quality work and to explain their judgements of quality. Indeed, much pedagogical development work in university education has focused on exploring strategies which set out to help equip students with the means by which to establish levels of performance and develop their powers of discrimination and judgement (see, for example, Boud *et al.*, 2010; Orsmond, Merry and Reiling, 2002; Rust, Price and O'Donovan, 2003; Sambell and McDowell, 1997).

It is important to reiterate and emphasize the point that many students need explicit help and support to develop the capacity to evaluate and manage their own learning, in the same way that they require our help and support to learn subject content. Research is making it clear that it may no longer be sufficient to leave students to learn by chance, or assume they already possess the requisite dispositions, skills and qualities to judge work (Defeyter and McPartlin, 2007; Norton, 1990; Rust *et al.*, 2003; Sambell, 2011). The development of learners' self-evaluation skills is too vital to leave to serendipity and a casual process of 'picking it up as one goes along'. Finding cost-effective strategies which help students become more assessment-literate in this way becomes even more crucial in the context of large class sizes and the accompanying reduction in small-group teaching in many university courses (Nicol, 2010b). The traditional chances for on-going dialogue and contextualized social interaction about expectations and standards have been eroded in many contexts.

Rust *et al.* (2003) amongst others have consistently proposed that we need to devote time and attention to developing students' peer and self-evaluation skills, so that students develop their assessment literacy and thereby are empowered to achieve and succeed in the university assignments they are expected to carry out. These influential researchers have, over a number of years, put forward strong and convincing arguments for helping students learn about assessment processes via *experience* and *participation* in relevant, highly contextualized communities of assessment practice, rather than simply being told what the assessment rules are (O'Donovan, Price and Rust, 2004). They suggest that students need to learn about assessment, as they do about anything else, through extensive social interaction and active involvement. From this perspective, being supported to participate actively in assessment communities is the only way that students can grasp what is truly required and how, therefore, to monitor and adapt their own approaches.

Thus it is incumbent on us to help make sure that, as far as we are able and within the constraints of our mass education system, our teaching and assessment environments support students' capacities to evaluate work and take deep approaches to assessment. The ideal aim is, then, to provide students with substantial evaluative experience as an integrated aspect of the design of our teaching (Sadler, 2009). In our view, active involvement in the complex and challenging business of making judgements about the relative worth of academic work is the *only* way students are able to learn, say, about the tacit local meanings that become implicitly attached to goals, standards and criteria in particular contexts. Research also shows that it is a mistake to believe that transparency about assessment can be achieved simply by writing things down (Orr and Blythman, 2005), or that 'messages' about assessment are sent to students and then received and assimilated in a straightforward manner (Sambell, 2011). More worryingly, some surveys of students' assessment experiences have even suggested that attempts to be explicit by publishing assessment criteria might unintentionally have quite damaging side-effects. Research by Gibbs and Dunbar-Goddet (2007), for example, implied that some universities' attempts to make goals and standards overt actually led to students narrowing 'their attention and their effort to those things they were told would be assessed' (2007: 24), in ways which were actually detrimental to learning.

From our viewpoint, students need to gradually 'see' and develop a feel for what standards and criteria might look like in practice and, crucially, in context, before they are in a position to co-construct and negotiate shared meanings of appropriate criteria and standards. Extensive dialogue, including focused discussion about the 'backstage' thinking academics use in the process of appraising a piece of work, is absolutely vital. This is likely to take time and considerable effort, on our part and from the students, so needs to be built incrementally into courses right from the start, and carefully handled in progressively more challenging ways.

The examples of AfL practice outlined in the following section revolve around students' experiences of getting involved, formally and informally, in the business of making and discussing judgements about the quality of work. We have chosen them to suggest and exemplify some of the diverse ways in which learning and teaching environments can be engineered to offer a range of opportunities for students to understand assessment more fully, so that they learn to play an active part within it.

Putting it into practice

There are many ways in which subject lecturers have tried to improve the manner in which their students experience the benefits of self-assessment. One way of doing this is to design activities which introduce students to the idea that the ability for self-critique and the capacity to make informed judgements are valuable qualities. This is especially important as students make the transition to university, but can also be fostered and progressively developed at later stages. Second, opportunities for students to participate as assessors and engage in meaningful dialogue with others about the assessment process are important features. Strategies which help learners practise and develop their assessment skills can also help develop good habits, such as taking up the mantle of responsibility for making judgements about one's own learning. Finally, strategies for helping students develop better understandings of standards, criteria and other assessment procedures can offer productive ways of putting AfL into practice and encouraging students to become members of our assessment communities.

This section of the chapter highlights three broad approaches to putting self-assessment into practice. These are:

- putting it into practice by inducting students into AfL assessment cultures and communities;
- putting it into practice by stimulating students' active involvement in the assessment process;
- putting it into practice by developing students' assessment literacy.

Under each of these broad approaches, we have selected a range of different examples to show some of the diverse ways in which assessment can be engineered to offer students a range of self-assessment experiences.

Putting it into practice by inducting students into AfL assessment cultures and communities

Designing assessment tasks to promote the importance of self-review and reflection

Haggis (2006) and Boud *et al.* (2010) argue that it is not uncommon for students to enter university with extremely varied levels of preparedness and understanding of what is entailed. This means that sustained work which inducts students into the assessment practices and cultures of our courses is often required. By setting specific assignment tasks and activities, lecturers can try and initiate vital self-regulation processes in their students. Arguably, especially for some students, this is extremely important in the early stages of study, when they are trying to get to grips with the new expectations and standards. This is an important time to establish expectations about the participatory roles students are expected to take within assessment communities.

'Springboards' to self-evaluation can be embedded in summative contexts in the early stages of a programme with powerful effects, where they embody a sort of 'hidden curriculum' of self-assessment, encouraging students to think critically about their role in the assessment process, rather than seeing assessment as solely the lecturer's job. This can be an effective strategy because, as we argued earlier, a student's actions can be seen as contingent on her or his individual interpretations of the specific context. So designing assessment tasks which explicitly endorse reflection, self-assessment or peer assessment in courses can help students realize that these processes are valued, and that it is important to develop the skills and dispositions associated with them.

This example illustrates this. The lecturer wanted her students to perceive that she valued a deep approach to assessment tasks, rather than an approach which simply recorded and regurgitated the lecture notes. She set her students a reflective essay as one of the first assignments they undertook. The aim was to open up dialogue about the tacit values she held with regard to assessment, and to instil appropriate approaches and self-monitoring habits of mind in her students.

Designing summative assessment to promote reflection on learning and progress

In an introductory year-long theory module in a Humanities degree, the lecturer set a reflective essay at an early stage, which was worth 30 per cent of the overall module marks. The essay required students to explain how their understandings had developed over the first semester of study and was designed to encourage students to begin to record and gauge their own learning, and to think about (and express) what learning and assessment meant in the context of the subject. Above all, it sought to seed communities in which dialogue about assessment performance became routine, and personal responsibility for reflection and decision-making about the quality of work achieved was fostered. The lecturer encouraged students to maintain reflective diaries throughout the learning and teaching activities on the module, reminding them to keep a record of their views, inter-pretations and conceptual understandings as they engaged with the course, materials and further reading.

Students were advised that the reflective essay should explain how far and in what ways they believed they had, at this stage, successfully met the module learning outcomes. Students were asked to include extracts from their reflective diaries as illustrative evidence to support any claims they made in their essay. This provided concrete examples of what students felt they had achieved on the module, together with reflections about what had helped them attain this.

When students submitted their reflective essays, they often included a 'before' and 'after' version of short writing tasks that were part of the module. This encouraged students to talk about what they had decided to improve upon and how they had sought to achieve that improvement. This kind of self-evaluation helped the lecturer see, and comment upon, the quality of students' self-evaluations and relate it to her own expectations and standards.

This approach to self-assessment also meant that, in order to prepare for the reflective essay, the students often discussed with each other and with the lecturer, what they believed they had learned about the subject from undertaking class-room activities, plus work they had engaged in beyond the classroom. This necessarily involved them in regular dialogue about the demands of the tasks and activities the lecturer set each week and helped to bring to the surface the lecturer's expectations about study and assessment at university level.

Encouraging students to evaluate what they already know and can do

Another way of encouraging students to develop the skills and disposition to monitor their own learning is to use self-evaluation checklists as a springboard for activity and dialogue. These can not only involve students in discussions about ideas that matter within the relevant community, but also usefully offer students a framework or alternative criteria by which to view and compare their own learning. In the early stages of university it can be helpful, for instance, to encourage students to undertake skills audits, or self-evaluations of their own approaches to learning and assessment, as the following example illustrates.

Enhancing self-evaluation skills via audits and inventories

A group of first-year students were asked to reflect upon a series of self-evaluation checklists, which helped them to identify for themselves aspects they needed to further develop. For instance, students were asked to audit their basic IT skills to identify areas in which they required additional support, which helped them decide into which support workshops they should enrol in the library. They were also asked to perform self-rating exercises which helped them to evaluate their existing study skills, such as setting oneself manageable goals, or knowing how to make the most of group work, or how to get started on an assignment. These were used to bring together the students' ideas about their current strengths, and the areas they wished to develop, into a prioritized development plan.

The course team developed the resources to highlight to students, from the outset of the course, the value of explicitly evaluating and expressing their achievements as useful preparation for job interviews, as well as fostering an important approach within university study itself. They encouraged their students, in regular guidance tutorials throughout the degree programme, to revisit their profiles. The process also helped students to perceive the need to develop practical experience beyond the course, as well as underlining the importance of 'soft' skills, such as oral communication, influencing others, and negotiation, which were developed as part of the course and highly prized by employers, but which students often forgot to consider in their curriculum vitae and job applications. As a result, many became encouraged to maintain and build curriculum vitae, using the tools available in the web-based e-portfolio system 'PebblePad,' which helped them make the links between the academic content of their degree and its application in practice. In this way the skills and dispositions of the effective lifelong learner, underpinned by the capacity to evaluate one's own work, were foregrounded.

Designing assessment tasks which encourage students to regard themselves as partners in assessment communities

Students need help to appreciate and develop the skills that they need to manage and monitor their own learning in the specific context of learning at university level. As previous chapters have made clear, learning is enhanced by formative assessment environments which encourage student participation in dialogue about different approaches to particular tasks and the opportunity to practise a task and reflect upon how successfully it was achieved and what next steps can be taken. Summative assessment formats can be designed to highlight and stimulate these kinds of academic–social integration (Nicol, 2009b), especially as learners are making the transition into Higher Education. In the following example, lecturers on a Study Skills module designed the assessment format of the whole module to encourage students to reflect on the quality of their own and others' work in an ongoing process in an attempt to foster the skills and dispositions of autonomous learning.

Stimulating self- and peer assessment using a log book

One hundred and fifty first-year Education students took a Study Skills module which was assessed on a pass/fail basis. The module had been designed to help them to make effective academic transitions to university-level study. Students were required to complete a log book which was designed around four formative short writing tasks. The tasks were targeted on issues which, in the past, the teaching team had realized were challenging for newcomers to university study, such as: tackling wider reading effectively; recognizing the relative authority of online material; avoiding plagiarism; developing an argument; referencing and drawing upon theory in one's own academic writing. Students undertook each task individually, and then took their writing to a series of seminars dedicated to the module.

In the seminars, students were asked to share their writing with the small group and discuss their work with the tutor and with the other students. Learners were assured that, whilst completing the log book was a course requirement, the booklet was a working document, so 'making mistakes' was to be expected and would be part and parcel of the learning experience.

Following each seminar, each student then completed other sections of the log book, which required them, in the light of the seminar discussions and the opportunity to hear what was said about the strengths and necessary improvements in everyone's work, to engage with self-review and produce a personal action plan. Students were encouraged to use their action plan as a working document, which might identify, for instance, anything an individual felt unsure about and wanted to ask someone's advice about at the next meeting, or strategies students planned to use in order to improve their work. Whatever students wrote in the action plan acted as discussion points at the start of each seminar meeting. In this way, although the log book would be handed in as partial evidence of meeting the module learning outcomes, it sought mainly to function as a formative discussion document. It signalled to students that reflection and discussion were important aspects of learning.

The sense of community, dialogue, action-planning and shared purpose that was forged in the seminar series discussions continued to be of value throughout the students' three-year degree programme, so that the guidance system itself subsequently began to act as an environment for self-assessment.

Reflection and self-evaluation for employability

In the following example, second-year students were encouraged to appreciate the need to foster and develop their self-assessment skills. This was done by redesigning the assessment format to focus upon the ways in which the course related to the world of work and future employment, and by supporting students to make informed decisions about the areas they might choose for dissertation work in the final year.

Encouraging students to reflect on the relevance of the degree

A group of Educational Studies undergraduates were required to reflect on the relevance of their degree by undertaking a summative assessment task. Because the students were in the second year, they would soon need to choose a dissertation topic of personal interest to explore in their final year. To this end they were offered a year-long module which was designed to introduce appropriate research methods, and help them develop suitable research areas and research questions.

The Research Methods module had two assignments, each divided into two stages across the year. The first task required students to:

- research possible employment opportunities within the field;
- compile a curriculum vitae and complete an application form for a job they might like to apply for in this field.

The second assignment task required students to:

- prepare a proposal to undertake fieldwork within a relevant setting which might strengthen their application in future.

These two interrelated assignments encouraged students to take stock of what they had learned to date, and think carefully about what debates, issues and contexts they wished to pursue in their final-year projects. The second assignment also prompted considerable discussion with course tutors about former students' dissertations and the ways in which 'good' dissertations threw light upon an issue or a theme, whilst weaker ones tended to cover too broad a territory and skimmed too much material. They looked at former students' dissertations to build a sense of appropriate standards and quality and discussed how far each would help the student to demonstrate capability in a job interview in the specific field.

This helped students engage at an early stage with the goals and criteria for evaluating final-year projects, in time to make informed decisions about choosing their own topic. The assessment format on the Research Methods module also helped students explicitly think about linking educational theory to the 'real world', as well as thinking laterally about the sorts of careers their particular degree might equip them for. It also encouraged them to build up their hands-on experience, via volunteering to work in schools and so on, if the sort of career they had in mind required it.

Developing online self-testing facilities to enhance student learning and foster self-monitoring

Whilst the above examples have focused on summative assessment designs to promote self-assessment, opportunities for active student involvement in self- and peer assessment activity can be part of formative assessment. Examples are informal or voluntary self-testing online, whereby self-testing facilities are offered as learning activities which allow students to test their understanding by tackling questions in a subject domain (McDowell *et al.*, 2006). Alternatively, as in the following example, students can be offered the opportunity to evaluate their own skills and identify their own needs.

Designing support materials which promote self-monitoring

In this example information specialists in the university library designed an electronic information skills auditing tool. This was made available via the library pages on the university website. Students were encouraged by their lecturers to undertake a series of online quizzes in their own time. The quizzes helped them evaluate their own information literacy needs, identifying any 'gaps' or mis-understandings.

The programme included self-testing at the end, which students could use to check their own understanding of key concepts and strategies. If students failed to answer any question appropriately, they gained access to rich qualitative feedback immediately, which appeared in a pop-up box. They were advised to seek further clarification from staff if they still did not understand where they were going wrong with their information-seeking skills. For example, the site advertised a series of hands-on workshops which students could sign up for to address specific areas of need they had identified by doing the audit.

Using informal peer review to promote self-monitoring

The disposition to monitor one's own achievements in an ongoing way can also be promoted via involvement in informal peer review processes. This kind of activity can help to seed social communities of learners, within and across year groups, and open up dialogue about assessment and learning based around self-assessment, as the following example illustrates.

Student mentoring to promote a process of self-review

Second- and third-year Guidance and Counselling students were offered the chance to support, as mentors, the induction process of 'new' first-year under-graduates. To help give some structure and focus to the initial meetings, the first-years were invited to engage in a self-evaluation activity. This was based on a board game, developed by second-year students. The game aimed to help the first-years identify aspects of study which they found challenging in the first few weeks at university and begin to think about ways forward. In this way, it focused the first-years on reflection and self-review.

The game used the basic idea of the board game 'Snakes and Ladders'. Working in small groups, students were asked to indicate and discuss their 'snakes' on the board. The snakes represented barriers and challenges the students found they faced. These typically included referencing, accessing journals online, knowing where to start with huge reading lists, worries about getting started with assignments and so on. Next, the groups were encouraged to identify and discuss their 'ladders'. Ladders represented strategies students had already used or heard about, which would offer support and development opportunities to overcome the 'snakes'. At this stage ladders typically included resources and people who could help, such as library staff, guidance tutors and information literacy resources online, as well as approaches to learning, such talking about one's ideas, active reading and note-taking strategies.

The mentors, as well as their mentees, found huge value in engaging in this type of informal self-evaluation. The social engagement with the first-years prompted the mentors to articulate what and how they had learned during their time at university. In fact, the ways in which the mentors talked about the experience of becoming a mentor evidenced many of the features of self-assessment, in the sense of developing evaluative expertise (Sadler, 1989) and the kinds of skills and dispositions required for effective lifelong learning (Falchikov, 2005a). Many claimed to suddenly realize how far they had come and what they *could* do, rather than, as was normally the case, simply focusing on what they had not yet achieved. One said, for example:

> "It was not until this point that I realized how far I had come, not just academically, but personally. Many of us were unaware as to how much progress we had made on our own development while at university."

Putting it into practice by stimulating students' active involvement in the assessment process

There is a growing body of research in Higher Education (for example, Boekaerts and Minnaert, 2003; Orsmond, Merry and Reiling, 1996; Rust, O'Donovan and Price, 2005; Sambell, McDowell and Sambell, 2006; Sluijsmans *et al.*, 2001), in which self-, peer and co-assessment is viewed as a way of engaging students in meaningful developmental activities aiming explicitly to open up the 'black box' of assessment to students. This concerns empowering students to become partners in our assessment communities, rather than passive recipients of the judgements we mete out.

Explicitly involving students as assessors

If we are serious about wanting students to become self-regulating learners, arguably they must overtly be offered an active role in assessment processes themselves. As we suggested earlier, empowering students via self-assessment does not necessarily mean getting students to award marks which count but it can be very powerful to involve students as markers, of their own work or, more usually, of their peers, as a means of preparing students for self-monitoring and self-regulation (Gielen *et al.*, 2011). A number of authors have all argued that the practice of student self-assessment can usefully help reduce the teacher's unilateral power over students; see Stefani (1998), McMahon (1999), Butcher and Stefani (1995), Somervell (1993) and Boud (1995).

Students are very well-placed to mark, say, individual contributions to a group project and many lecturers feel confident in setting aside some marks for students to award, as the following example shows.

Peer assessment of group processes

A lecturer in Law felt that it was important to assess the process involved in students' assessed group work, rather than simply the product, so that valuable skills were being recognized and rewarded. She felt that in group work a range of relevant skills are deployed in the process of producing the group product. As well as the ability to work with others, these include self-management and organizational skills, research skills, communication and intellectual skills. She wanted, therefore, to capture these, but worried that they were not particularly visible to herself as the teacher. She decided that allowing students to assess the performance of other group members offered a viable means of assessing the group processes, so negotiated suitable assessment criteria with the students, which they subsequently used to evaluate the contributions of their peers and allocate marks for individuals. The student-generated marks represented 20 per cent of the overall assessment.

The lecturer felt that it was important to involve students in making judgements about each others' contributions, because this was something that occurred in professional life. Several students could see these benefits, too. But while they felt it was useful, many expressed concerns about the fairness of receiving marks from other students, and felt that their peers did not have the experience or expertise to mark reliably. The lecturer had to spend time persuading students to accept this approach. Allaying their anxieties and taking care to ensure that students were trained to use the criteria appropriately took a lot of the lecturer's time. Again, she felt this was a worthwhile use of her time, because it opened up important dialogue about standards and criteria, and helped students learn to apply them.

When we are designing self- or peer assessment strategies we need to remain acutely aware of the 'risks' associated, from the student viewpoint, with expecting students to allocate marks which 'count'. Students may worry, for example, about fairness (Falchikov,

2005b; Smith, Cooper, and Lancaster, 2002) or about the effect of giving a 'bad' mark, or even critical feedback, to a friend (Cartney, 2010). Whilst these sorts of issues are not impossible to overcome, they present resistances which, again, are likely to take time and effort to address. That is why, according to Bloxham and West (2007), involving students explicitly in peer marking, and even in offering candid peer feedback, can take a fair degree of confidence and courage on the lecturer's part.

Research has shown that, from a lecturer's viewpoint, the term 'self-assessment' can, in fact, be variously understood. It can be seen to span a spectrum from students' self-marking at one end, through to fairly informal reflection and self-review at the other (McDowell and Sambell, 1999; Tan, 2004). Attempts to include students in making high-stakes decisions at one end of this spectrum, where they actually become responsible for awarding grades and marks, whether to their own work or that of others, needs careful thinking through and extensive preparation. Many studies have found that students can indeed be supported to develop peer and self-assessment skills to the extent that they are able, by and large, to achieve a close correspondence between lecturer and peer marks (Falchikov, 1995). This is, of course, very empowering, when it works well, as it offers a means for students to gain a measure of power or control in the assessment process. Some researchers such as Taras (2001) argue that the control dynamics in play between tutor and students are never really challenged if students are excluded from summative graded assessment.

Sometimes lecturers use procedures for 'moderating' student-allocated marks to encourage self- and peer assessment.

Using a tool to support peer assessment

WebPA is an open-source automated online tool that facilitates peer-moderated marking of group work. The tutor sets a group task and assesses the overall performance of the group. However, a 'weighting factor' is generated for each individual group member. This is derived from each student's input against defined criteria. The weighting factor is then used to moderate marks, reflecting an individual student's contributions and providing an individual mark for each student. Students value the process of identifying peers' strengths and weaknesses, because it helps them improve their approaches in subsequent assignments (Loddington *et al.*, 2009).

Using peer review to involve students in the assessment process

Peer review is used to stimulate students' engagement in, and learning about, the assessment process, rather than using it to generate marks which 'count'. In the following example, for instance, students were involved in peer review (Nicol, 2010b), in which they were required to make evaluative judgements about the quality of peers' work, and offer suggestions for improvement, at different stages of a group project. The emphasis was on encouraging students to generate useful feedback, rather than marks. This was done on the basis that, as Nicol suggests, actively producing feedback is a highly demanding cognitive enterprise which involves meaning-making and knowledge construction in ways that connect with what students already know. It also requires students to actively engage with criteria in a powerful and compelling way. In short, it means seeing assessment from the point of view of the assessor and making evaluative judgements in the context of specific subject material. This is a high-order skill which takes time and practice to develop.

As we have discussed, students need access to ample opportunity to 'see' what counts as achievement in a specific context so that they are empowered to perceive where they are, where they need to be, and to close the gap between the two, if necessary. Engaging in discussions about disciplinary concepts, ideas and ways of thinking and practising 'naturally' involves students in a process of informal self- and peer evaluation, these methods may develop a belief in students that they are in a position to exert significant control of their learning and improve their own performance. However, if students are also explicitly encouraged by the lecturer to make frequent evaluative judgements, the 'natural' effect of discussion within the academic–social community can be heightened dramatically.

Peer evaluation of group work

In this example a lecturer in Electrical and Electronic Engineering redesigned the whole of a second-year module by asking his undergraduates to conduct independent pieces of research on a range of related topics. By getting students to work in groups he hoped this process would encourage learners, within the social context of each individual group, to:

- rehearse the process of understanding, condensing and presenting information;
- practise using the analytical skills they need; and
- discuss their thinking.

Halfway through the term, the lecturer asked each group to present their interim findings to the rest of the students on the module. The presentations were informally peer and tutor evaluated, mainly to drive home to students the value of self-assessment. The lecturer asked students who were listening to others' team presentations to evaluate the work of the presenting team. Every student in the audience was expected to record his or her feedback on peer evaluation sheets designed specifically for the activity. To prepare students for this, the lecturer ran a workshop session which opened up dialogue about 'What makes a good project report?' This stimulated lengthy student–teacher discussions about the demands of the specific task and the workshop was used to generate assessment criteria and agree some broad headings for the peer evaluation sheets.

The lecturer explained: *"I particularly wanted them to reflect on what makes a good piece of work in this area, and we had a lot of discussion about this, and the criteria, before and after the presentation."* He felt that by encouraging his students to view assessment from his point of view as an assessor, he had helped his students engage with his expectations, and the requirements of the final submission, more fully then might otherwise have been the case. He also included a requirement to self review in the final project report, by explicitly asking students to highlight as an element of the report anything they had learned from the process of evaluating the other groups' presentations.

Indeed, the students themselves appreciated the insights that being involved in the process of peer review afforded them. Even though they found the presentations challenging, and didn't always enjoy doing them, they felt that evaluating other teams' presentations helped them to see what was really required. As one said: *"It gives you the gist of what is going to be asked and the level they expect you to be at."* Another explicitly referred to a process of self-evaluation when he talked about how being involved in making judgements about others' work had alerted him to a gap in his own understanding: *"I learned quite a lot about what I needed to improve on. I thought I'd got {x} right, but found out that I hadn't. It made me think, well, I'd better check up on that, work it out a bit better."* For other students, being required to make a judgement about their peers' efforts heightened their awareness of the strengths and weaknesses of their own work:

> *"Having to comment on somebody else's presentation makes you think a lot more, made you more aware. You started to compare your presentation to other people, so . . . you were seeing what you are good at and what you need to improve on, by comparing."*

In other words, being able to see the ways in which other students tackled work, and to judge and discuss the relative merits and shortcomings of different approaches to the subject-matter, helped students refine their understandings of what counted as quality work in this domain.

Encouraging active participation in self-review

Another way of encouraging students to engage actively with the assessment process is to provide comment-only marking. In the following example, this was used to stimulate students' engagement with the assessment process by encouraging students to consider assessment from the point of view of the marker. This approach was based on the work of Taras (2001).

Comments first on assessed work

In this example, students received a tutor-marked assignment which was handed back with the feedback comments on the script and the front sheet, but the mark was temporarily withheld. Students were asked to re-read the work they had submitted and reflect upon their performance, especially in the light of the feedback comments it had received. They were then asked to consider what mark they thought had been allocated by the tutor.

Students were then asked to attend a tutorial during which they proposed the grade they felt had probably been awarded to the work. This process allowed the tutor to reveal to each student what grade had actually been awarded and, most importantly, to open up discussion about any discrepancies between the students' self-evaluation and the teacher's grade. The ensuing dialogue supported students to adjust any misapprehensions they had about criteria and standards, and allowed them to re-calibrate the basis for their self-evaluations, if necessary. It also enabled productive dialogue about the situated meanings of the tutor's feedback comments, ensuring that, as far as possible, students understood what tutors meant by specific feedback language. The tutors felt this helped the students reflect on their current performance, and the actual meanings of the assessment criteria and standards, in more subtle and contextualized ways than had hitherto been achieved.

Fostering students' involvement with assessment by thinking about the meanings of criteria

Research has shown that the standards and criteria for judging work often remain a mystery to students, preventing learners from making effective evaluations for themselves (Carless, 2007b). Strategies which encourage students to actively engage with, and take some ownership of, assessment criteria can help induct them into the relevant assessment community. One very powerful approach is to ask students to put assessment criteria into their own words. For instance, as the following example shows, students can usefully become involved in formulating and co-designing assessment criteria, which can subsequently be used to evaluate work they are asked to produce.

Negotiating assessment criteria

One lecturer involved her second-year Joint Honours students in a process suggested by Race, Brown and Smith (2002). Halfway through the module, she helped learners gradually generate, negotiate and agree on things one would look for in an excellent submission on the module. As students generated their lists, the lecturer realized they were missing some important elements and failing to recognize the need to develop critical analyses of the material in question. After lengthy discussions about the learning outcomes of the module, which focused on understanding principles and concepts, the students were prompted to work further on aspects relating to critical approaches in the area. Eventually the students generated a more comprehensive set of criteria which related more closely to what the lecturer had in mind (and, hence, would receive high marks).

Finally, the students' lists were collated to generate an overall criteria sheet which was formulated in the students' own words. Whilst these focused more pointedly on concepts, theory-into-practice issues and the interpretation of findings, one 'new' criterion ('shows creativity in getting the message across') was included, as the students convinced the lecturers of the importance of this feature. All the agreed criteria were ultimately used to inform the lecturers' and external examiner's appraisals of the work submitted. The main benefit, though, was that staff and students' understandings of what 'counted' as good work had been enhanced through extensive dialogue and joint deliberation.

Involving students in assessment communities: seeing from the point of view of the assessor

Another strategy involves enabling students to take some level of responsibility for assignment setting, as the following example illustrates.

Enabling students to practise setting assignments

In an engineering-related subject area, students were encouraged to think about assessment from the assessors' viewpoint by being invited to become involved in an exam question-setting exercise. Students were expected to undertake an end-of-year exam. To help them to prepare for the exam, the lecturer ran a workshop in which he asked students to design a set of exam questions that would test students' understandings of the topics covered by the module. The questions that students generated were discussed in class.

This procedure encouraged students' active engagement with assessment criteria and standards. Lengthy discussions were opened up about the nature of 'good' questions and the type of learning they would foster. This helped learners identify for themselves whether they had understood the learning goals they would be expected to achieve in the actual exam. Questions which sought to elicit mere facts, for instance, were highlighted by the lecturer as far less effective than questions which tested understanding and application.

Thinking about the exam from the lecturer's viewpoint enabled students to realize, sooner rather than later, what type of questions they would need to be prepared to address. It also allowed the lecturer to open up productive discussions about his expectations, and, hence suitable revision strategies. The feedback they gained from being involved in this self-evaluation activity subsequently informed the way students went about studying for the exam.

Enabling students to practise applying assessment criteria

It is worth bearing in mind that it is simply not enough to throw students in at the deep end as assessors, especially if they are expected to mark work. It takes a lot of careful preparation, practice and effort to develop student confidence and expertise in such high-stakes assessment contexts. Extensive training of the student assessors is vital

(Sluijsmans *et al.*, 2001). The following example illustrates a strategy for helping students who, as first-year undergraduates, were at that stage on the periphery of the relevant assessment community. The approach aimed to induct students into a deeper engagement with criteria and standards.

Running assessment workshops to increase student engagement with criteria and standards

Working with first-year students prior to the hand-in of a graded assignment, students were provided with two sample assignments. One was a good response and one was a merely satisfactory response. The scripts, which were on a related topic to the students' actual assignment, were accompanied by sheets which included assessment criteria and grade definitions.

First, students were asked to mark the assignments in their own time, and to complete the mark sheets, providing a grade, marks and feedback for each assignment. They then came to a two-hour workshop where they worked in small groups to discuss the marks and feedback they awarded to the sample scripts, and agree a group mark and rationale. Each group then fed back their results in a plenary session. The tutor then discussed the students' results with the assessment criteria, offering detailed explanations for each criterion and referring extensively to examples of 'good' and less effective ways each sample script had exemplified each criterion. Following this discussion, student groups reviewed their original assessments and reported these back in another plenary discussion. Finally, the tutor provided copies of tutor-annotated and marked versions of the two sample assignments and discussed the reasons for these.

When students came to submit their own assignment a few weeks later they were asked to complete a self-review of their work using the criteria sheet that had been discussed in the workshop. Staff found that students' approaches to the assignment improved when students had been involved in the workshop activities.

Involving students in self- or peer marking is unlikely to be a feasible means of saving lecturers' time by cutting down the time academics spend on their marking. Instead, it is more likely, because of the need for time spent intensively training students to undertake the process adequately, to simply change the use of academics' time. So whilst the pay-offs in terms of learning are likely to be high, it is vital to bear in mind the time and expertise required to equip students to become effective and confident members of our assessment communities.

Furthermore, as the following section makes clear, it is important to recognize that students benefit from the chance to make repeated, highly context-specific discriminations about the quality of work, and the opportunity to discuss the rationales for any judgement in the context of the particular learning community. Insights into, say, the 'real' demands of an assessment task, are rarely gained in a one-off manner, but gradually develop over time, as students' understanding of a subject grows.

Putting it into practice by developing students' assessment literacy

Activities designed to enhance students' appreciation of assessment processes and criteria

Rust *et al.* (2003) conducted research which indicated that active methods of engaging students with the process of making, rather than simply receiving, judgements on academic work significantly improved students' grades in similar assignments. However, their research also revealed that novice markers (first-years) had a tendency to focus exclusively on the 'visible' criteria (aspects of presentation, such as structure or referencing), rather than using the more 'invisible', arguably more important, criteria, such as analysis. This suggests students need time and opportunity, ideally embedded in the context of the module and working closely with the teaching team, to develop the skills of assessment (Defeyter and McPartlin, 2007). Bloxham and West (2007), amongst others, argue that involving novice learners explicitly in the assessment of peers' work can help engage students with the more complex, 'invisible' aspects of assessment, thus aiding their understanding of the 'rules of the game' in university assessment.

If it is accepted that learning is an active, constructive process, then essentially *learners* set goals for their learning, and monitor, regulate and control their behaviour, guided and constrained, of course, by their personal goals and their interpretations of where they need to be and what counts as good work in a given context. But when it comes to assessment in Higher Education, students often report feeling unsure about what their lecturers really expect (McCune and Hounsell, 2005). For example, Hartley and Chesworth (2000) found that 'difficulties with knowing what was wanted' was one of the most widespread student complaints.

Discussing and applying criteria

In this example from Psychology, students were involved in a range of discussions, activities and peer assessment tasks threaded throughout the content of a module, rather than offered as a stand-alone workshop.

In one teaching session, for instance, students were invited to try to rank ten criteria (such as 'argument'; 'understanding'; 'organization', 'relevant information') according to the way they thought lecturers would rank them. After these had been discussed at length, they were then asked to apply the criteria to evaluate sample assignments. Students were asked specifically to note two positive and two negative aspects of each sample assignment.

Activities like these helped students to appreciate when their views of what mattered most were out of line with their tutors' expectations. Furthermore, many said that this had been the first time that they had discussed the assessment process with peers, beyond discussing what mark they had been awarded for a piece of work. In sum, the activities provoked them to discuss and debate the essential differences between the 'better' and 'worse' essays, thus heightening their awareness of quality responses. The whole process opened up dialogue between the students and their lecturer about the learning goals, task requirements and what student achievement looked like in a concrete sense. Importantly, it thereby focused students' attention holistically on issues of quality in the context of the discipline, carried in the use of evidence and wider reading, rather than on more general or superficial 'essay-writing' skills (Harrington *et al.*, 2006).

Further, seeing and making judgements about others' work helped them to see the kinds of things they were doing in their own work. As one said: *"Whoa! The things the 2.2 piece of work is doing, it's just like me!"* Seeing this helped her *"know how to go about getting a better mark"*, by taking a deep approach to learning and privileging understanding.

Simply issuing students with guidelines, written instructions or grids of criteria will not be enough to help students understand what counts as quality in a given context. Furthermore, and on a fairly straightforward level, students often do not understand the language in which university assessment criteria are typically couched. They often do not adequately appreciate, for instance, what 'critical analysis' or 'developing an argument' actually means and looks like, in practice. Moreover, they may not have had enough opportunity to practise moving from abstract criteria to concrete implementations and back again.

Developing students' discriminative awareness by exposing them to a range of standards

Another strategy to engage students actively in assessment was used in Sports Sciences. Students were asked to identify suitable criteria for appraising a piece of work. Next, students were invited to read, compare and contrast samples of good and poor assignments submitted by previous cohorts, using their criteria to explain which they felt was better and why.

Here, as in many of our most successful AfL examples, students had the chance to evaluate 'weak', as well as exemplary work. This is useful, because, whilst much can be learned by seeing how to tackle a task well, even more can be learned by seeing how not to do it. In fact, Sadler (1989) maintains that exposing students to a range of exemplars is the most effective strategy for sharing task requirements, as criteria are tacit, emergent and often unarticulated even in the minds of tutors. So the more students actively engage with goals and exemplifications of quality the more likely they are to internalize a task's requirements.

In fact, our research showed that by looking at 'good' pieces of work students often appear to believe they could take steps to improve their own learning by becoming clearer about tutors' expectations, and thus get a 'feeling' for how they can apply criteria to their own work, in time to improve it. As one said: *"You learn to see what the module tutor is doing – how they mark."* But, as the following students also observed, a full appreciation of quality typically stems from having access to a diverse range of responses, including 'poor' ones, because that forces the process of making decisions about which is 'better' and why: *"You are in that position where you are making decisions, making judgements: who is better at what? That helps you get a feeling for what the tutor is looking for when they are judging you."*

Voicing the issues revisited: a case study on developing self-assessment

Involving students with exemplars in the context of the discipline

In order to support students' induction into the literacy practices which are required for the purposes of assessment, Lillis (2001) advocates a model of 'talkback'. This requires ample space for novice–expert dialogue during the actual course of the students' production of their assessed writing. By focusing on writing conventions embodied in draft texts produced by students, Lillis proposes that lecturers, as subject-experts who 'feel' what the conventions are, seek to 'talk their students into' the specific ways of meaning-making that are privileged within the specific context. They do this, for example, by drawing attention to the student's intended meanings, referring to wordings from the question set, and helping the student make their meanings textually explicit within the given context. Such 'dialogues of participation' provide a mediating role, helping students see, feel and ask questions about what is really valued in specific writing practices, rather than simply correcting or intervening in the production of a student's script. In this way 'talkback' emphasizes the mediating importance of novice–expert dialogue as a vital means of helping students move from being outsiders to insiders in university writing practices. It epitomizes the principles of AfL.

But Lillis's model is highly resource-intensive. It assumes, for instance, that lecturers have the chance to work with students in small group seminars or tutorials, which may no longer be the case in many university contexts (Nicol, 2011). The lecturers in this final example were unable to work in small groups. Instead, they needed to look for alternative strategies to enhance dialogue and interaction about assessment in the context of working with groups of over a hundred students.

They found that one feasible way of enabling large groups of students to work out their tacit expectations was the pedagogic use of exemplars. These are examples of student writing selected to illustrate a range of assessment standards in a given domain. They aim to act as a medium through which to help students actively develop a 'feel' for task requirements and what counts as quality work. Sadler (cited in Handley *et al.*, 2008: 44) defines exemplars as 'key examples chosen so as to be typical of designated levels of quality or competence. The exemplars are not standards themselves, but are indicative of them . . . they specify standards implicitly'. Exemplars can take many forms. They may be complete assignments or excerpts. They may be authentic pieces of student work, or constructed by academics to illustrate specific pedagogic points in as transparent a manner as possible.

The first-year students were only in the ninth week of study on a large introductory theory module which introduced them to the concept of the social construction of childhood. The two lecturers teaching the module prepared interactive activities which aimed to engage students with four 500-word exemplars of previous students' responses to a short writing task. The exemplars were carefully chosen by the lecturers to exemplify a range of effective through to ineffective work in relation to the task. One was picked because it demonstrated a common conceptual mistake that students frequently make in the early stages of study, as the lecturers felt it was important to raise this mistake to visibility for their students, before similar misconceptions had a negative impact on their own assessed work. All the exemplars were anonymized and copied, ready to share with the class during one two-hour teaching session scheduled as part of the lecture series.

How the exemplars were used

Before students attended the two-hour session, the lecturers asked them to write their own response to the written task, which they brought along to reflect upon after taking part in discussion of the exemplars. By asking students to explain a key concept and then evaluate their own response, tutors hoped to raise learners' awareness that the domain contains various challenging elements which they need to tackle in the summative assignment.

The session itself ran in three phases.

Phase 1

In the first forty-five minutes of the lecture students were asked to work in small groups, reading, discussing and ranking the exemplars by making holistic judgements about which exemplars they felt addressed the task most/least effectively. Students discussed and negotiated in groups, debating what they saw as the strengths and weaknesses of each exemplar, guided by criteria which had been negotiated with the students and were displayed on a PowerPoint slide.

Phase 2

Next, tutors revealed their views of the rankings they would award, together with their rationales. They talked particularly about how each exemplar met, or failed to meet, particular learning outcomes and the assessment criteria. Students were not required to reveal whether they were 'right' or 'wrong' in their rankings (although actually, a surprising number were wrong, and some even muddled the best and the worst exemplars). Instead, they were invited to ask questions or share observations about good and weak approaches.

Phase 3

Student groups were then invited, in the light of the lecturers' dialogue, to generate feedback which would help the writer of each exemplar to improve their work. This involved students working again on exemplars for another forty-five minutes, refining their original appraisals, if need be. The groups' ideas were pooled and discussed in plenary, with tutors finally advising students to apply the insights they had gained to evaluate the quality of their own piece of work with a view to improving it. In practice, during this phase many students who had failed to rank the exemplars in the same order as the tutors re-read the exemplars in the light of the tutors' discussions and tried to see the strengths and weaknesses afresh, discussing, adjusting and recalibrating their evaluations accordingly.

How the students responded

Students valued the insights that being involved in the activity offered. As one claimed: *"You can see things that the lecturers, the people who are marking it, don't view as being that great."* Many referred to the value of seeing and trying to evaluate concrete examples of work. For example, one said: *"Seeing it just makes you understand it more. Like, someone can stand there and say, 'You shouldn't do this and that' but until you've actually seen it then you don't know what that looks like."* And another observed: *"I think it's harder if you just get a list of rules and have to figure out for yourself how to apply it."* In summary, most felt that as a result of becoming involved in relatively informal low-stakes peer review activities, they were better placed to make informed decisions about the quality of their own work, during the course of actually producing it. These decisions, importantly, were embedded in disciplinary material, involved participation and enabled dialogue which involved various members of the subject community.

Key questions to think about

The following key questions are designed to help course and module teams develop their practice. They could, alternatively, be used for personal reflection.

- **Do students have opportunities to engage in the assessment of their own or others' work and act as assessors?** Throughout this book we have emphasized the importance of students seeing academic work other than their own because it helps them to develop their understanding within the discipline. Here we particularly consider the practice of evaluating disciplinary practices and products, such as student writing. Where in your programme are students given specific guidance on ways of reviewing and evaluating? Where are the rationale, process and difficulties for this type of activity systematically addressed and subsequently reinforced as part of the 'normal' ways of doing things?

- How are your students helped to develop the skills of self-evaluation and self-monitoring that are required in settings beyond the point of graduation? Self- and peer assessment are often used in combination but there is a tendency to regard self-assessment as the 'easy' part because it does not involve some of the social difficulties that may arise in assessing the work of fellow students. However, self-assessment requires particular attention because it is in some ways the most difficult component. Students have to be able to 'see' their own work from a different viewpoint and to make changes to habitual, probably reasonably successful, ways of working. How does your programme engage students in self-assessment through specific tasks and requirements, going beyond general encouragement to review and reflect? Is there a general ethos promoting habits of critical self-review and continual improvement rather than hitting targets and moving on?

- How do you induct your students into what counts as quality, standards and criteria in your subject area? It is widely recognized that students only develop their fluency in handling quality, standards and criteria in relation to a specific context, perhaps the broad discipline within which they are studying but also specific subjects and the types of task in which they engage. How are opportunities to develop in this way embedded throughout your programme and modules, not just as one-off or occasional activities? Is this taken further to encourage students to become the types of graduates who look for and can understand the assessment environment in new contexts in their professional careers?

An Assessment for Learning manifesto

Throughout this book we have emphasized that AfL is an integrated approach to teaching, assessment and supporting student learning. Our view of assessment is broad. It includes summative assessment activities but also assessment which plays a vital role in improving students' progress and attainments and is embedded in teaching.

In each chapter we have stressed that AfL is not just a set of techniques to be dropped into a module or programme. There are underpinning principles and considerations which we have presented in the form of questions for course and module teams or individuals to address in relation to specific aspects of AfL. In this final chapter we present a manifesto built on the overall ethos of AfL as an integrated whole and we address the key foundations of AfL.

The three foundational elements that we discuss are:

- *Risk* – if we want good AfL we need to be prepared to take some (calculated) risks. Risk avoidance does not lead to the kinds of good learning, teaching and assessment that comprise AfL.
- *Power* – AfL shifts the balance of power between teachers and students as control is shared. AfL can also help the voices of students *and* teachers to become more powerful in institutional and broader contexts.
- *Reconceptualizing teaching* – AfL gives us a different perspective on the practice of learning, teaching and assessment. Most important is integration of these three familiar components and thus a reconceptualization leading to forms of integrated practice.

These foundations lead us to a manifesto for taking AfL forward. We focus on the overarching principles of AfL and ways in which teachers can build practice around these. The key foundations of AfL can be used to guide reflection on current practice and lead to an emerging agenda which requires transformed roles, relationships, sense of responsibilities and new ways of thinking that are needed to bring a culture of AfL about.

Risk

AfL offers students opportunities that are not normally available in conventionally designed modules and programmes. Perhaps more often than we like to admit, we may rely upon the routine ways of teaching and assessing students to ensure that students carry out required tasks, spend their time appropriately and produce expected kinds of outcomes. AfL is used quite differently but, as a result, can be seen as high risk.

The assessment practices that we design for our students are deeply connected with how much we trust them to act responsibly, to want to learn, to be capable of getting involved and immersed in genuine, worthwhile learning and so on. If we mistrust students on this score, we are likely to be fearful of moving away from assessment practices which, for example, ensure that students jump through the hoops to simply gain the marks we believe they want. By contrast, if we trust students, we can set them tasks which are genuinely challenging, thought-provoking and stimulating, and which can be tackled in a whole host of novel, creative and interesting ways. When it comes to the issue of feedback, if we mistrust our students we may seek to use teacher feedback as a means of 'teaching to the test', so our feedback is actually designed to steer students clearly and unequivocally in particular directions. If we trust them, we are more prone to offer feedback which opens up dialogue, highlights further questions and next steps, and which is far less directive and controlling. From this viewpoint it might be useful to ask ourselves: where and how do our assessment practices imply that we trust the students for whom they are designed? Do students interpret our systems and procedures simply as means of controlling and regulating their behaviour?

The perceived risk from trusting students is one key influence in the design and delivery of assessment practice. A second risky issue is the use of assessment approaches that move away from the conventional. In routine practice, tests and assignments are of a standard type, and their design, the production of responses by students, and the marking process conform to a routine, predetermined process and set of outcomes. AfL may disrupt this, allowing for uncertain outcomes and prioritizing meaningful assessment over 'standard' assessment which sticks to the norm. Instead of producing a nice pile of very similar assignments answering the same questions in the required ways, legitimate responses to an AfL task may be very different. We argue that this is often a great benefit to students but it could be seen as very risky in managerial systems driven by quality assurance considerations. The demand for consistency and predictability can create a difficult context for AfL. We may be faced by institutional expectations about the forms of assessment and requirements of teaching. For example, it may be stated that all modules have a one-hour weekly lecture and a monthly seminar and will be assessed by an assignment of 2,000 words and a two-hour exam. These might be seen as maintaining quality through consistency. We need to promote other perspectives on quality assurance with a reduced emphasis on consistency and more emphasis on 'fitness for purpose'. The idea that assessment should be designed so that genuine learning objectives can be fostered and evaluated in a way that is appropriate for the specific objective, the subject, the level and so on, can be regarded as a 'fitness for purpose' approach. However, it also has a long pedigree in educational thinking in the form of constructive alignment.

Of course quality assurance is a means of managing risk and valuing predictability. Teaching that proceeds in a transmission form without very much dialogue or participation from students is likely to result in predictable behaviour and outcomes. This is also true for assessment. If we engage students in many of the ways discussed in this book we are likely to find ourselves treading different pathways to help students to attain the learning outcomes. We may not be certain of exactly where we will get to and how we will get there.

If innovative teachers appear to threaten the regime in place they may find that they are not trusted and supported by their institution. Moreover, if we feel that our assessment actions and judgements are not going to be accepted, or may be seen as untrustworthy, we are likely to act defensively, and 'play safe'. For instance, if we are worried that our authority may be called into question, or if we feel we will not be supported if something 'goes wrong' or leads to a student complaint, then our practices may well be driven by attempts to shore ourselves up against that possibility, rather than by adventurous or creative thinking.

It is worth asking ourselves where we feel that we are practising assessment in particular ways to minimize risk, or, alternatively, how we practise more positive assessment approaches because we feel we are trusted to do so. Doing what everyone else does and what is expected is not likely to draw attention to yourself as a teacher – but keeping your head below the parapet like this might be short-changing your students. To cope with uncertainty and risk, it's best not to go it alone but have supportive colleagues along with you such as a module or programme team. You also need the support of students, so keep them informed, encourage active participation and be open with them. You also probably need to 'start small' – unless you have a genuine opportunity to begin from scratch. Another key strategy is to learn from what others have done, their success and the problems they faced, drawing on examples from your own discipline and beyond. Finally, in turn, ensure that you evaluate your practices, tell other people about your successes and your difficulties, and most important of all, demonstrate the impacts on student learning.

Power

Assessment, particularly summative assessment, embodies the power of our national educational systems, individual institutions, disciplinary groups and teachers in their role of assessors. Assessment systems have the power to determine how learning is constructed by determining what is to be learned and the forms in which capability must be demonstrated. Academics, individually and collectively, such as through the External Examiner system, determine and label the quality of student attainments. However, many aspects of AfL practice require us to cede some of that power to students.

The extent to which we feel able to cede or 'share' power with our students reveal our 'unspoken' values, attitudes and assumptions about what students are like, and what students need. In other words our assessment designs tend to imply a certain view of the student. Often our approaches seem to suggest that students are 'problems', or lacking in some way. For instance, students may be seen as potential 'cheats' who need to comply with the rules, or as people who should not be given too much information and guidance for fear that they will take advantage of the system. If students ask too many questions or seem to want 'too much' help do we complain and regard this as a demand for 'spoon feeding'? In short, it's worth asking ourselves how far might our students experience our overall way of talking, discussing and writing about our assessment as practices that have a hidden message: the popular myth that they are in deficit? Does the emphasis on procedures and penalties (about, for example, hand-in times, word limits, putting written work through the Turnitin 'plagiarism check') suggest to students that these prominent aspects of assessment and the conformity they demand are more important than learning, understanding and communicating?

Assessment for Learning offers a way of thinking about the student which doesn't see them so negatively but positions them as people who, while inexperienced, have the potential to contribute, learn and improve, no matter what their starting point. Are there places where our assessment practices imply a more positive view of the student? In AfL we aim to develop informed students who are in a much more powerful position when it comes to asking pertinent questions, directing their own learning and making judgements about the quality of their work. But do the tasks, guidelines, assignment briefings and so on that we 'publish' for students in our handbooks frame the student as an interested learner capable of communicating interesting ideas? Do we discuss assessment, and the thinking behind it, openly with our students?

Students should be helped to realize that taking control of assessment, rather than being governed by it, is a vital aspect of worthwhile learning. They should be aware that they need to think about assessment from a variety of viewpoints, including that of the assessor. Becoming involved as an assessor, rather than waiting for someone else to assess your work for you, is an important aspect of being a graduate who takes responsibility for their own learning. Ideally students should actively seek feedback from a variety of sources and consider it, deciding whether and how it might be useful, and then use it to improve their work. In this book we have illustrated a range of ways in which students can be more in control of assessment, ranging from exercises to help them understand assessment criteria to full participation in self- or peer assessment in a summative context.

It is unrealistic and indeed undesirable to think that the power of assessment can be 'handed over' to students. First, students need to learn what assessment is about and how to be an assessor. Second, for good reasons, there will always be limits to the student assessor role. This will be most obvious when considering, say, engaging students in the marking of work that contributes to final degree results. But every step we take to inform students, communicate with them and develop their assessment literacy means that they become more knowledgeable, active and competent and we will therefore need to engage with them in a different way. Assessment will necessarily become more of a partnership rather than a source of power embodied in the teacher alone. Teaching teams will need to be more open with students and engage them in negotiation.

Reconceptualizing teaching

It has become commonplace to talk about 'teaching, learning and assessment' sometimes even using the acronym TLA. These are seen as a linked set of activities but often in the form of a linear path or a cycle where *teaching* leads to *learning* which is then *assessed*. Although convenient because it makes planning and documenting modules or programmes easy, this standardized form has its limitations. Along with this viewpoint we tend to find an account of teaching as 'content' delivery, where content might be described as another threesome: skills, knowledge and understanding. A prevalent concern that often arises within this viewpoint is that of 'coverage'. Since there is never enough time to fit all of the desired content into a module and the learning trajectory is founded on teaching this leads to further concern about 'over-assessment'. Because assessment is identified as purely for testing and grading there are frequent demands to reduce time spent on it in order to give more time to teaching and learning. In some institutions there are set limitations on the amount of time that can be spent on assessment.

From an AfL perspective we argue that the division outlined above is not helpful. Broadly defined, assessment is at the core of learning. It is not just about tests, assignments and marks but, for example, ensuring that students make the most of every opportunity to collaborate and discuss their work, with staff or fellow students. Learners should be active in trying things out, seeing the results and receiving feedback during the actual process of doing it. AfL challenges and blurs the boundaries between assessment and teaching. Some of the most useful 'teaching' that lecturers can do takes the form of reviewing what students are doing and offering advice and guidance. Similarly some of the most valuable student learning takes place when engaged in assessment perhaps by interpreting and using feedback or by engaging in judgements of the quality of academic work. AfL sees teaching, learning and assessment as integrated, with no hard and fast lines between them.

At institutional level, breaking down the conventional view of teaching–learning–assessment may not be straightforward. Teaching–learning–assessment is widely embedded into various institutional practices such as the structure of the academic year ('exam weeks'); the descriptions of modules; the nature of spaces provided for 'teaching' and 'learning'; and the analysis of staff workloads – often based on 'teaching hours' with a separate set of hours for assessment, if indeed any formal acknowledgement of assessment is included.

Fortunately, many AfL approaches can be implemented at module level without the need for specific institutional sanction, opening up much more fluid spaces in the classroom and beyond. Teachers may become aware of new opportunities opening up and enabling them to move between teaching, learning and assessment. To some this blurring of boundaries can seem alien at first. Students however normally have few problems in negotiating the new AfL context. As long as they are active, positively engaged, and supported in their learning they have little need to worry about terminologies.

Finally . . .

Institutions should ensure that processes, procedures and assessment regulations support Assessment for Learning. There should be opportunity for well-founded, well-planned 'calculated' risks. It should never be the case that innovations and good practice are turned down because the regulations do not permit them. The regulations need to serve student learning.

Lecturers should act on the basis that predictability may feel safe but it is not inspiring. Think about giving your standard lecture on Topic X (just slightly updated), or marking the same responses to exam questions year on year. It is not inspiring for students either to feel that they are doing the same tasks as hundreds of students before them.

Students should realize that assessment can be an opportunity for learning, rather than just something to be endured and suffered. Active participation in assessment will lead to increased confidence, responsibility and competence within and beyond Higher Education.

If we reduce assessment to a form of drudgery for teachers and students we are mis-representing what learning at university within academic disciplines is. We are failing to acknowledge the relevance of curiosity and the importance of asking and answering pertinent questions. Instead, assessment should be the point where knowledge, ideas and understanding are generated and exchanged – a process that is at the very heart of the university.

References

Angelo, T.A. and Cross, P. (1993) *Classroom assessment techniques: A handbook for college teachers*, 2nd edn, San Francisco, CA: Jossey Bass.

ASKe (2007) *How to make your feedback work in three easy steps!* Oxford: Oxford Brookes University. Online. Available: <http://www.brookes.ac.uk/aske/documents/Make%20FeedbackWork.pdf> (accessed 15/05/12).

Askew, S. and Lodge, C. (2000) 'Gifts, ping-pong and loops: Linking feedback and learning', in Askew, S. (ed.) *Feedback for learning*, London: Routledge, pp. 1–18.

Barrie, S. (2007) 'A conceptual framework for the teaching and learning of generic graduate attributes', *Studies in Higher Education*, 32: 439–458.

Baxter Magolda, M.B. (2001) *Making their own way: Narratives for transforming Higher Education to promote self-development*, Sterling, VA: Stylus.

Beetham, H. (2007) 'An approach to learning activity design', in Beetham, H. and Sharpe, R. (eds) *Rethinking pedagogy for a digital age*, London: Routledge, pp. 26–38. Also in JISC (2009) *Effective practice in a digital age: A guide to technology-enhanced learning and teaching*, HEFCE. Online. Available: <http://www.jisc.ac.uk/media/documents/publications/effectivepractice digitalage.pdf> (accessed 25/03/12).

Biemans, H., Nieuwenhuis, L., Poell, R., Mulder, M. and Wesselink, R. (2004) 'Competence-based VET in the Netherlands: Background and pitfalls', *Journal of Vocational Education and Training*, 56: 523–538.

Biggs, J. (1996) 'Assessing learning quality: Reconciling institutional, staff and educational demands', *Assessment and Evaluation in Higher Education*, 21: 5–15.

Biggs, J. and Tang, C. (2007) *Teaching for quality learning at university*, 3rd edn, Maidenhead: Open University Press.

Biggs, J. and Tang, C. (2011) *Teaching for quality learning at university*, 4th edn, Maidenhead: Open University Press.

Black, P. (2007) 'Full marks for feedback', *Make the Grade (Journal of the Institute of Educational Assessors)*, 2: 18–21.

Black, P. and McCormick, R. (2010) 'Reflections and new directions', *Assessment and Evaluation in Higher Education*, 35: 493–499.

Black, P. and Wiliam, D. (1998a) 'Assessment and classroom learning', *Assessment in Education: Principles, Policy and Practice*, 5: 7–74.

Black, P. and Wiliam, D. (1998b) 'Inside the black box: Raising standards through classroom assessment', *Phi Delta Kappan*, 80 (2): 139–148.

Black, P. and Wiliam, D. (2009) 'Developing the theory of formative assessment', *Educational Assessment, Evaluation and Accountability*, 21: 5–31.

Black, P., Harrison, C., Lee, C., Marshall, B. and Wiliam, D. (2003) *Assessment for learning: Putting it into practice*, Maidenhead: Open University Press.

Bloomer, M. (1997) *Curriculum making in post 16 education: The social conditions of studentship*, London: Routledge.

Bloxham, S. (2008) 'Assessment in teacher education: Stakeholder conflict and its resolution', *Practitioner Research in Higher Education*, 2: 13–21.

Bloxham, S. (2009) 'Marking and moderation in the UK: False assumptions and wasted resources', *Assessment and Evaluation in Higher Education*, 34: 209–220.

Bloxham, S. and Boyd, P. (2007) *Developing effective assessment in higher education: A practical guide*, Maidenhead: Open University Press.

Bloxham, S. and West, A. (2007) 'Learning to write in Higher Education: Students' perceptions of an intervention in developing understanding of assessment criteria', *Teaching in Higher Education*, 12: 1, 77–89.

Boekaerts, M. and Minnaert, A. (2003) 'Assessment of students' feelings of autonomy, competence and social relatedness: A new approach to measuring the quality of the learning process through self and peer assessment', in Segers, M., Dochy, F. and Cascallar, E. (eds) *Optimising new modes of assessment: In search of qualities and standards*, Boston, MA: Kluwer Academic Publishers.

Boud, D. (1995) *Enhancing learning through self assessment*, London: Kogan Page.

Boud, D. (2000) 'Sustainable assessment: Rethinking assessment for the learning society', *Studies in Continuing Education*, 22 (2): 151–167.

Boud, D. (2006) 'Foreword', in Clegg, K. and Bryan, C. (eds) *Innovative assessment in Higher Education*, London: Routledge, pp. xvii–xix.

Boud, D. (2009) 'How can practice reshape assessment?', in Joughin, G. (ed.) *Assessment, learning and judgement in Higher Education*, Dordrecht: Springer, pp. 29–43.

Boud, D. and Falchikov, N. (2006) 'Aligning assessment with long-term learning', *Assessment and Evaluation in Higher Education*, 31: 399–413.

Boud, D. and Falchikov, N. (eds) (2007) *Rethinking assessment in Higher Education: Learning for the longer term*, London: Routledge.

Boud, D. and Hawke, G. (2004) *OVAL Research Working Paper 03–17*, Sydney: The Australian Centre for Organisational, Vocational and Adult Learning (OVAL), University of Technology, Sydney.

Boud, D. and Middleton, H. (2003) 'Learning from others at work: Communities of practice and informal learning', *Journal of Workplace Learning*, 15 (5): 194–202.

Boud, D., Cohen, R. and Sampson, J. (1999) 'Peer learning and assessment', *Assessment and Evaluation in Higher Education*, 24 (4): 413–426.

Boud, D. *et al.* (2010) *Assessment 2020: Seven propositions for assessment reform in Higher Education*, Sydney: Australian Learning and Teaching Council. Online. Available: <http://www.assessmentfutures.com> (accessed 26/03/12).

Bowden, J., Hart, G., King, B., Trigwell, K. and Watts, O. (2000) *Generic capabilities of ATN university graduates*, Canberra: Australian Government Department of Education, Training and Youth Affairs. Online. Available: <http://www.clt.uts.edu.au/ATN.grad.cap.project.index.html> (accessed 03/04/12).

Brew, A. (2006) *Research and teaching: Beyond the divide*, London: Palgrave Macmillan.

Broadfoot, P. (2007) *An introduction to assessment*, London: Continuum.

Brooks, R. (2005) 'The impact of extra-curricular activities on young people's understandings of citizenship', *British Educational Research Association Research Intelligence*, 93: 8–11.

Brown, G., Bull, J. and Pendlebury, M. (1997) *Assessing student learning in Higher Education*, London: Routledge.

Brown, J.S. and Adler, R.P. (2008) 'Minds on fire: Open education, the long tail, and Learning 2.0', *EDUCAUSE Review*, 43 (1): 2–19.

Brown, J.S., Collins, A. and Duguid, P. (1989) 'Situated cognition and the culture of learning', *Educational Researcher*, 18: 32–42.

Brown, S. and Knight, P. (1994) *Assessing learners in Higher Education*, London: Kogan Page.

Bull, J. and McKenna, C. (2004) *Blueprint for computer-assisted assessment*, London: RoutledgeFalmer.

Butcher, A.C. and Stefani, L.J. (1995) 'Analysis of peer, self- and staff-assessment in group project work', *Assessment in Education*, 2(2): 165–186.

Carless, D. (2006) 'Differing perceptions in the feedback process', *Studies in Higher Education*, 31: 219–233.

Carless, D. (2007a) 'Conceptualizing pre-emptive formative assessment', *Assessment in Education: Principles, Policy and Practice*, 14: 171–184.

Carless, D. (2007b) 'Learning-oriented assessment: Conceptual bases and practical implications', *Innovations in Education and Teaching International*, 44: 57–66.

Carless, D. (2011) 'Developing sustainable feedback practices', *Studies in Higher Education*, 36: 395–407.

Carless, D., Joughin, G. and Mok, M.M.C. (2006) 'Learning-oriented assessment: Principles and practice', *Assessment and Evaluation in Higher Education*, 31: 395–398.

Cartney, P. (2010) 'Exploring the use of peer assessment as a vehicle for closing the gap between feedback given and feedback used', *Assessment and Evaluation in Higher Education*, 35: 551–564.

Chanock, K. (2000) 'Comments on essays: Do students understand what tutors write?', *Teaching in Higher Education*, 5: 95–105.

Chickering, A.W. and Gamson, Z.F. (1987) 'Seven principles for good practice in undergraduate education', *AAHE Bulletin*, 39: 3–7.

Chinn, C.A. and Brewer, W.F. (1993) 'The role of anomalous data in knowledge acquisition: A theoretical framework and implications for science instruction', *Review of Educational Research*, 63: 1–49.

Claxton, G. (2010) 'Higher Education as epistemic apprenticeship', Keynote Address to the 9th Annual Galway Symposium and NAIRTL 5th Annual Conference on Higher Education: Engaging Minds: Active Learning, Participation and Collaboration in Higher Education, National University of Ireland Galway, 9–11 June, 2010.

Cleary, M., Flynn, R., Thomasson, S., Alexander, R. and McDonald, B. (2007) *Graduate employability skills: Prepared for the Business, Industry and Higher Education Collaboration Council*, Canberra, ACT: Department of Education, Science and Training.

Collins, A., Brown, J.S. and Newman, S.E. (1989) 'Cognitive apprenticeship: Teaching the craft of reading, writing and mathematics', in Resnick, L.B. (ed.) *Knowing, learning and instruction: Essays in honour of Robert Glaser*, Hilldale, NJ: Erlbaum.

Crook, C., Gross, H. and Dymott, R. (2006) 'Assessment relationships in Higher Education: The tension of process and practice', *British Educational Research Journal*, 32 (1): 95–114.

Dahlgren, L.O., Fejes, A., Abrandt-Dahlgren, M. and Trowald, N. (2009) 'Grading systems, features of assessment and students' approaches to learning', *Teaching in Higher Education*, 14: 15–194.

Davison, G. (2011) 'Investigating the relationships between authentic assessment and the development of learner autonomy', unpublished DPhil thesis, Northumbria University.

Dawes, L., Mercer, N. and Wegerif, R. (2004) *Thinking together*, 2nd edn, York, UK: Imaginative Minds.

Deane, M. and Borg, E. (2011) *Critical thinking and analysis*, London: Pearson.

Defeyter, M.A. and McPartlin, P.L. (2007) 'Helping students understand essay marking criteria and feedback', *Psychology Teaching Review*, 13: 23–33.

Denton, P. (2001) 'Generating coursework feedback for large groups of students using MS Excel and MS Word', *University Chemistry Education*, 5: 1–8.

Dweck, C.S. (2000) *Self theories: Their role in motivation, personality and development*, Philadelphia, PA: Psychology Press.

Ecclestone, K. (2002) *Learner autonomy in post-16 education: The politics and practice of formative assessment*, London: RoutledgeFalmer.

Elton, L. (2010) 'Academic writing and tacit knowledge', *Teaching in Higher Education*, 15: 151–160.

Elwood, J. and Klenowski, V. (2002), 'Creating communities of shared practice: The challenges of assessment use in learning and teaching', *Assessment and Evaluation in Higher Education*, 27: 243–256.

Entwistle, N., Tait, H. and McCune, V. (2000) 'Patterns of response to an approach to studying inventory across contrasting groups and contexts', *European Journal of Psychology of Education*, 15: 33–48.

Falchikov, N. (1995) 'Peer feedback marking: Developing peer assessment', *Innovations in Education and Teaching International*, 32: 175–187.

Falchikov, N. (2001) *Learning together: Peer tutoring in Higher Education*, London: RoutledgeFalmer.

Falchikov, N. (2005a) *Improving assessment through student involvement: Practical solutions for aiding learning in Higher and Further Education*, London: RoutledgeFalmer.

Falchikov, N. (2005b) '"Unpacking" peer assessment', in Schwartz, P. and Webb, G. (eds) *Assessment: Case studies, experience and practice from Higher Education*, London: Kogan Page.

Flint, N.R.A. and Johnson, B. (2011) *Towards fairer university assessment: Recognizing the concerns of students*, London: Routledge.

Gibbs, G. (2006) 'How assessment frames student learning', in Bryan, C. and Clegg, K. (eds) *Innovative assessment in Higher Education*, London: Routledge, pp. 23–36.

Gibbs, G. (2010) *Using assessment to support student learning*, Leeds: Leeds Metropolitan University.

Gibbs, G. and Dunbar-Goddet, H. (2007) *The effects of programme assessment environments on student learning*, report submitted to the Higher Education Academy: Oxford Learning Institute, University of Oxford. Online. Available: <http://www.tlrp.org/themes/seminar/daugherty/docs/grahamgibbspaper.pdf> (accessed 26/03/12).

Gibbs, G. and Simpson, C. (2004) 'Conditions under which assessment supports students' learning', *Learning and Teaching in Higher Education*, 1: 3–31.

Gielen, S., Dochy, F. and Dierick, S. (2003) 'Evaluating the consequential validity of new modes of assessment: The influence of assessment on learning, including pre-, post-, and true assessment effects', *Innovation and Change in Professional Education*, 1: 37–54.

Gielen, S., Dochy, F., Onghena, P., Struyven, K. and Smeets, S. (2011) 'Goals of peer assessment and their associated quality concepts', *Studies in Higher Education*, 36: 719–735.

Glover, C. (2006) 'Report of research carried out at Sheffield Hallam University for the Formative Assessment in Science Teaching Project (FAST) for the period 2002–2003. Online. Available: <http://www.open.ac.uk/fast/FASTProject/Publications.htm> (accessed 26/03/12).

Gulikers, J. (2006) *Authenticity is in the eye of the beholder: A five dimensional framework for authentic assessment*, Heerlen, the Netherlands: The Open University.

Haggis, T. (2006) 'Pedagogies for diversity: retaining critical challenge amidst fears of "dumbing down"', *Studies in Higher Education*, 31 (5): 521–535.

Handley, K., Price, M. and Millar, J. (2008) *Engaging students with assessment feedback: Final report for FDTL5 Project 144/03*, Oxford: Oxford Brookes University. Online. Available: <http://www.brookes.ac.uk/aske/documents/FDTL_FeedbackProjectReportApril2009.pdf> (accessed 26/03/12).

Handley, K., Szwelnik, A., Ujma, D., Lawrence, L., Millar, J. and Price, M. (2007) 'When less is more: Students' experiences of assessment feedback', Paper delivered to the Higher Education Academy Annual Conference, June 2007.

Harrington, K., Elander, J., Lusher, J., Norton, L., Aiyegbayo, O., Pitt, E., Robinson, H. and Reddy, P. (2006). 'Using core assessment criteria to improve essay writing', in Bryan, C. and Clegg, K. (eds), *Innovative assessment in Higher Education*, London and New York: Routledge, pp. 110–119.

Hartley, J. and Chesworth, K. (2000) 'Qualitative and quantitative methods in research on essay writing: No one way', *Journal of Further and Higher Education*, 24 (1): 15–24.

Hattie, J., Biggs, J. and Purdie, N. (1996) 'Effects of learning skills intervention on student learning: A meta-analysis', *Review of Educational Research*, 66: 99–136.

HEFCE (2011) *National student survey: Findings and trends 2006–2010*, Bristol: HEFCE. Online. Available: <http://www.hefce.ac.uk/pubs/hefce/2011/11_11/> (accessed 26/03/12).

Herrington, J., Reeves, T.C. and Oliver, R. (2002) 'Patterns of engagement in authentic online environments', *Australian Journal of Educational Technology*, 19 (1): 59–71.

Higgins, R., Hartley, P. and Skelton, A. (2002) 'The conscientious consumer: Reconsidering the role of assessment feedback in student learning', *Studies in Higher Education*, 27 (1): 53–64.

Hinett, K. and Thomas, J. (eds) (1999) *Staff guide to self and peer assessment*, Oxford: Oxford Centre for Staff and Learning Development.

Hounsell, D. (2003) 'Student feedback, learning and development', in Slowey, M. and Watson, D. (eds) *Higher Education and the lifecourse*, Buckingham: SRHE/Open University Press, pp. 67–78.

Hounsell, D. (2007) 'Towards more sustainable feedback to students', in Boud, D. and Falchikov, N. (eds) *Rethinking assessment in Higher Education: Learning for the longer term*, London: Routledge, pp. 101–113.

Hounsell, D., Hounsell, J. and Tai, C.M. (2010) *Enhancing feedback*, University of Edinburgh. Online. Available: <http://www.tla.ed.ac.uk/feedback/index.html> (accessed 26/03//12).

Hounsell, D., McCune, V., Hounsell, J. and Litjens, J. (2008) 'The quality of guidance and feedback to students', *Higher Education Research and Development*, 27: 55–67.

Hughes, G. (2011) 'Towards a personal best: A case for introducing ipsative assessment in Higher Education', *Studies in Higher Education*, 36: 353–367.

Hyland, P. (2000) 'Learning from feedback on assessment', in Hyland, P. and Booth, A. (eds) *The practice of university history teaching*, Manchester: Manchester University Press, pp. 233–247.

Kahn, P. and O'Rourke, K. (2005) 'Understanding enquiry-based learning', in Barrett, T., MacLabhrainn, I. and Fallon, H. (eds) *Handbook of enquiry and problem-based learning: Irish case studies and international perspectives*, Dublin: Centre for Excellence in Learning and Teaching, NUI Galway and All Ireland Society for Higher Education (AISHE). Online. Available: <http://www.aishe.org/readings/2005-2/contents.html> (accessed 26/03/12).

Knapper, C.K. (1990) 'Lifelong learning and university teaching', in Moses, I. (ed.), *Higher Education in the late twentieth century: A festschrift for Ernest Roe*, Kensington, New South Wales: Higher Education Research and Development Society of Australasia.

Knapper, C. and Cropley, A. (2000) *Lifelong learning and Higher Education*, 3rd edn, London: Kogan Page.

Knight, P. (2006) 'The local practices of assessment', *Assessment and Evaluation in Higher Education*, 31: 435–452.

Knight, P.T. and Yorke, M. (2003) *Assessment, learning and employability*, Maidenhead: SRHE/Open University Press.

Knights, P. (2006) 'Responding online: A starter activity for e-discussion boards', *MEDAL Casebook*. Online. Available: <http://medal.unn.ac.uk/learning_resources/signs_of_child hood.htm> (accessed 26/03/12).

Kuh, G.D., Kinzie, J., Schuh, J.H. and Whitt, E.J. (2005) *Student success in college: Creating conditions that matter*, New York: Jossey Bass.

Kvale, S.A. (2008) 'A workplace perspective on school assessment', in Havnes, A. and McDowell, L. (eds) *Balancing dilemmas in assessment and learning in contemporary education*, New York: Routledge, pp. 197–208.

Laurillard, D. (2002) *Rethinking university teaching: A conversational framework for the effective use of learning technologies*, 2nd edn, London: RoutledgeFalmer.

Lave, J. and Wenger, E. (1991) *Situated learning: Legitimate peripheral participation*, Cambridge: Cambridge University Press.

Lea, M.R. and Street, B.V. (1998) 'Student writing in higher education: An academic literacies approach', *Studies in Higher Education*, 23: 157–172.

Light, R.J. (2001) *Making the most of college: Students speak their minds*, Cambridge, MA: Harvard University Press.

Lillis, T. (2001) *Student writing: Access, regulation, desire*, London: Routledge.

Lillis, T. and Turner, J. (2001) 'Student writing in Higher Education: Contemporary confusion; traditional concerns', *Teaching in Higher Education*, 6: 57–68.

Liu, N.F. and Carless, D. (2006) 'Peer feedback: The learning element of peer assessment', *Teaching in Higher Education*, 11 (3): 279–290.

Loddington, S., Pond, K., Wilkinson, N. and Willmot, P. (2009) 'The development and evolution of an online peer-moderated marking tool: WebPA', *British Journal of Learning Technology*, 40: 329–341.

Lombardi, M.M. (2007) 'Authentic learning for the 21st century: An overview', ELI Paper 1, Educause. Online. Available: <http://www.educause.edu/ELI/AuthenticLearningForthe21st Cen/156769> (accessed 05/05/12).

McCune, V. and Hounsell, D. (2005) 'The development of students' ways of thinking and practising in three final-year biology courses', *Higher Education*, 49: 255–289.

McDowell, L. (2008) 'Negotiating assignment pathways: Students and academic assignments', *Teaching in Higher Education*, 13 (4): 423–435.

McDowell, L. and Sambell, K. (1999) 'Students' experiences of self-evaluation in Higher Education: Preparation for lifelong learning?', paper presented at the 8th European Conference for Research on Learning and Instruction, Gothenburg, Sweden, August 24–28.

McDowell, L., Smailes, J., Sambell, K., Sambell, A. and Wakelin, D. (2008) 'Evaluating assessment strategies through collaborative evidence-based practice: Can one tool fit all?', *Innovations in Education and Teaching International*, 45: 143–153.

McDowell, L., Wakelin, D., Montgomery, C. and King, S. (2011) 'Does assessment for learning make a difference? The development of a questionnaire to explore the student response', *Assessment and Evaluation in Higher Education*, 36 (7): 749–765.

McDowell, L., Sambell, K., Bazin, V., Penlington, R., Wakelin, D. and Smailes, J. (2006) 'Assessment for Learning exemplars: The foundations of CETL AfL', CETL AfL Occasional Paper 3. Newcastle: Northumbria University.

McMahon, T. (1999) 'Using negotiation in summative assessment to encourage critical thinking', *Teaching in Higher Education*, 4 (4): 549–554.

Maina, F.W. (2004) 'Authentic learning: Perspectives from contemporary educators', *Journal of Authentic Learning*, 1: 1–8.

Marshall, B. and Drummond, M. (2006) 'How teachers engage with assessment for learning: Lessons from the classroom,' *Research Papers in Education*, 21 (2): 133–149.

Marton, F., Hounsell, D. and Entwistle, N. (eds) (1997) *The experience of learning*, 2nd edn, Edinburgh: Scottish University Press.

Mayes, T. and de Freitas, S. (2004) 'JISC e-Learning models desk study. Stage 2: Review of e-learning theories, frameworks and models'. Online. Available: <http://tinyurl.com/3xqeq3> (accessed 26/03/12). Also in JISC (2009) *Effective practice in a digital age: A guide to technology-enhanced learning and teaching*, Bristol: HEFCE. Online. Available: <http://www.jisc.ac.uk/media/documents/publications/effectivepracticedigitalage.pdf> (accessed 26/03/12).

Merry, S. and Orsmond, P. (2008) 'Students' attitudes to and usage of academic feedback provided via audio files', *Bioscience Education*, 11. Online. Available: <http://www.bioscience.heacademy.ac.uk/journal/vol11/beej-11-3.aspx> (accessed 26/03/12).

Meyer, J.H.F. and Land, R. (2005) 'Threshold concepts and troublesome knowledge: Epistemological considerations and a conceptual framework for teaching and learning', *Higher Education*, 49: 373–388.

Mitchell, S. (2010) 'Thinking writing: A guide to writing intensive courses'. Online. Available: <http://www.thinkingwriting.qmul.ac.uk/> (accessed 26/03/12).

Moon, J. (2005) *A new perspective on the elusive activity of critical thinking*, Bristol: ESCalate.

Nicol, D. (2009a) 'Assessment for learner self-regulation: Enhancing achievement in the first year using learning technologies', *Assessment and Evaluation in Higher Education*, 34: 335–352.

Nicol, D. (2009b) *Transforming assessment and feedback: Enhancing integration and empowerment in the first year*, Mansfield: Scottish Quality Assurance Agency for Higher Education.

Nicol, D. (2010a) 'From monologue to dialogue: Improving written feedback processes in mass higher education', *Assessment and Evaluation in Higher Education*, 35: 501–517.

Nicol, D. (2010b) 'The foundation for graduate attributes: Developing self-regulation through self and peer assessment', Glasgow: Quality Assurance Agency for Higher Education. Online. Available: <http://www.reap.ac.uk/reap/public/papers//DN_The%20foundation%20for%20 Graduate%20Attributes.pdf> (accessed 26/03/12).

Nicol, D. (2011) The peer project. Online. Available: <http://www.reap.ac.uk/peer.aspx> (accessed 26/03/12).

Nicol, D. and Macfarlane-Dick, D. (2006) 'Formative assessment and self-regulated learning: A model and seven principles of good feedback', *Studies in Higher Education*, 31: 199–218.

Nicol, D.J. and Milligan, C. (2006) 'Rethinking technology-supported assessment in terms of the seven principles of good feedback practice', in Clegg, K. and Bryan, C. (eds) *Innovative assessments in Higher Education*, London: Routledge.

Northedge, A. (2003) 'Rethinking teaching in the context of diversity', *Teaching in Higher Education*, 8: 17–32.

Norton, L. (1990) 'Essay writing: What really counts?', *Higher Education*, 20: 411–442.

O'Donovan, B., Price, M. and Rust, C. (2004) 'Know what I mean? Enhancing student understanding of assessment standards and criteria', *Teaching in Higher Education*, 9 (3): 325–335.

O'Donovan, B., Price, M. and Rust, C. (2008) 'Developing student understanding of assessment standards: A nested hierarchy of approaches', *Teaching in Higher Education*, 13: 205–217.

Orr, S. (2007) 'Assessment moderation: Constructing the marks and constructing the students', *Assessment and Evaluation in Higher Education*, 32 (6): 645–656.

Orr, S. and Blythman, M. (2005) 'Transparent opacity: Assessment in the inclusive academy', in Rust, R. (ed.) *Improving student learning: Diversity and inclusivity, Proceedings of the 2004 12th International Symposium*, Oxford: Oxford Centre for Staff and Learning Development, pp. 175–187.

Orrell, J. (2006) 'Feedback on learning achievement: Rhetoric and reality', *Teaching in Higher Education*, 11 (4): 441–456.

Orsmond, P. and Merry, S. (2009) 'Processing tutor feedback: A consideration of qualitative differences in learning outcomes for high and non-high achieving students', paper presented at Fostering Communities of Learners: 13th EARLI Conference, Amsterdam, 25–29 August.

Orsmond, P., Merry, S. and Reiling, K. (1996) 'The importance of marking criteria in the use of peer assessment', *Assessment and Evaluation in Higher Education*, 21 (3): 239–251.

Orsmond, P., Merry, S. and Reiling, K. (2002) 'The use of exemplars and formative feedback when using student-derived marking criteria in peer and self-assessment', *Assessment and Evaluation in Higher Education*, 27: 309–323.

Price, M., Handley, K. and Millar, J. (2011) 'Feedback: Focusing attention on engagement', *Studies in Higher Education*, 36 (8): 879–896.

Price, M., Handley, K., Millar, J. and O'Donovan, B. (2010) 'Feedback: All that effort, but what is the effect?', *Assessment and Evaluation in Higher Education*, 35: 277–289.

QAA (2006) *Code of practice for the assurance of academic standards and quality in higher education. Section 6: Assessment of students*. Online. Available: <www.qaa.ac.uk> (accessed 10/04/12).

Race, P. (2001) *Learning through feedback*, York: HEA.

Race, P. (2005) *Making learning happen: A guide for post-compulsory education*, London: Sage.

Race, P. (2007) *How to get a good degree: Making the most of your time at university*, 2nd edn, Maidenhead: Open University Press and McGraw-Hill.

Race, P., Brown, S. and Smith, B. (2002) *500 tips on assessment*, London: Routledge.

Ramsden, P. (2003) *Learning to teach in Higher Education*, 2nd edn, London: RoutledgeFalmer.

Rule, A.C. (2006) 'The components of authentic learning', *Journal of Authentic Learning*, 3 (1): 1–10.

Rust, C. (2000) 'A possible student-centred assessment solution to some of the current problems of modular degree programmes (opinion piece)', *Active Learning in Higher Education*, 1 (2): 126–131.

Rust, C. (2007) 'Towards a scholarship of assessment', *Assessment and Evaluation in Higher Education*, 32 (2): 229–237.

Rust, C., O'Donovan, B. and Price, M. (2005) 'A social constructivist assessment process model: How the research literature shows us this could be best practice', *Assessment and Evaluation in Higher Education*, 30 (3): 231–240.

Rust, C., Price, M. and O'Donovan, B. (2003) 'Improving students' learning by developing their understanding of assessment criteria and processes', *Assessment and Evaluation in Higher Education*, 28: 147–164.

Sadler, D.R. (1989) 'Formative assessment and the design of instructional systems', *Instructional Science*, 18: 119–144.

Sadler, D.R. (1998) 'Formative assessment: Revisiting the territory', *Assessment in Education*, 5 (1): 77–84.

Sadler, D.R. (2009) 'Indeterminacy in the use of preset criteria for assessment and grading in higher education', *Assessment and Evaluation in Higher Education*, 34: 159–179.

Sadler, D.R. (2010) 'Beyond feedback: Developing student capability in complex appraisal', *Assessment and Evaluation in Higher Education*, 35: 535–550.

Sambell, K. (2009) *Seeing the signs: Involving students as researchers across the disciplines via a research-based teaching framework*, Red Guide 60, Newcastle: Northumbria University.

Sambell, K. (2011) *Rethinking feedback: An assessment for learning perspective*, Bristol: ESCalate.

Sambell, K. and McDowell, E. (1997) 'The value of self and peer assessment to the developing lifelong learner' in Gibbs, G. (ed.) *Improving students as learners*, Oxford: OCSLD, pp. 46–56.

Sambell, K. and McDowell, L. (1998) 'The construction of the hidden curriculum: Messages and meanings in the assessment of student learning', *Assessment and Evaluation in Higher Education*, 23 (4): 391–402.

Sambell, K., McDowell, L. and Brown, S. (1997) '"But is it fair?": An exploratory study of student perceptions of the consequential validity of assessment', *Studies in Educational Evaluation*, 23 (4): 349–371.

Sambell, K., McDowell, L. and Sambell, A. (2006) 'Supporting diverse students: Developing learner autonomy via assessment', in Clegg, K. and Bryan, C. (eds) *Innovative assessment in Higher Education*, London: Routledge, pp.158–168.

Segers, M., Dochy, F. and Cascaller, E. (eds) (2003) *Optimising new modes of assessment: In search of qualities and standards*, Dordrecht: Kluwer Academic.

Shepard, L.A. (2000) 'The role of assessment in a learning culture', *Educational Researcher*, 29: 4–14.

Sluijsmans, D., Moerkerke, G., Van Merriënbor, J. and Dochy, F. (2001) 'Peer assessment in problem-based learning', *Studies in Educational Evaluation*, 27: 153–173.

Smith, H., Cooper, A. and Lancaster, L. (2002) 'Improving the quality of undergraduate peer assessment: A case for student and staff development', *Innovations in Education and Teaching International*, 39: 71–81.

Snyder, B.R. (1970) *The hidden curriculum*, New York: Alfred A. Knopf.

Somervell, H. (1993) 'Issues in assessment, enterprise and higher education: The case for self-, peer and collaborative assessment', *Assessment and Evaluation in Higher Education*, 18 (3): 221–233.

Stefani, L. (1998) 'Assessment in partnership with learners', *Assessment and Evaluation in Higher Education*, 23 (4): 339–350.

Storey, E. (2007) *A catalogue of assessment for learning essentials for Higher Education staff*, Red Guide 33, Newcastle: Northumbria University.

Tan, K. (2004) 'Does student self-assessment empower or discipline students?', *Assessment and Evaluation in Higher Education*, 29: 651–662.

Taras, M. (2001) 'The use of tutor feedback and student self-assessment in summative tasks: Towards transparency for students and for tutors', *Assessment and Evaluation in Higher Education*, 26: 605–614.

Taras, M. (2010) 'Student self-assessment: Process and consequences', *Teaching in Higher Education*, 15: 199–209.

Tinto, V. (1993) *Leaving college: Rethinking the causes and cures of student attrition*, Chicago, IL: University of Chicago Press.

Torrance, H. (ed.) (1994) *Evaluating authentic assessment: Problems and possibilities in new approaches to assessment*, Buckingham: Open University Press.

Torrance, H. (2007) 'Assessment as learning? How the use of explicit learning objectives, assessment criteria and feedback in post-secondary education and training can come to dominate learning', *Assessment in Education: Principles, Policy and Practice*, 14: 281–294.

Trowler, V. and Trowler, P. (2010) *Student engagement evidence summary*, York, Higher Education Academy. Online. Available: <http://www.heacademy.ac.uk/assets/documents/student engagement/StudentEngagementEvidenceSummary.pdf> (accessed 05/05/12).

Tuckman, B.W. and Jenson, M.A.C. (1977) 'Stages of small-group development revisited', *Group and Organization Management*, 2: 419–427.

Tudor, J., Penlington, R. and McDowell, L. (2010) 'Perceptions and their influence on approaches to learning', *Engineering Education: Journal of the Higher Education Subject Centre*, 5 (2): 69–79.

van de Ridder, J.M.M., Stokking, K.M., McGaghie, W.C. and Ten Cate, O.J.J. (2008) 'What is feedback in clinical education?', *Medical Education*, 42: 189–197.

Wake, B. and Watson, H. (2007) *Assessment for learning: A student survival guide*, Red Guide 32, Newcastle: Northumbria University.

Watkins, D., Dahlin, B. and Eckholm, M. (2005) 'Awareness of the backwash effect of assessment: A phenomenographic study of the views of Hong Kong and Swedish lecturers', *Instructional Science*, 33 (4): 283–309.

Whitelegg, D. (2002) 'Breaking the feedback loop: Problems with anonymous assessment', *Planet*, 3: 7–8. Online. Available: <http://www.gees.ac.uk/planet/p5/dw.pdf> (accessed 26/03/12)

Wiliam, D. (2011) 'What is assessment for learning?', *Studies in Educational Evaluation*, 37: 3–14.

Winter, R. (2003) 'Contextualizing the patchwork text: Addressing problems of coursework assessment in HE', *Innovations in Education and Teaching International*, 40: 112–122.

Zhao, C. and Kuh, G.D. (2004) 'Adding value: Learning communities and student engagement', *Research in Higher Education*, 45 (2): 115–138.

Index